Hermeneutics
and the Voice
of the Other

SUNY series in Contemporary Continental Philosophy
Edited by Dennis J. Schmidt

HERMENEUTICS AND THE VOICE OF THE OTHER

Re-reading Gadamer's Philosophical Hermeneutics

James Risser

STATE UNIVERSITY OF NEW YORK PRESS

Published by
State University of New York Press, Albany

For information, address State University of New York Press,
State University Plaza, Albany, N.Y., 12246

Permissions are listed on page x.

Production by Cathleen Collins
Marketing by Theresa Abad Swierzowski

Library of Congress Cataloging in Publication Data

Risser, James, 1946–
    Hermeneutics and the voice of the other : re-reading Gadamer's philosophical
hermeneutics / James Risser.
        p.   cm. — (SUNY series in contemporary continental philosophy)
    Includes bibliographical references and index.
    ISBN 0-7914-3257-2 (alk. paper). — ISBN 0-7914-3258-0 (pbk. : alk. paper)
    1. Gadamer, Hans Georg, 1900—Contributions in hermeneutics.
2. Hermeneutics. I. Title. II. Series.
B3248.G34R575   1997
193—dc20   96-22787
                                                                       CIP

10 9 8 7 6 5 4 3 2 1

In memory of my brother
Richard J. Risser
1943–1991

Not understood are the sufferings.
Neither has love been learned,
and what removes us in death

is not unveiled.
Only song over the land
hallows and celebrates.

—Rilke, *Sonnets to Orpheus*

Contents

Acknowledgments

This study spans a decade of research that began with a dissatisfaction with the available commentaries on Gadamer's project of a philosophical hermeneutics. It appeared to me that, although some excellent work on Gadamer's philosophy had been published, little of this published work had either taken account of the philosophical sources from which a philosophical hermeneutics is derived, or taken account of the full range of Gadamer's writings. In part the latter could be attributed to the fact that a collected edition of Gadamer's writings has only recently appeared. Still, much of this work had been previously published. Drawing on the full range of Gadamer's writings, I have attempted here to produce an assessment of Gadamer's philosophy that continually draws on the philosophical sources that Gadamer himself incorporates into his project. I have also attempted to assess the project of a philosophical hermeneutics in its post–*Truth and Method* expressions. This entails a sustained account of hermeneutics in relation to deconstruction and, perhaps more importantly, to the role and function of the poetic word for the experience of understanding.

In the course of the years during which the various chapters of this book were written, I was greatly aided by colleagues at the yearly symposium on Gadamer's philosophy held in the Philosophisches Seminar at the University of Heidelberg. In particular I am thankful to Lawrence Schmidt, Dennis Schmidt, Richard Palmer, and Jean Grondin. I am especially thankful to Professor Hans-Georg Gadamer, who attended the symposium and who always found time for our questions and conversations. In addition, this book owes much to colleagues from my own university who were generous enough to read and criticize various chapters: MaryLou Sena, Patrick Burke, Paulette Kidder, and David Madsen.

I am most grateful for the support of my family, especially my wife Jean, who with her grace made all my writing possible.

Some of the material in this book has previously been published in earlier versions. The following presses and journals have kindly consented to allow this material to be reprinted. Chapter 3 contains parts of "Hermeneutic Experience and Memory: Rethinking Knowledge as Recollection," published in *Research in Phenomenology* 16 (1986): 41–56. Chapter 4 contains parts of "Hermeneutics of the Possible: On Finitude and Truth in Philosophical Hermeneutics," in *The Specter of Relativism*, ed. Lawrence K. Schmidt (Evanston: Northwestern University Press, 1995). Chapter 5 contains parts of "The Remembrance of Truth: The Truth of Remembrance," in *Hermeneutics and Truth* (Evanston: Northwestern University Press, 1994). Chapter 6 contains parts of "Two Faces of Socrates: Gadamer/Derrida," in *Dialogue and Deconstruction*, ed. Diane Michelfelder and Richard Palmer (Albany: SUNY Press, 1989). Chapter 7 contains parts of "Poetic Dwelling in Gadamer's Hermeneutics," published in *Philosophy Today* 38 (Winter 1994): 369–79.

Abbreviations

The following abbreviations are used in the body of the text. All citations of Gadamer's work will be given with the English translation, where available, and to the corresponding text in his *Gesammelte Werke*.

DD   *"Destruktion* and Deconstruction." *Dialogue and Deconstruction: The Gadamer-Derrida Encounter.* Edited by Diane Michelfelder and Richard Palmer. Albany: SUNY Press, 1989.

DDP   *Dialogue and Dialectic: Eight Hermeneutical Studies on Plato.* Translated by P. Christopher Smith. New Haven: Yale University Press, 1980.

EPH   *Hans-Georg Gadamer on Education, Poetry, and History: Applied Hermeneutics.* Edited by Dieter Misgeld and Graeme Nicholson. Albany: SUNY Press, 1992.

GW1   *Hermeneutik I: Wahrheit und Methode: Grundzüge einer philosophischen Hermeneutik.* Gesammelte Werke Band 1. Tübingen: J. C. B. Mohr: 1986.

GW2   *Hermeneutik II: Wahrheit und Methode: Ergänzungen/Register.* Gesammelte Werke Band 2. Tübingen: J. C. B. Mohr: 1986.

GW3   *Neuere Philosophie I: Hegel—Husserl—Heidegger.* Gesammelte Werke Band 3. Tübingen: J. C. B. Mohr: 1987.

GW4   *Neuere Philosophie II: Problem—Gestalten.* Gesammelte Werke Band 4. Tübingen: J. C. B. Mohr: 1987.

GW5   *Griechische Philosophie I.* Gesammelte Werke Band 5. Tübingen: J. C. B. Mohr: 1985.

GW6   *Griechische Philosophie II.* Gesammelte Werke Band 6. Tübingen: J. C. B. Mohr: 1985.

GW7   *Griechische Philosophie III: Plato im Dialog.* Gesammelte Werke Band 7. Tübingen: J. C. B. Mohr: 1991.

GW8   *Ästhetik und Poetik I: Kunst als Aussage.* Gesammelte Werke Band 8. Tübingen: J. C. B. Mohr: 1993.

GW9   *Ästhetik und Poetik II: Hermeneutik im Vollzug.* Gesammelte Werke Band 9. Tübingen: J. C. B. Mohr: 1993.

GW10   *Nachträge und Verzeichnisse.* Gesammelte Werke Band 10. Tübingen: J. C. B. Mohr: 1994.

IG   *Idea of the Good in Platonic-Aristotelian Philosophy.* Translated by P. Christopher Smith. New Haven: Yale University Press, 1986.

HW   *Heidegger's Ways.* Translated by John Stanley. Albany: SUNY Press, 1994.

LP   *Literature and Philosophy in Dialogue: Essays in German Literary Theory.* Translated by Robert H. Paslick. Albany: SUNY Press, 1994.

PHC   "The Problem of Historical Consciousness." Translated by Jeff L. Chose. *Graduate Faculty Philosophy Journal* 5.1 (1975).

PH   *Philosophical Hermeneutics.* Translated and edited by David E. Linge. Berkeley: University of California Press, 1976.

PDE   *Plato's Dialectical Ethics.* Translated by Robert Wallace. New Haven: Yale University Press, 1991.

RAS   *Reason in the Age of Science.* Translated by Frederick Lawrence. Cambridge, MA: MIT Press, 1981.

RB   *Relevance of the Beautiful and Other Essays.* Edited by Robert Bernasconi. Cambridge: Cambridge University Press, 1986.

TI   "Text and Interpretation." *Dialogue and Deconstruction: The Gadamer-Derrida Encounter.* Edited by Diane Michelfelder and Richard Palmer. Albany: SUNY Press, 1989.

TM   *Truth and Method*. 2nd revised ed. Translated by Joel Weinsheimer and Donald Marshall. New York: Crossroad Publishing, 1989.

SZ   Heidegger, Martin. *Sein und Zeit*, 7th ed. (Tübingen: Niemeyer, 1963). English translation by John Macquarrie and Edward Robinson, *Being and Time* (New York: Harper & Row, 1962). Page references to the German text are found in the margins of the English translation.

R   Kierkegaard, Soren. *Fear and Trembling/Repetition*. Translated and edited by Howard Hong and Edna Hong. Princeton: Princeton University Press, 1983.

Introduction

The Determination of the Problematic of Philosophical Hermeneutics

The work of Hans-Georg Gadamer, brought to prominence in 1960 with the appearance of *Truth and Method* and now synonymous with the name philosophical hermeneutics, by now would appear to need little introduction. In the years since the publication of his major work not only have numerous critical and expository accounts of this work appeared, but Gadamer himself has continued to give lectures and to write, providing us with an expansion and a further interpretive perspective of his work. Because of this expansion and of some of the accounts of philosophical hermeneutics that have been given, accounts that read Gadamer in terms of a narrowly defined project, there is a need for further exposition and appraisal of Gadamer's hermeneutics. The present study proposes to take up such a task.

The evidence that the intervening years have added complexity to the project of a philosophical hermeneutics when compared with the description of this project found at the outset of *Truth and Method* is hard to ignore. Gadamer himself, in compiling his *Gesammelte Werke*, titled both volumes one and two "*Wahrheit und Methode*" to indicate that the work of volume 1 (which contains the text initially published in 1960) extends to the material in volume 2. Contained in volume 2 are some of the essays initially published in his *Kleine Schriften* (1967–77), essays such as "What is Truth?" (1957) and "On the Problem of Self-Understanding" (1961) that supplement particular themes found in *Truth and Method*. But the volume also contains

1

more recent essays, such as "Text und Interpretation"(1981), in which Gadamer clarifies the very scope and intentions of his project. Along this same line, Gadamer's major writings after *Truth and Method* appear to place the primary emphasis within the project of philosophical hermeneutics on issues and concerns that were not overtly placed at the center in *Truth and Method* itself. With the publication of *Reason in the Age of Science* (1974), a compilation of essays resulting, in part, from Gadamer's confrontation with Habermas and the problem of social reason, one could argue that the Greek notion of $\phi\varrho\acute{o}\nu\eta\sigma\iota\varsigma$ is really the key to the entire project. With the publication of *The Idea of the Good in Platonic and Aristotlean Philosophy* (1978), a work that extends Gadamer's initial work in Greek philosophy, one could just as well argue that the key to Gadamer is to be found in his reading of Plato, a claim that in more recent years Gadamer himself seems willing to make.[1] More recently, with the publication of *Wer bin Ich, und wer bist Du?* (1986 revised ed.), his commentary on the poetry of Paul Celan, Gadamer brought his ongoing interest in issues in poetry to the forefront. If one couples this work with all the material on art and poetry in volumes eight and nine of his *Gesammelte Werke*, the question must be asked whether the key to understanding philosophical hermeneutics is actually found in that same gesture that orients the reader of poetry.

Even if one wanted to disregard the importance of these other writings in determining the project of a philosophical hermeneutics and to state that project solely on the basis of a reading of *Truth and Method*, the complexity still remains. We now know on the basis of a comparison with the original draft of *Truth and Method*, a manuscript of approximately one hundred pages, that Gadamer made significant changes along the way to the publication of the text of 1960.[2] Looking carefully at the development of the themes through the various sections in the text of 1960, one can detect, for example, that the section "The Rediscovery of the Fundamental Hermeneutical Problem" was added to the original text. The beginning of the section which immediately follows, "The Analysis of Effective Historical Consciousness," not only fits better thematically with the section preceding "The Rediscovery of the Fundamental Hermeneutical Problem," but actually refers back to this preceding section as if the reader had just turned from it. We also know that in its original form the first part on aesthetics was not included. Undoubtedly, the transformation of the text from the original draft to the version published in 1960 clearly reflects the long gestation period of approximately ten years that it took Gadamer to produce "Truth and Method." During this period of time in which Gadamer taught at the

University of Leipzig and began his long career at the University of Heidelberg, Gadamer was occupied mainly with teaching duties that focused to a large extent on the work of German Idealism. These duties included giving seminars on Kant's aesthetics and may account for the fact that the first part of *Truth and Method* on the question of truth in art was added to the original draft and why his long preoccupation with Greek philosophy is underplayed in the final version of the text. But the addition of part one of *Truth and Method* is only part of the complexity. The relation of part 3 to part 2 is no less significant for the determination of the project. Clearly, in the published text of 1960 the themes in part 1 and part 2 all point to part 3, and the questions announced at the outset of the book that guide the development of the themes are answered in part 3. Nevertheless, part 3 ("The Ontological Shift of Hermeneutics Guided by Language") represents something of a break in comparison with part 2 ("The Extension of the Question of Truth to Understanding in the Human Sciences").

Amidst all this complexity, it is nonetheless possible to identify in a decisive manner precisely what Gadamer's project is about. To state the matter simply and in the broadest terms, the concern of a philosophical hermeneutics is with the problematic of understanding. This problematic is presented in *Truth and Method* in terms of a shift from a methodological hermeneutics to a philosophical hermeneutics, a shift from understanding as a methodology of the human sciences to the universality of understanding and interpretation. The claim to universality speaks primarily to the scope rather than the conditions of understanding. That is to say, the claim to universality is not about an unconditional validity relative to Gadamer's "theory" of understanding, for in fact the actual condition for understanding that Gadamer posits (viz., the historicity of understanding) runs counter to any claim to universality. In a philosophical hermeneutics the scope of understanding is broadened by virtue of its ontological determination; that is, following Heidegger's analysis in *Being and Time*, understanding is a determination of human existence that is prior to a functioning in methodological research. This "hermeneutics of *Existenz*" is what allows Gadamer to posit a claim to universality. For philosophical hermeneutics, understanding takes place in all aspects of experiencing: "the way we experience one another, the way we experience historical traditions, the way we experience the natural givenness of our existence and of our world, constitute a truly hermeneutic universe, in which we are not imprisoned, as if behind insurmountable barriers, but to which we are opened" (TM xxiv/GW1 4).

The question for Gadamer then is quite simple: How does understanding at this fundamental level in fact occur? What he proceeds to show is that understanding is foremost an act of repetition where interpretations, which always remain a limited instance of understanding, are continually placed back into the process of understanding. More specifically, he shows that understanding is an open historical process in which the interpreter stands within an already constituted interpretation. The mediation of interpretation in this process, Gadamer insists, is fundamentally dialogical. What is other to the interpreter draws the interpreter into an exchange in which a new understanding occurs. The dialogical character of understanding is most evident in the description of understanding in part 3 of *Truth and Method*. There Gadamer tells us that the process of understanding is linguistic: "that which can be understood is language" (TM 475/GW1 479). But language is for Gadamer always the language of conversation where the other encounters the interpreter in dialogue. The distinctive mark of this process of understanding accordingly runs counter to the spirit of modern philosophy. It is a process in which there is a fundamental restraining of subjectivity relative to its determining grasp and hold on the world. The shift from a methodological hermeneutics is also a shift from the reach of subjectivity.

Already we can see that in way the problematic of understanding shifts, there occurs a certain development of that problematic. This development, from which we will take our interpretive perspective of Gadamer's work, can be characterized in terms of a threefold determination of philosophical hermeneutics.

Philosophical Hermeneutics as a Hermeneutics of the Humanities

Philosophical hermeneutics is first of all a *hermeneutics of the humanities*.[3] By Gadamer's own account, the starting point in the development of a philosophical hermeneutics was from the practice of hermeneutics as it occurs in the humanities, specifically, the humanities as they emerge out of German Romanticism. In this context a philosophical hermeneutics wants to clarify, in the name of the humanities, the very self-understanding of the humanities as historical human sciences. The problem as Gadamer sees it is that, in line with the attempt to save the scientific character of the humanities, the nineteenth-century humanist tradition modeled itself on the natural sciences. The effect of this was to narrow down the parameters of human knowledge. When Dilthey formulates a distinct methodology for the human sciences—the methodology of *Verstehen*—he remains caught in this same narrowing down of the parameters of human knowledge, viz., objectivity secured by methodological research. Gadamer deliberately begins with the experience of art in *Truth and Method* because it is for him a mode of experience that confronts this theoretical orientation toward objectivity with its own limitation.[4] In art (and ultimately in history and philosophy as well) the originary experience that is mediated through it simply cannot be grasped in the manner of scientific objectivity and methodological research.

Unfortunately for Gadamer, as we know from the preface to the second edition of *Truth and Method*, the critique of method that orients the analysis of the humanities at the outset of *Truth and Method* was not made clear enough for his critics.[5] In proposing an alternative to the *way* of understanding in the historical human sciences, his initial readers assumed he was presenting an alternative method (Greek ὁδός = way). The title of the book did nothing to dispel the confusion. The title does not mean that truth and method are mutually exclusive, nor does it mean that Gadamer is proposing a methodology for the human sciences that has its own truth (Dilthey's project). It simply means that there are modes of experience in which a truth is communicated that is not a matter of verification though the methodological procedure of modern empirical science. The critique of method is directed against the self-conception of the historical human sciences that, according to Gadamer, has concealed "the orienting, ideological determination of their interests behind the method-consciousness of their scientific procedure" (GW2 496).[6] Perhaps Gadamer should have insisted, against his publishers wishes, on the title that he initially proposed for the book, the title still found in the German subtitle of the book, namely, "Grundzüge einer philosophischen Hermeneutik" ("Fundamentals of a Philosophical Hermeneutics").[7]

The philosophical basis for Gadamer's critique of method is drawn from several sources, the principal one being, of course, Heidegger's hermeneutics of facticity, in which for the first time the problematic of understanding turns from epistemological to ontological considerations. For the hermeneutics of the humanities, the hermeneutics of facticity means, in the most general terms, that the concept of understanding is a fundamental categorical determination of human existence. Accordingly, the question of the possibility of understanding is a question that precedes an action of understanding on the part of subjectivity, and this includes the methodological activity of the human sciences. Gadamer's use of the term "hermeneutics" throughout *Truth and Method* will retain its indebtedness to Heidegger's employment of this term. Hermeneutics "denotes the basic being-in-motion [*Grundbewegtheit*] of Dasein that constitutes its finitude and historicity, and hence embraces the whole of its experience of the world" (TM xxx/GW2 440).

But, as we know from the story of Gadamer's own education and influences, this indebtedness to Heidegger is itself quite complex, even here at the outset where it appears that Gadamer has simply taken over the fundamental assumptions of *Being and Time* and applied them to the problem of understanding in the humanities. As a young man Gadamer first met Heidegger in 1923 when Heidegger was still at Freiburg and Gadamer had already received his doctorate from Marburg under the Neo-Kantian Paul Natorp. Gadamer recalls how Heidegger's seminar on Aristotle's *Nicomachean Ethics* had a tremendous influence on his own thinking.[8] The study of the Ethics, and in particular Aristotle's notion of $\phi\rho\acute{o}\nu\eta\sigma\iota\varsigma$, enabled Gadamer to penetrate more deeply into the hermeneutic situation.[9] He saw in the Ethics that the notion of $\phi\rho\acute{o}\nu\eta\sigma\iota\varsigma$ allowed for a "critique of the abstract and universal that—without being driven to a dialectical extreme, as in the manner of Hegel, and hence without the untenable consequence presented by the concept of absolute knowledge—has become essential for the hermeneutic situation after the rise of historical consciousness" (TM 450/GW2 422–23).

When Heidegger came to Marburg shortly thereafter, as a result of his penetrating work in Aristotle,[10] Gadamer had a further opportunity to learn from Heidegger and to be "filled with the passion of his thinking." During this time Heidegger gave a number of lectures and seminars on phenomenology in which its fundamental concepts were linked to concepts in Greek philosophy. Eventually, Gadamer, under Heidegger's direction, wrote his *Habilitationschrift* on Plato's ethics.[11] One gets a vivid picture of this time in Germany from several sources.[12] It was, by Gadamer's own account, a "tension-filled time," a time of crisis in theology and transition in philosophy. Neo-Kantianism, which had so decisively shaped the problem of epistemology and methodology in the sciences, was on the wane. Phenomenology was now attracting attention, especially with Heidegger's arrival. From the phenomenology of Max Scheler it became clear that ethical phenomena could not be accounted for merely from the consciousness of the "ought," and from Husserl and Heidegger one came to see that behind scientific experience there was to be found the "natural experience of life." In theology, Bultmann's critique of myth has taken issue with the claims of "objectifying thinking." All of this profoundly shaped the mind of this young classics scholar concerned with issues in the humanities.

We can readily see how the main argument of a hermeneutics of the humanities in *Truth and Method* is formed as a result of this shaping influence on Gadamer's thought. The concern of the book is to articulate what a methodological dispute in the humanities would only conceal, that is, the conditions for the possibility of understanding anything. Such conditions are derived from Heidegger's insight that understanding is first a mode of being before it is a mode of knowing (life understands itself from out of itself). This self-interpretation of life entails a peculiar circularity: understanding remains permanently determined by the anticipatory movement of the fore-structure of understanding. This means that the hermeneutic situation is constituted by the fact that there is no zero point from which hermeneutical consciousness is able to stand, and even less so, that the hermeneutical situation can ultimately be dissolved in perfect understanding. The lack of a presuppositionless stance—which speaks to a certain relation of self to other—is presented in terms of a renewed understanding of prejudice that in turn allows Gadamer to speak of the hermeneutical circle as the interplay of the movement of tradition and the movement of the interpreter. The anticipation of meaning that guides understanding "proceeds from the commonality that binds us to tradition" (TM 293/GW1 298). Once understanding in the historical human sciences is seen in terms of the movement of tradition and its interpretation, objectivity in the human sciences, as this is understood by methodological research, is no longer possible. The hermeneutical consciousness in the historical human sciences is always an "historically effected consciousness" (*wirkungsgeschichtliche Bewußtsein*). Such a consciousness, which Gadamer claims is more being than consciousness, is at once a consciousness effected by history and a consciousness of these effects.

The insight gained in Gadamer's reformulation of the hermeneutical circle is not simply about the limitation of objectivity in the human sciences; it is also about the character of understanding as an event (*Geschehen*). As a movement of tradition and its interpretation, understanding has the character of a process that one participates in rather than something constructed (by a subject): "Understanding is to be thought of less as a subjective act than as participating in an event of tradition, a process of transmission in which past and present are constantly mediated" (TM 290/GW1 295). The self-understanding of the humanities—reflected in the questions of understanding historical events and the interpretation of classical texts, for example—must come to see how this event structure is at work in it.

Finally, the shaping influence on Gadamer's thought tells us that there is yet another component in addition to Heidegger's hermeneutics of facticity that comes to bear on the problematic of understanding within a hermeneutics of the humanities. This component is the tradition of practical philosophy that Gadamer finds in Greek philosophy. Of course, this component is not so utterly different from Heidegger's hermeneutics of facticity. As we know from looking at the courses Heidegger gave in the early twenties, the hermeneutics of facticity is itself shaped from a reading of Aristotle's practical philosophy. The model of practical philosophy, like the hermeneutics of facticity, does not start at a zero point or end in infinity. The model of practical philosophy, which concerns the knowing with respect to action, starts from the fact that one is first formed by one's education and citizenship. Accordingly, the reasonability in practical philosophy, unlike the reasonability at work in the methodological thinking of anonymous science, does not sever the connection between knowledge and life. In this return to the model of practical philosophy, Gadamer is attempting in effect to reconstruct the humanist tradition in its broader perspective beyond the questions of method and objectivity. Gadamer is convinced that the Aristotelian project of practical science offers the only scientific-theoretical model that can do justice to what in fact is going on in the human sciences.

But it is not just a matter of what is going on in the human sciences. Following this model, which is eventually broadened by Gadamer to include the "practical" philosophy of Plato, Gadamer wants to confront the general problem of contemporary social life.[13] For Gadamer this is the problem of the way in which scientific rationality comes to form all aspects of human life. When a calculating, technical rationality is applied to the problems of human organization and living, the sphere of practical reasoning—the sphere of judgment—effectively disappears. The issue is whether in that which binds us all together we can forego the proper exercise of judgment.

Philosophical Hermeneutics as a Hermeneutics of Experience

But philosophical hermeneutics is not simply a hermeneutics of the humanities. Although the problematic of understanding in *Truth and Method* is developed in terms of the historical human sciences, that analysis is intended as a starting point in order to discover the conditions for understanding anything at all.[14] The intention of a philosophical hermeneutics is not to ask how understanding occurs in the human sciences, but to ask the question of understanding relative to the entire human experience of the world and the practice of life. The human sciences, in other words, are to be connected with the modes of experience that lie outside science—the experience of philosophy, art, and history itself—and in doing so connect the human sciences "with the totality of our experience of the world." In articulating the conditions for hermeneutic practice as such, a philosophical hermeneutics is effectively a hermeneutics of experience.

That a philosophical hermeneutics is a hermeneutics of experience should be apparent to any careful reader of *Truth and Method*. In part 1 of *Truth and Method* on the question of truth in art, Gadamer is mainly concerned with a critique of the subjectification of art (that has its beginnings in Kant's aesthetics) whereby aesthetic consciousness, under the restraint of a scientific conception of truth, takes the artwork as a simple possession of aesthetic culture. Against this view Gadamer wants to defend the experience of truth that comes to us through the artwork by taking the concept of experience more broadly than Kant did. The question of truth in art depends on being able to take aesthetic experience as experience (*Erfahrung*). As experience, art is not regarded an object of aesthetic enjoyment, but an encounter in the manner of play (*Spiel*) with an unfinished event. When Gadamer lays out the elements of a theory of hermeneutic experience in part 2, he is trying to develop a conception of truth and knowledge that "corresponds to the whole of our hermeneutical experience" (TM xxiii/GW1 3). To see what this is we can repeat with some variation the main argument of *Truth and Method* outlined above. A theory of hermeneutic experience begins by taking over the fundamental insight of a hermeneutics of facticity: there is no zero point from which an understanding consciousness can proceed in its attempt to hear what the object of interpretation has to say. This does not mean, however, against the impossibility of pure objectivity, that interpretation is subjective. It means precisely that interpretation is always caught up in sorting out anticipations of meaning in order to let the alterity of the object of interpretation present itself. Gadamer then applies this insight to the experience of historical tradition as the object of investigation for the human sciences as a whole. Here the lack of a zero point means that the hermeneutical consciousness is always subject to history, which itself effects the horizon in which the object of interpretation stands. Hermeneutical consciousness is a consciousness of history's effects and a consciousness effected by history.

Gadamer's argument does not end here. What remains to be seen is precisely how knowledge and effect belong together. What we find in the chapter where Gadamer takes up this question, the chapter that according to the preface takes on a systematic and key position in the investigation, is an analysis of experience itself. Gadamer's claim is that historically effected consciousness has the structure of experience, which is to say that hermeneutical experience is not fundamentally different from the pattern of experience itself. What is the pattern of experience? When properly understood, Gadamer insists the pattern of experience displays how knowledge and effect belong together. Every experience, which is always that in which one already is, entails an openness to new experience that happens when experience is led by its own negative instances. In this configuration lies a fundamental connection between experience and insight: through experience we are confronted with the insight that are insights are finite and limited. This insight, in one form or another, is repeated by Gadamer throughout his writings and stands as the determining mark of his philosophical hermeneutics.[15]

When Gadamer then turns specifically to find in hermeneutical experience the elements of experience in general, he begins by introducing in the most provisional way the distinctive features of his fully developed philosophical hermeneutics, that is, the linguisticality (*Sprachlichkeit*) of hermeneutical experience and the dialogical character of hermeneutical experience. Hermeneutical experience, Gadamer tells us,

> is concerned with *tradition*. This is what is to be experienced. But tradition is not simply a process [*Geschehen*] that experience teaches us to know and govern; it is *language*—i.e., it expresses itself like a Thou. (TM 358/GW1 363–64)

To say that tradition expresses itself like a Thou does not mean that what is experienced in tradition is the opinion of another person. It simply means, in this reformulation of his already reformulated hermeneutic "circle" (see TM 293), that "tradition is a genuine communication partner [*Kommunikationspartner*] with which we belong, as does the I with the Thou" (TM 358/GW1 364). To experience tradition truly as a Thou means precisely that the claim from the other is not to be overlooked; it means that the other really has something to say when one is able to listen. Here we begin to see for the first time that hermeneutical experience is not really about the assimilation of meaning any more than it is simply an appropriation of meaning by a subject. Rather, hermeneutical experience pertains, again as in experience itself, to openness whereby the word of the other can be understood. The logical structure of this openness Gadamer finds in the dialectic of question and answer. Every genuine question, which opens up possibilities of meaning, entails that the matter to be understood is brought into the open, and the art of asking questions is the art of dialectic. Gadamer concludes part 2 of *Truth and Method* by relating the dialectic of question and answer to the earlier analysis of historically effected consciousness.

> The dialectic of question and answer disclosed in the structure of hermeneutical experience now permits us to state more exactly what kind of consciousness historically effected consciousness is. For the dialectic of question and answer that we demonstrated makes understanding appear to be a reciprocal relationship of the same kind as conversation. It is true that a text does not speak to us in the same way as does a Thou. We who are attempting to understand must ourselves make it speak. But we found that this kind of understanding, "making the text speak," is not an arbitrary procedure that we undertake on our own initiative but that, as a question, it is related to the answer that is expected in the text. Anticipating an answer itself presupposes that the questioner is part of the tradition and regards himself as addressed by it. This is the truth of historically effected consciousness. It is the historically experienced consciousness that, by renouncing the chimera of perfect enlightenment, is open to the experience of history. (TM 377–78/GW1 383)

If to this point Gadamer has shown the significance of the question for the hermeneutical phenomenon in the essence of conversation, what remains to be seen is the linguisticality of conversation, which is taken as a basis for the question. The thematic of tradition that so dominates the theory of hermeneutical experience shifts to the thematic of language, to the hermeneutical event as language-bound. Understanding tradition is a communication event, the event that happens in "the conversation that we are." Part 3 of *Truth and Method*, on the ontological shift of hermeneutics guided by language, does indeed present a "break" from the analysis in part 2, but it does not represent a departure from the task of articulating the conditions for hermeneutical experience. In language—in living language (i.e., in the language of conversation, the language of speaking of one to another)—*is* the experience of the world.

In view of this way in which Gadamer stakes out his own position, his indebtedness to Heidegger is not as simple as it first appears. When Gadamer explicitly acknowledges this indebtedness in laying out the elements of a theory of hermeneutical experience, it appears that a philosophical hermeneutics is simply an extension of the hermeneutics of *Being and Time* and that *Truth and Method* is accordingly a variation on a Heideggerian theme. Such a view is inaccurate on two accounts. First of all, in light of Gadamer's emphasis on art and the turn to language, it would be inaccurate to say that what influences Gadamer's project is merely the Heidegger of *Being and Time*. In his "Reflections on My Philosophical Journey," in which he comments on his relationship to Heidegger, Gadamer notes that the focus on the concept of historically effected consciousness gave the appearance that he remained completely captive to the standpoint of the early Heidegger which took Dasein as its starting-point. But in fact his intention was to adhere to the line of questioning of the later Heidegger and to make it available in a new way. Gadamer does not want to hold fast to Heidegger's transcendentally conceived fundamental ontology of *Being and Time*, but to respond in his own way to the new trajectories in thought opened by the *later* Heidegger on the themes of the artwork, the thing, and language. The concept of historically effected consciousness in Gadamer's eyes is not about a modification of self-consciousness, which is conceptually linked to a philosophy of subjectivity, but about the limitation placed on consciousness by history having its effect. One could make this same argument for Gadamer's use of the hermeneutic circle. The very mention of a hermeneutic circle gives the appearance that Gadamer remains captive to the circularity of understanding, to the movement of interpretation from implicit to explicit, that Heidegger himself later rejects. But in fact the dialogical character of the hermeneutic encounter is more appropriate to the hermeneutic relation of belonging which characterizes the later Heidegger's reformulation of his hermeneutics.[16]

Secondly, the view is inaccurate because it fails to take note of the originality of Gadamer's thought which emerges in identifying his departure from the Heideggerian project. Commenting on Heidegger's "*Kehre*" in which the notion of hermeneutics was no longer trusted "to keep his thinking free from the consequences of a transcendental theory of consciousness," Gadamer writes:

But to me, it seemed, fell precisely the task of speaking on behalf of the happening that resides in understanding and of the overcoming of modern subjectivism in an analysis of the hermeneutic experience that has become reflectively aware of itself. So already in 1934 I began with a critical analysis of aesthetic consciousness, concerning which I sought to prove that it did not do justice to the truth claim of art; and accompanied by a constant intercourse with the Greek classics, especially with Plato, I sought to overcome the historical self-estrangement with which historical positivism deflated ideas into opinions and philosophy into doxography. (RAS 43–44)

And, in another context, Gadamer tells us:

But where I . . . still appeal to Heidegger—in that I attempt to think of "understanding" as an "event"—is turned however in an entirely different direction. My point of departure is not the complete forgetfulness of being, the "night of being," rather on the contrary . . . the unreality of such an assertion.[17]

Quite simply, Gadamer's question is not the question of being, but, indeed in making the line of questioning of the later Heidegger available in a new way, of accounting for the communicative event in which we share in a common meaning. The distinctive task of a philosophical hermeneutics is to explicate the practice of hermeneutics in life, a practice that takes its orientation from the Socratic dialogue where speaking never encounters what Heidegger calls the "language of metaphysics." For Gadamer the question of language is the question of our becoming-at-home in the world. In this, language knows no restrictions since it holds infinite possibilities of speaking within it. Certainly there are concepts in metaphysics whose content is determined by the usage of these words, and Heidegger rightly uncovers, relative to their ontological implications, their prejudicial character. But for Gadamer the concepts in which our thinking moves are no more governed by a fixed givenness than the words used in everyday language. Sounding more Hegelian than Heideggerian, Gadamer asks, "Are the universality of objectifying reason and the eidetic structure of linguistic meanings really bound to these particular historically developed interpretations of *subjectum* and *species* and *actus* that the West has produced? Or do they hold true for all languages?" (HP 78–79/GW3 237).

Of course, one must ask whether this departure from Heidegger merely serves to "domesticate" what is most challenging in Heidegger's thinking, and whether in the end Gadamer is successful in distinguishing his position substantially from that of Heidegger's.[18] However this question is ultimately answered, it is certainly true that Gadamer has not so much urbanized the Heideggerian province, as Habermas describes it, but that Gadamer, somewhat ironically, has existentialized the Heideggerian project. The hermeneutic aspect of human life is not limited to history and texts, but pertains to everything about which one seeks to communicate. Hermeneutic understanding is, in the end, a matter of communication in which the task of understanding is to find a common language so that the one who speaks can be heard by the other.

Philosophical Hermeneutics and the Voice of the Other

By attending more carefully to this description of hermeneutic understanding, the third determination of philosophical hermeneutics comes into view. As a communicative event, hermeneutic understanding is framed by the dynamics of conversation. Accordingly, it is not enough to say that for philosophical hermeneutics the experience of meaning is linguistic; one must immediately add to this the specificity of this linguisticality that this experience of meaning takes shape in the language of *speech,* in living language. In this context it can be said that a philosophical hermeneutics is a hermeneutics of the voice. At one place Gadamer actually describes hermeneutics precisely in these terms: hermeneutics is letting that which is far and alienated speak again "not only in a new voice but in a clearer voice."[19] In setting philosophical hermeneutics off in this way we can, at the same time, see more precisely how Gadamer separates himself from those thinkers closest to him who come to bear on the project of philosophical hermeneutics. Hegel's dialectic is now reoriented toward the art of living dialogue and Heidegger's project of overcoming metaphysics is continued in the dynamics of a language, not of metaphysics, but "which we speak with others and to others."[20] If one were to ask for a justification for locating the experience of meaning in the voice one could only assume that it follows from the context of that Socratic-Platonic mode of thinking that comes to bear on the project of philosophical hermeneutics precisely as that corrective to the formalism of Hegelian dialectic and to the Heideggerian preoccupation with the overcoming of metaphysics. This context insists that understanding is only found in the living word, in the word of memory (Μνημοσύνη). The hermeneutic turn toward conversation seeks to go back to the very presupposition in Socratic inquiry, that is, "the ἀνάμνησις sought for and awakened in λόγοι." The recollection that Gadamer has in mind here is "not only that of the individual soul but always that of the 'spirit that would like to unite us'—we who are a conversation" (DD 110/GW2 369). In taking over the model of Socratic dialogue for hermeneutic understanding, Gadamer will insist that logical demonstration must yield to the power of communication in language where one must find the right word to convince the other. The communicative event is essentially a rhetorical phenomenon.

But the real significance of this determination of philosophical hermeneutics is yet to be seen. It is not just that philosophical hermeneutics is a hermeneutics of the voice. The dialogical element of hermeneutic understanding means that what is brought to speech again is the voice of the *other*. This emphasis on the other has always been present in Gadamer's writings. Again, in recounting his own philosophical itinerary Gadamer tells us that one of the motivations for his philosophical hermeneutics was the crisis of idealism that during his youth erupted with the Kierkegaardian critique of Hegel. In this critique the meaning of understanding takes its orientation from the other who breaks into my ego-centeredness and gives me something to understand. This "Kierkegaardian motif" of the special autonomy of the other (person) guided Gadamer "from the beginning." This motif is clearly present in *Truth and Method* not only where one would expect to find it, that is, in the analysis of conversation that is structured by definition as a relation of self and other. It is also found early in the text as we notice in his discussion of the reformulation of the hermeneutic circle:

> A person trying to understand something will not resign himself from the start to relying on his own accidental fore-meanings, ignoring as consistently and stubbornly as possible the actual meaning of the text until the latter becomes so persistently audible that it breaks through what the interpreter imagines it to be. Rather, a person trying to understand a text is rather prepared for it to tell him something. That is why a hermeneutically trained consciousness must be sensitive to the other of the text from the beginning. (TM 269/GW1 273)

What is at stake in understanding is the otherness of the text and its ability to assert its truth against one's own fore-meanings. In effect this is precisely what is repeated in the analysis of hermeneutic experience near the end of part 2 of *Truth and Method*, where he shows how hermeneutical experience is comparable to the experience of the Thou in the I-Thou relation. The openness to experience means that one does not overlook the claim of the other, whereby one must accept some things that are against the one who seeks to understand.

If we grant that there has been an emphasis from the outset on the other as the direction from which understanding occurs, it is also the case, perhaps as a result of his contact with deconstruction but certainly as a result of his contact with the poetry of Paul Celan, that the voice of the other is not to be regarded as a voice to be assimilated. In the writings that resulted from this contact with the poetry of Celan, the language of unity that dominates *Truth and Method* in notions such as "fusion of horizons" and (the all encompassing nature of) "tradition" recedes into the background. In defending himself against Derrida's charge of logocentrism in "Text and Interpretation," for example, Gadamer repeats a claim made in *Truth and Method*, namely, to the extent that understanding is successful it is always understanding differently: In every experience of meaning there is a "potentiality for being other that lies beyond every coming to agreement about what is common" (TI 26/GW2 336). Understanding is not a mere assimilation into identity where what is foreign is made near again as a return to identity in a subject. The dialogical character of language is such that it leaves behind any starting point in the subjectivity of the subject. As a relation of self-to-other then the process of understanding is one in which "one is capable of stepping into the place of the other in order to say what one has there understood and what one has to say in response."[21] In hermeneutic conversation the performance of meaning necessarily demands that one be exposed to the rejoinder of the other. It is to think with the other and to come back to oneself as if to another.

What Gadamer learns from his reading of Celan is that the conversation with the poetic word is by no means a simple communication. Celan's poetry is a particularly interesting case of the non-identity of communication where the "message in the bottle," as Celan describes his poetry, cannot be made completely transparent. The poetic word holds within itself a breathless stillness, that point where the breath turns (*Atemwende*) between inhaling and exhaling. The reader of a text, especially a poetic text, must be prepared to encounter this otherness, this non-communication of the poetic word. For hermeneutic understanding in general, this means of course that the rupture in communication, that fact that the word may be untranslatable, is deeply embedded in hermeneutic experience. What is so different about Gadamer's position here is subtle. For the Gadamer of *Truth and Method* the lack of communication should not deter one in the optimism that communication can still be achieved. For Gadamer as a reader of Celan's poetry, however, the task of understanding is not to make poetry transparent, but to enter into that space of transparency and non-transparency. Here the task of understanding is to be attentive to what is demanded by the text, to be attentive to the voice of the other. The last word for philosophical hermeneutics is not the communication of meaning as such, but the open-endedness of communication in which we continually gain access to the world in which we live. In the end a philosophical hermeneutics is about self-understanding; but this, as Gadamer insists, has little to do with a philosophy of subjectivity. Rather, it has to do with our being at home in the world that we are awakened to in the voice of the other.

The Aim of the Book

In being able to identify a development in the problematic of understanding through a threefold determination of philosophical hermeneutics, the intention has not been to suggest that Gadamer's own thinking undergoes a number of turns such that one could introduce a Gadamer I and II (or III) into the reading of the project. The hermeneutics of the voice already animates the discussion of hermeneutic understanding in the humanities. Or, to say the same thing: the hermeneutics of the humanities is found in a hermeneutics of experience, and the hermeneutics of experience, as dialogical, is found in a hermeneutics of the voice (of the other). The determinations of philosophical hermeneutics simply serve as marks that lay out Gadamer's position, a position that is complex as we have said, not only because he brings so many resources and contexts to bear on his project, but also because his philosophical writings themselves span the full range of twentieth-century philosophical history. Despite the complexity, the character of understanding for philosophical hermeneutics is unmistakable. Understanding is a communicative event in which question and answer constitute the basic hermeneutic relationship. Gadamer's hermeneutics is a dialogical hermeneutics. Taking account of this complexity, the problematic of understanding, situated by its own historical context, is directed initially to issues in the humanities framed by the particular problematic of the *Geisteswissenschaften*. After *Truth and Method* the problematic of understanding is directed more and more to the unique situation of the eminent text, to poetry and literature where language emerges "in its full autonomy." But here too, Gadamer has not left behind his guiding insight that is obviously in play even in his reconstruction of the humanist tradition, namely, that all our attempts at speaking concern the practice of living where the openness to the other becomes a way of confronting ourselves. It is for this reason that Gadamer concludes his "Selbstdarstellung" by pointing out that his reflections have served to remind him "that Plato was no Platonist and that philosophy is not scholasticism" (GW2 508). In Plato Gadamer saw how it is that the philosopher is concerned with life. Plato, for Gadamer, is not a forerunner of onto-theology, but is the one who provided the initial insight through his creation of the Socratic dialogue that the monological claim of scientific consciousness never permits philosophical thought to fulfill its intended purpose. In following the spirit of Plato philosophy cannot be scholasticism.

The aim of this book, as stated at the outset, is to treat philosophical hermeneutics in a more encompassing way, in a way that takes account of the complexity and breadth of the project of philosophical hermeneutics. Having outlined this complexity and breadth in the threefold determination of philosophical hermeneutics, the treatment called for is one that first of all can establish the real *philosophical* conversation in which philosophical hermeneutics is rooted. This means showing not only thematically the immediate philosophical background that motivates Gadamer's project as it develops in *Truth and Method*, that is, the project of phenomenology in the context of a critique of Neo-Kantianism, but also where and how Gadamer's conversational partners—Plato, Aristotle, Hegel, Kierkegaard, Celan, Heidegger—enter into and shape the determination of philosophical hermeneutics. Gadamer's relation to Heidegger is of course a special case. It is surprising how little has been said about the precise nature of this indebtedness.[22] Perhaps this is due to the fact that Gadamer himself has said so much.[23] In exploring some of the aspects of this indebtedness throughout this book, it should become readily apparent that it is insufficient to say, for example, that Gadamer's position in *Truth and Method* is built around an explication of sections 31 and 32 of *Being and Time*. Even if such a claim were substantially true, its sense could only be determined through a more detailed analysis of Heidegger's hermeneutics of facticity in its initial formulation in the early 1920s where its relation to Greek philosophy is more apparent.

In this treatment of philosophical hermeneutics that wants to be more faithful to the multiple sources of philosophical hermeneutics, the aim of the book is also to make certain readings of Gadamer's project questionable. These are the readings that either approach philosophical hermeneutics with too narrow a focus—and thereby distort its intention—or challenge the operative principles in a philosophical hermeneutics.[24] The criticism in the former reads Gadamer as an apologist for tradition, and, more often than not, as a Hegelian who still pays homage to Heidegger. Undoubtedly, Gadamer is indebted to Hegel as well as Heidegger in the formulation of his project. Does this mean, as it has been claimed, that a philosophical hermeneutics is simply a Hegelianism without its dialectical completion in absolute knowledge? If it were so, a philosophical hermeneutics could easily be characterized, following the principle of Hegelian dialectical advancement, as monological in its foundation—still a unity of spirit, but one whereby the end keeps on delaying its arrival. Such a claim must then distort the professed dialogical character of philosophical hermeneutics, reducing the dialogical to simply the self-referential. Is it really the case that Gadamerian dialogue, according to one commentator, is that "in which subjects become present to themselves in each other and remain identical with themselves in every difference"?[25] If such were the case how does one account for Gadamer's claim that "to reach an understanding in a dialogue is not merely a matter of putting oneself forward and successfully asserting one's own point of view, but being transformed into a communion in which we do not remain what we were" (TM 379/GW1 384). Or is it really the case, as John Caputo has argued, that "Gadamerian hermeneutics, moved as it is by its Hegelian mainsprings, is preoccupied with digestion";[26] that is, that Gadamer's hermeneutics is monological insofar as the life of the one is consumed into the life of the other? But then, how does one account for Gadamer's claim, ironically embedded in his reading of Hegel, that "the other must be experienced not as the other of myself grasped by pure self-consciousness, but as a Thou" (TM 343/GW1 349), that is, as precisely that which is not to be consumed, appropriated? If it is the case that the experience of the Thou is always to be related to oneself, that is because Gadamer insists that, by virtue of finitude, one cannot extricate oneself out of the interpretative situation.

In another context Caputo has also claimed that Gadamer's hermeneutics is nothing but a traditionalism. That is to say, Gadamer's hermeneutics, as a simple repetition of the standpoint of *Being and Time*, links itself to the most conservative element in Heidegger's philosophy whereby it seeks to keep the deep unity of the tradition safe.[27] To take up this criticism is to see precisely how tradition is understood within the historicity of existence where in fact "preservation" of the tradition has little to do with the ordinary understanding of "preserving" as maintaining the continuity of culture and with it the preservation of cultural values. Such criticism, moreover, deflects one away from what descriptively is actually taking place in the movement of tradition. The movement of tradition expresses the way in which the rational is at work in human life.[28] Again, along this same line of criticism, it has been claimed by Gianni Vattimo that a philosophical hermeneutics is a "simple acceptance of collective consciousness" in which there is a "risk of being reduced to an apology for what already exists."[29] But this claim, as with the others, tends to read Gadamer from the position of his hermeneutics of the humanities only where the notions of tradition and the historicity of consciousness dominate. It fails to see precisely how nuanced Gadamer's position is in the broader scope of his writings. Not only does this claim fail to take account of the central section in the "Elements of a Theory of Hermeneutic Experience" in *Truth and Method* on experience where being experienced means to be exposed to the unexpected. It also fails to take account of Gadamer's remarks in "Text and Interpretation" where it is apparent that a collective consciousness is nowhere to be found in philosophical hermeneutics.

But even if one claims that Gadamer presents us with merely a hermeneutics of the humanities, the various claims are difficult to hold. Tradition for Gadamer is certainly not a collective subject. Hermeneutics is not a reproduction of prior meaning. The dialogical element in hermeneutic conversation is not a monological relation of self to self. On the contrary, the event of understanding is a production of meaning by performing that meaning in the encounter with the other. The event of understanding as dialogical encounter is a sharing in and through the other. Gadamer concludes his essay "The Diversity of Europe" on a note that expresses what I take to be at the very center of Gadamer's project. In the context of a discussion on the future of Europe as a community, Gadamer says,

> Where one is not concerned with learning how to control something, we will always and again learn through experiencing our own biases, the otherness of the other in its other-being. To participate with the other and to be part of the other is the most and the best that we can strive for and accomplish. So it may not be unjustified to conclude from our discussion a final political consequence. We may perhaps survive as humanity if we would be able to learn that we may not simply exploit our means of power and effective possibilities, but must learn to stop and respect the other as an other, whether it is nature or the grown cultures of peoples and nations; and if we would be able to learn to experience the other and the others, as the other of our self, in order to participate with one another. (EPH 235–36)

The sentiment expressed in this occasional piece is expressed philosophically in philosophical hermeneutics. Philosophical hermeneutics maintains that the act of understanding is constituted in relation to the other; it asks about the conditions under which one is able to hear the voice of the other.

For the most part, the criticisms and the responses to them are taken up in the course of the development of the problematic of understanding that moves from the question of tradition, through the central analysis of experience, to the analysis of language in the chapters that follow. The analysis of language is tied directly to the explicit engagement with criticism in part 2 of this book. This placement of the analysis of language is due to the fact that the question of language becomes the focus for Gadamer in responding to the criticism by deconstruction. Gadamer's encounter with Derrida in 1981 raised the question of hermeneutics's logocentrism, of whether philosophical hermeneutics stands within the tradition of a metaphysics of presence. This question is what allows Gadamer to really clarify how, as a description of understanding, philosophical hermeneutics is an engagement in the effort to bring to speech again, how philosophical hermeneutics is expressly about listening to the voice of the other.

PART ONE

The Voice of Tradition

CHAPTER ONE

The Philosophical Background
of Philosophical Hermeneutics

§ 1. Phenomenology as a Movement beyond Neo-Kantianism

It would be insufficient for the purpose of establishing the background of philosophical hermeneutics to simply trace the development of hermeneutic theory from Schleiermacher through Dilthey and Heidegger. Although one cannot fully understand Gadamer's position without some recognition of this development—a development that Gadamer himself traces out in various essays and, in part, in *Truth and Method*—the *philosophical* background of Gadamer's thought requires that we follow a different line of development. We have already indicated that, along with his reading of the Greeks, it was Heidegger's hermeneutics of facticity that shaped so decisively Gadamer's thinking in his own studies in Marburg in the 1920s.[1] This was the time of the full flowering of phenomenology as a philosophical movement in Germany. Not only was Heidegger drawing worldwide attention with his lectures in Marburg, but Husserl was still in Freiburg and Scheler continued to determine the course of intellectual currents from his position in Cologne. Even Nicolai Hartmann, who succeeded Paul Natorp in Marburg, pro-claimed to be doing the work of phenomenology.[2] This was also the time when phenomenology established itself more clearly here than elsewhere in opposition to the then dominant philosophical tradition of Neo-Kantianism. The crisis in foundations that gave rise to phenomenology as a rigorous science was due in part to the unclarified presuppositions in the theoreti-cal framework of Neo-Kantianism. In the discoveries of intentionality,

25

categorical intuition, and a new sense of the apriori—not to mention the concept of life-world—phenomenology engaged in a conceptual effort at overcoming the "theoretical attitude" of Neo-Kantianism that was rooted in Cartesianism and the restriction of consciousness to its own content.

Generally speaking, Neo-Kantianism refers to the philosophical movement that turned back to the philosophy of Kant in reaction to the dissatisfaction with the philosophy of Absolute Idealism that was prominent in the middle of the nineteenth century. In particular, what distinguished Neo-Kantianism from other "back to Kant" movements was the emphasis on the "critical" foundation to philosophy that is obtained in privileging the theory of knowledge. No longer was the foundation of philosophy to be provided by formal logic or logic in Hegel's sense. But Neo-Kantianism was by no means a single unified philosophical movement. In Marburg, Neo-Kantianism took shape initially with the work of Friedrich Lange and then by his successor Hermann Cohen, who is attributed with founding the Marburg school of Neo-Kantianism. Cohen emphasized the logical rather than the physiological in reading Kant's first Critique in that the object of knowledge is not given, but is constructed by apriori subjectivity. The rival to this school was the South-West German School of Neo-Kantianism that was associated with the work of Wilhelm Windelband and his student, Heinrich Rickert, and was known principally for working out the relation between knowledge and values. What was held in common for both schools was the "critical way," that is, the transcendental method in which reality is generated by pure thinking.[3]

This effort at overcoming the theoretical attitude (as understood by Neo-Kantians) is true of Husserlian phenomenology at least initially, and it is this same effort that defines Gadamer's own project, not withstanding the fact that Paul Natorp, Gadamer's teacher, was himself a Neo-Kantian. It is not surprising then that Gadamer, despite the fact that he draws so decisively on Heidegger's hermeneutics of facticity for his theory of understanding, and thus wants to separate himself from Husserl's transcendental phenomenology, reads Husserl in a considerably favorable light.[4] The phenomenology of both Husserl and Heidegger will call into question the form of modern ontology found in Neo-Kantianism. Accordingly, the philosophical background of Gadamer's thought begins here in phenomenology in its opposition to Neo-Kantianism.

Nowhere is this opposition of phenomenology to Neo-Kantianism more evident than in Heidegger's 1925 lecture course on "The History of the Concept of Time,"[5] a course at which Gadamer was present. The title of the lecture course is somewhat misleading for there is little said in this course on the concept of time itself; instead, Heidegger is concerned with establishing the conditions for a "phenomenology of history and nature," which is the announced subtitle of the course. In the long preliminary part of this published lecture Heidegger lays out the central insights of phenomenology; it amounts to what the translator of the text calls "a phenomenological reflection upon the history of phenomenology designed to point to the need for Heidegger's own problematic of Dasein, being, and time."[6] More to the point, Heidegger uses this as an occasion to present the merits of Husserlian phenomenology against Neo-Kantianism and at the same time to criticize Husserl for failing to move phenomenology in its proper direction. Heidegger charges that in the end Husserl falls back into the conceptual framework of Neo-Kantianism.

The preliminary part begins with a brief consideration of the situation of philosophy in the second half of the nineteenth century. The collapse of the idealistic systems in the second half of the nineteenth century allowed philosophy to align itself with the situation of science as a whole which was dominated by the worldview of natural science. Philosophy, now defined in opposition to speculation and empty concepts, has the essential character of a theory of science, in which it is constantly oriented to the factual conduct of the sciences themselves. This renewal of philosophy takes place "not in an original return to the matters at issue," but in a return to Kant, which is to say to a positivistic interpretation of Kant. Neo-Kantianism interprets Kant's *Critique of Pure Reason* as a theory of experience that is nothing other than scientific experience. But in carrying out a theory of scientific experience along Kantian lines, this scientific research gets caught up in a return to consciousness. According to Heidegger, "even though consciousness became a theme in scientific psychology and in epistemology in completely different ways, it nevertheless remained and until now has remained the tacit thematic field of consideration."[7] Thus, despite the fact that Neo-Kantianism launched a strong opposition to psychology regarded as a natural science, this did not prevent the elevation of psychology, as a theory of consciousness, to the basic science of philosophy. When the work of Cohen, who had initially looked to Kant for a theory of scientific experience, was taken up by the South-West German School of Neo-Kantianism in the work of Windelband and Rickert, the theoretical clarification of science was pushed more and more in the direction of the logical structure of scientific representation. It was reduced, in Heidegger's words, "to an empty methodology."[8]

It is in this context that we encounter Husserl. Under the influence of his teacher Brentano, Husserl extended his initial research in the logic of mathematics to the fundamental concepts of thinking as such. The results of his work on the problem of a scientific logic produced the two volume *Logical Investigations.* This ground-breaking work in phenomenology appears as a challenge to Neo-Kantianism in a double sense. Phenomenology not only corrects the false priority of self-consciousness, it also reorients the task of philosophy away from theoretical construction and the transcendental justification of scientific knowledge in particular. Gadamer's comments on this in his essay "The Phenomenological Movement" are strikingly parallel to Heidegger's analysis in *The History of the Concept of Time.* Gadamer writes:

> In contrast to [the position of Neo-Kantianism], Husserl's phenomenological approach meant from the very beginning the posing of a new task. Instead of the constructive mastery of reality, which has its ideal in the mathematical formalism of the natural science, the ideal of knowledge for Husserl was intuition, the concrete givenness of what is perceived. Thus he had the "natural attitude" of "immediately living" consciousness in view just as much as the convincing certainty of mathematical deductions. What interested him about the knowledge of the world in the "natural attitude" was certainly neither the fact actually encountered nor even the factical performance [*faktische Vollzug*] in which it was perceived. Rather, he was interested exclusively in the "phenomenon" in its essential nature and the corresponding apprehension of that essence by acts of consciousness. (PH 152/GW3 124)

Without directly saying so, the above passage indicates what the correction to the priority of self-consciousness is, namely, the priority of self-givenness in intuitive self-evidence. The significance of this emphasis on self-givenness cannot be overstated, for in it lies the challenge to any representational view of knowledge. For Husserl, we do not refer to things in terms of inner representation; knowing is not at all a matter of a subject existing for itself that then chooses its objects. The apprehension of the phenomenon in acts of consciousness is always of a consciousness correlated with the phenomenal objects. This correlation expresses what is meant by intentionality.

In the 1925 lecture course Heidegger explicitly defends Husserl's concept of intentionality against its Neo-Kantian misinterpretation. He begins by pointing to the way in which intentionality, as the manner in which I am directed toward objects, structures lived experience (*Erlebnisse*). In every lived experience I am directed toward something. In natural perception— for example, in the perception of a chair which I find upon entering a room—I move about my world not in detached perception, but "in order to orient myself, to pave the way in dealing with something."[9] It is a mistaken interpretation of intentionality to say that it is the coordination of a psychic occurrence inside with a physical thing outside. Such an interpretation could easily be refuted by the fact of hallucinations in which case intentionality, as directing itself toward something, is not true of every perception. Heidegger asks us to consider the interpretation more pointedly. Is it not the case that even in hallucinations the deceptive perception as such remains a directing-itself-toward? The point is that intentionality is not a property that adheres to perception, but that perception is "intrinsically intentional." Every attempt at retaining the distinction between psychical and physical, consciousness and reality, spirit and nature hinders the efforts at arriving at the original thematic field of phenomenological investigation. It is precisely this that is misinterpreted by the Neo-Kantian Rickert. He reserves intentionality for the comportment relating to judgment, but drops it for representing. Heidegger insists that he maintains this position because he is trapped in the dogma that representing does not get out to the object. For Rickert, representing is not knowing.

It is only when Heidegger pursues the matter of intentionality further that the problem of Husserl's falling back into Neo-Kantianism emerges. After discussing the basic character of phenomenology in § 9 "The Clarification of the Name 'Phenomenology' " in which one can already see Heidegger's distinctive interpretation of phenomenology emerging,[10] Heidegger asks: How is intentionality as the structure of lived experience first given? How, in other words, are the comportments in which the structure of intentionality is read accessible? According to Husserl, the accessibility of the comportments is through the phenomenological field of pure consciousness, which is for Husserl the sphere of absolute being. In positing pure consciousness as the sphere of absolute being, Heidegger accuses Husserl of failing to take up the question of the being of intentional acts and the question of the meaning of being which would naturally follow in a genuine turn to the matters themselves. Husserl's falling back is consequently attributable to a lack of genuine radical inquiry into the matters themselves. In connection with this, Heidegger is more than suspicious of Husserl's further refinement of the task of phenomenology in the *Ideas*. Husserl saw the need for a further reduction beyond the eidetic reduction that would achieve for the first time an idealism of a really transcendental character. The ultimate foundation for a rigorous science is obtained through a transcendental reduction, grounded in a transcendental ego. The transcendental reduction suspends or brackets all posited reality for the sake of the phenomena and thus provides science with a new clarified basis. In its fundamental outline, this position remains close to Neo-Kantianism. In *The Basic Problems of Phenomenology*, a lecture course given two years later, Heidegger writes: "The view [of Neo-Kantianism] that knowledge equals judgment, truth equals judgedness equals objectivity equals valid sense, became so dominant that even phenomenology was infected by this untenable conception of knowledge, as appears in the further investigation of Husserl's works, above all, in the *Ideas toward a Pure Phenomenology and Phenomenological Philosophy* (1913)."[11] Heidegger insists in the 1925 lecture course that it was Dilthey who was a major contributor to the further advancement of phenomenology. Heidegger goes so far as to say that Dilthey was the first to understand the aim of phenomenology. What Heidegger means here is that Dilthey is credited with formulating a psychology that is concerned with life itself in its structure, as the basic reality of history, and that this psychology stands in marked contrast to a psychology fashioned after natural science.[12] "Man" is not regarded for Dilthey as a thing of nature to be explained by other universal laws of events, but is understood as a living person actively involved in history. Heidegger wants to credit Dilthey for moving in the direction of his own project. Phenomenology, reinterpreted by Heidegger, is to take as its subject matter not just the theoretical but also the practical, and this means the factical life, the great "fact of life."[13]

Ironically, for the same general reason that Heidegger wants to give credit to Dilthey in this lecture course, namely, because Dilthey is concerned with factical life, Gadamer wants to do the same for Husserl. In the concept of the life-world (*Lebenswelt*) Husserl is seen to be continuing his project of getting at the pre-reflective givenness of things; in this case, the concept of the life-world serves to get behind the objectivism that has its roots in Galilean science. Gadamer is well aware that the turn to the life-world has its precedence in the earlier philosophy of life that is found in the works of Nietzsche, Simmel, Bergson, and Dilthey. Nevertheless, Gadamer can still read Husserl favorably because of this explicit thematization of the concept of the life-world.

The issue for Gadamer is not the place of Husserl's *The Crisis of the European Sciences* (1936) (in which the concept of the life-world is explicitly made thematic) within the phenomenological movement; that is, it is not a question of whether or not Husserl is changing his position late in his life under the influence of Heidegger's analytic of Dasein in *Being and Time*. There is evidence to suggest that the concept of the life-world was already formulated by Husserl in the 1920s.[14] For Gadamer, the issue of the life-world is Husserl's insight "that the task of justifying knowledge did not mean scientific knowledge as much as it did the totality of our natural experience of the world" (PH 152/GW3 124). In this sense the introduction of the concept of the life-world must be seen in the context of the movement beyond Neo-Kantianism.

But Gadamer is by no means blinded to the inherent difficulties in Husserl's analysis of the life-world. Because Husserl's style of thinking blurs the distinction between self-correction and self-criticism, Gadamer feels that the concept of the life-world can be read in an ambiguous way. On the one hand, the concept of life-world describes the originary phenomenological approach that Husserl chose for his phenomenological investigation that distinguishes him and his philosophical interest from the dominant Neo-Kantianism and positivistic scientism (PH 182/GW3 147). In this sense the concept of the life-world is interpreted broadly by Gadamer to indicate the intention of phenomenology to get behind the whole of scientific experience to a wide field of everyday experience. It is a return to a pre-given world that does not abandon reason per se, but only the objectivistic reason that reductively extends positive science to the whole of life. On the other hand, it is "a new self-criticism" that would appear to make Husserl's goal to found philosophy as a rigorous science attainable. Husserl's description in the *Crisis* of the history of objectivism that arises out of the influence of Galilean science simply serves to bring Husserl's phenomenological program into explicit historical relief.

Gadamer recognizes, however, that the old goal of a transcendental phenomenology, based on the transcendental ego, is never left behind. When Husserl notes in the *Crisis* that the "dream is over" for philosophy as a rigorous science, Gadamer insists that we interpret this as a view that Husserl did not share. Actually, Husserl is challenged by this pronouncement to renew his reflections—in this case, it is historical reflection that is needed to offset that danger of the very future of philosophy. And it is in this context that Gadamer interprets the *Crisis* to be concerned with carrying out a really defensible transcendental reduction.

When we view the volume as a whole, the principle of its composition is unmistakable. It is concerned with carrying out a really

> defensible transcendental reduction. The elaborate survey of the history of objectivism serves the purpose primarily of bringing his own phenomenological program into explicit historical relief. A "transformation of the task of knowledge" is achieved through phenomenology. There is no more assumed experiential basis for it. Even that universal belief in the world, which, as the natural reflective life of man, supports the ground of experience in every case of doubt regarding the contents of experience must be suspended and must find its constitution in the transcendental ego. To that extent, the method of phenomenology, in contrast to all scientific methods, is a method dealing with that which has no foundation, the way of a "transcendental experience," not an empirical induction. For it must first create its ground for itself. (PH 159–60/GW3 130)

The doctrine of the life-world, which points to the original horizon of lived meanings, is intended to make the transcendental reduction flawless.

The question in Gadamer's mind is whether this attempt to secure transcendental phenomenology as the final meaning of the history of philosophy, through historical self-clarification, can really be successful. Gadamer is most suspicious at the point at which Husserl attributes historical considerations to transcendental phenomenology. For Husserl, the self-reflection that is tied to this new form of science would culminate in a "universal praxis" of humanity. To the extent that Husserl retains the connection between philosophy and science in this new form of science in which there is a universal account of things derived from life interests, this is indeed the promise. Gadamer wants to know if there is not an illusion present in the claim "that from science—in whatever style—rational decisions can be derived that would constitute a 'universal praxis' " (PH 196/GW3 158). The mistake is to think that behind our practical decisions there lies a knowledge based on the application of science. Gadamer does not think that the gulf between practical judgment, which characterizes human activity in the life-world, and the anonymous validity of science can be bridged in this way.

But Gadamer's suspicion at this point is not so overwhelming that the fundamental significance of the life-world is overlooked. "What confronts us here is not a synthesis of theory and practice nor science in a new style, but rather the prior, practical political limitation of the monopolistic claims of science and a new critical consciousness with respect to the scientific character of philosophy itself" (PH 196/GW3 158). The issue for Gadamer becomes the issue of an account of hermeneutic experience that will address the problem of "reason in the age of science." In connection with this Gadamer will link the older tradition of practical philosophy to the "moral impulse" that lies at the basis of Husserl's idea of a new kind of life-world praxis.

§ 2. Kierkegaard's Philosophy of Existence

When Gadamer concludes his essay "The Science of the Life-world" with the claim that what confronts us in the notion of the life-world is "a new critical consciousness with respect to the scientific character of philosophy itself," we could say, with proper qualifications, that this is also true of the Kierkegaardian philosophy of existence. In its own way, it too emerges as a corrective to the one-sidedness of the scientific methodologism of Neo-Kantianism.[15] In following the development of phenomenology to Heidegger's hermeneutics of facticity, and ultimately Gadamer's own project, we must recongnize that one of the strands that weaves itself into the phenomenological movement, broadly understood, is Kierkegaard's philosophy of existence. This is not to suggest that *Being and Time* represents a philosophy of existence, for everything Heidegger has said about his own work contradicts such a claim.[16] At the same time, there would be something insufficient in an account of hermeneutic phenomenology if the Kierkegaardian influence is denied by substituting Dilthey for Kierkegaard. This is especially true considering that it is Gadamer's position that we are ultimately moving toward. Not only does he claim that the philosophy of existence is decisive for Heidegger, that Heidegger was influenced by Kierkegaard early on with the appearance of the German translation of the Danish, and is thus essential to the whole development of a hermeneutics of facticity;[17] but, more importantly, it is decisive for Gadamer himself. Gadamer tells us that early on in his life his reading of Kierkegaard's *Either-Or* had a profound impression upon him; the second part of the book in particular, he notes, "awoke in me a sympathy for Judge Wilhelm and, unsuspectingly, for historical continuity."[18] Elsewhere, in commenting on his own point of departure for an analysis of hermeneutic experience, Gadamer indicates how Kierkegaard's theory of contemporaneity helped in the conceptual labor of posing a counter-position to understanding at a distance.[19]

What is it, though, that is so decisive for Heidegger and Gadamer in Kierkegaard's philosophy of existence? Interestingly enough, it is a concept that

Kierkegaard ultimately traces to Aristotle, namely, repetition (*Gjentagelse*).[20] There is no exaggeration in John Caputo's remark that what we call hermeneutics "defends the view that repetition is possible and indeed that everything in hermeneutics turns on its possibility."[21]

In the broadest terms, the character of hermeneutics in Heidegger's hermeneutic phenomenology of the 1920s pertains to the opening of life, from within life, toward itself. Hermeneutics is about the awakening of life toward itself. Repetition, quite simply, is the name for this movement of life. What is called repetition by Kierkegaard becomes for Heidegger *Wiederholung*, the opening of life that occurs by retrieving, literally fetching-back, possibilities in life. In *Being and Time* there are several senses in which this repetition is in play. We see it in the hermeneutic situation of the "hermeneutic circle" as the projective stretch in existence in which Dasein makes its way about. More importantly, we also see it in Heidegger's analysis of the temporal determination of the Being of Dasein. In terms of temporality, Dasein's resolve manifests itself as a retrieval: Dasein takes over its past through repetition by fetching back time and again its possibilities. In its fullest sense, in retrieval/repetition Dasein comes *toward* its authentic potentiality for Being when it comes *back* to itself, when it comes back to that which it has been all along.[22]

Now, if it is the case that Gadamer's philosophical hermeneutics does indeed take over as its starting-point the historicity of understanding gained from a hermeneutics of facticity, then we should expect to find repetition here as well. Certainly one does not have to look far to see how repetition is a feature of hermeneutic experience. The activity of understanding—the task of appropriating the self-same message of the transmitted text to the situation of the present—is nothing less than an exercise in repetition. Philosophical hermeneutics recognizes that temporality demands a creative repetition in all our projects.

In order to see precisely how repetition is in play in hermeneutics, we have to see, first of all, how it is understood by Kierkegaard. The concept of repetition is the focus of Kierkegaard's analysis in the book *Repetition, An Essay in Experimenting Psychology*. The pseudonymous author of *Repetition*, Constantin Constantius, reports on a conversation with a young man who is madly in love with a young girl. As it turns out, the young man's love for the girl is "poetic," he has turned this relationship with the girl into an "ideality." The love for the girl is a love that he recollects but cannot repeat, he cannot make the relationship real by living in the ongoing faithfulness of hard work that the relationship demands. As a consequence of this situation, the young man is melancholic, he is most unhappy.

> He was deeply and fervently in love, that was clear, and yet a few days later he was able to recollect his love. He was essentially through with the entire relationship. In beginning it, he took such a tremendous step that he leaped over life. If the girl dies tomorrow, it will make no essential difference; he will throw himself down again, his eyes will fill with tears again, he will repeat the poet's words again. What a curious dialectic! (R 136)

As one would suspect from Kierkegaard, the issue here is not limited to the characters in this mini-drama; it is not really about just this young man and his willingness to commit to the relationship, reversing the course of his love for the girl that at this point in the story is such that it essentially leaps over life. For Kierkegaard the story is an occasion to make a point about existence itself, about the ability to move forward *in* life as such. All life is repetition, and the question of living is about the extent to which real repetition is possible. This question is, for Kierkegaard, *the* question of modern philosophy.

> [T]his question [whether repetition is possible] will play a very important role in modern philosophy, for *repetition* is a crucial expression for what "recollection" was to the Greeks. Just as they taught that all knowing is a recollection, modern philosophy will teach that all life is a repetition. . . . Repetition and recollection are the same movement, except in opposite directions, for what is recollected has been, is repeated backward, whereas genuine repetition is recollected forward. Repetition, therefore, if it is possible, makes a person happy, whereas recollection makes him unhappy. (R 131)

This passage tells us several things. First of all, repetition for Kierkegaard is not recollection, but the contrast is subtle inasmuch as repetition and recollection "are the same movement." Here recollection is equivalent to Platonic recollection understood in its traditional sense as a speculative grasp of existence that is itself a movement away from existence. Recollection wants to solidify becoming, to see the present in terms of the past by repeating backwards to what was already—an existence finished, in a sense already at its end. In the case of the young man, he recollects his love by retreating backward to poetic eternity. Recollection thus pertains to the peculiar relation between time and eternity where temporal existence is the repetition of eternal pre-existence. But this Platonic recollection could just as well be Hegelian recollection. Kierkegaard tells us that "repetition proper is what has mistakenly been called mediation" (R 148). If mediation as recollective movement brings to unity thought and being, ideality and reality, existence as a movement of repetition keeps the two separate. This is most evident in ethical existence that is characterized by Kierkegaard as the "volitional activity in which [the individual] struggles to become a living expression of the ideal he has reflectively conceived."[23] For Kierkegaard the struggle for this identity of thought and being is the real constant, for ethical life is essentially historically emergent.

With respect to the claim in the above passage then that recollection takes place in the order of knowledge whereas repetition is in the order of existence, it appears that Kierkegaard does indeed have Hegel in mind. Existence—temporal becoming—cannot adequately be explained by the logical process of mediation, for logic itself, Kierkegaard insists, cannot admit of movement. The order of knowledge is timeless and Hegel's Logic in particular, in which the logical and the real are closely associated in a way that Aristotle could not imagine, interprets reality as a timeless, rational process where logical necessity rules. But Kierkegaard argues, specifically in *Concluding Unscientific Postscript*, a logical system of existence is impossible, for in such a system existence itself is lost; the process of mediation cannot account for the temporal movement of self toward its possibilities. Kierkegaard thinks the Greeks knew better than Hegel that mediation does not explain movement.

> There is no explanation in our age as to how mediation takes place, whether it results from the motion of two factors and in what sense it is already contained in them, or whether it is something new that is added, and if so, how. In this connection, the Greek view of the concept of κίνησις [motion, change] corresponds to the modern category " transition" and should be give close attention. (R 149)

The Greeks, in other words, either denied movement, or claimed that all is movement, but did not presume to account for movement in mediation.

In his *Papers*, Kierkegaard provides a more explicit account of what he means here. Mediation, he contends, helped to make the *transcendence* of movement—real movement (κίνησις)—illusory, but this transcendence of movement that is, in effect, the sphere of freedom is precisely what is to be captured by repetition.

> When movement is allowed in relation to repetition in the sphere of freedom, then the development becomes different from the logical development in that the *transition becomes* [*vorder*]. In logic, transition is movement's silence, whereas in the sphere of freedom it becomes. Thus, in logic, when possibility, by means of the immanence of thought, has determined itself as actuality, one only disturbs the silent self-inclosure of the logical process by talking about movement and transition. In the sphere of freedom, however, possibility remains and actuality emerges as a transcendence. Therefore, when Aristotle long ago said that the transition from possibility to actuality is a κίνησις [motion, change], he was not speaking of logical possibility and actuality but of freedom's and therefore he properly posits movement. (R 309–10)[24]

Genuine repetition then is the movement of transcendence from potentiality to actuality in the sphere of freedom. But strictly speaking, repetition is not something that occurs in freedom, it is freedom itself.[25] To become a self, as defined by freedom, requires then repetition, that renewal of a commitment one has made before.[26] For the young man to be happy he must have a "resolve" through which his love is made real.[27] In the end the young man is not capable of this and he *flees* in the face of it.

In characterizing repetition in this way, as the work of selfhood and existence, the scope of the category of repetition within Kierkegaard's philosophy becomes apparent. As we already mentioned, the category of repetition, first of all, enters into the choosing of oneself that is demanded of ethical existence. But here Kierkegaard is not alone. This repetition of choosing of oneself runs parallel to the activity of practical excellence in Aristotle's analysis of practical life.[28] According to Aristotle repetition appears in the work of living (well) insofar as it is practice that brings to fruition the natural potential for virtue: "we did not acquire the faculty of sight or hearing by repeatedly seeing or repeatedly listening, but the other way about—because we had the sense we began to use them . . . the virtues on the other hand we acquire by first having actually practiced them."[29] For Aristotle the virtues are not acquired by nature but by nature there is the capacity for virtue which is them brought to maturity by practice, and practice toward the good is something engendered out of a lifetime.

Of course this original potentiality for excellence may or may not be realized in one's life just as in Kierkegaardian fashion one can fail to become a self. There is, however, a fundamental difference between Kierkegaard and Aristotle that should be noted. In Aristotle's model of ethical development the repetition is linked to the formation of habits which affect future choices. Kierkegaard, on the other hand, makes no provision for habit; the resolute choice is repeated anew on each occasion.[30]

Within Kierkegaard's philosophy, the category of repetition, as an expression of the proper relation between being and becoming, also pertains to the proper character of Christian existence. The question of repetition for Christian existence is how the relation between time and eternity is thought differently when eternity is the goal of existence and not something behind (prior to) existence as the original for the image. Kierkegaard's Christian perspective, unlike the Platonic perspective, does not move backwards from time to eternal pre-existence and to find the theological self as recollected presence. Rather, the individual moves forward to a presence yet to be realized, to a self that is not yet. In recollecting forward, in this temporal movement of the self towards its future possibilities, one recommits oneself to the possibilities that are recognized as one's own. Such recommitment/repetition is metaphysical as the "moment" in which one is contemporaneous with Christ. To be in the moment means to be present in the presence of the eternal in time. For religious existence the moment is not an abstraction from time as it is for aesthetic existence. That is to say, for religious existence the moment is not simply a succession of moments which are disconnected from one's past and future, and neither is it disconnected from the eternal. "Eternity is a qualification of existence which transfigures the temporality of the self in the moment of decision."[31] The eternal intersecting the temporal is of course a paradox, but this is precisely what Christian experience entails for Kierkegaard. The point is that the repetition will move through time without negating time. Past possibilities of action become future possibilities and are repeated in the moment of decision.

From what has been said, one can understand why Kierkegaard speaks about a possibility of repetition, for it requires courage to will repetition. One can also understand why Kierkegaard would say that if repetition is possible, it makes one happy. It is the "unhappy consciousness" that has its identity with itself separated by the beyond of eternity. In repetition one escapes the condition of longing for the "other" of one's self.[32]

Finally, in linking repetition to the future, to freedom itself, it should be apparent that genuine repetition is fundamentally dynamic and should be distinguished from a static sense of repetition. A static repetition repeats the same; it is a literal recurrence analogous to recollection as the reproduction of life. A dynamic repetition, on the other hand, is creative as the production of life itself. For Kierkegaard, as we have seen, the dynamic repetition is the very production of self. Moreover, this dynamic repetition is inseparable from the character of truth in ethico-religious existence. Recall how Kierkegaard describes this truth in the *Postscript*: "an objective uncertainty held fast appropriation process of the most passionate inwardness."[33] As an objective uncertainty, truth is not the identity of thought and being; it is rather an appropriation process in which the individual continually approximates the ideal (of its own being), and thus truth is the "self-activity of personal appropriation." Static repetition does not belong here. When repetition is static it is, at best, related to truth as an indicator of something being true. The test of scientific objectivity, for example, displays the feature of repeatability, but what it repeats is always the same; the repeatability is an indication that something is the case. Dynamic repetition, on the other hand, as a feature of ethico-religious existence is more closely connected to the very emergence of truth. Dynamic repetition is what must be gone through in order to arrive at the true: truth is in the "how" (truth is subjectivity).

This distinction between dynamic and static repetition will prove to be decisive in a consideration of hermeneutic experience. It is by virtue of human finitude that I subject everything to review and revision, and consequently, a dynamic repetition would seem to be universal for the kind of knowledge at issue in hermeneutic experience. Gadamer's claim that understanding is always understanding differently makes sense from the from the point of view of dynamic repetition. In dynamic (hermeneutic) repetition, what is understood is not merely repeated. The event of understanding is not a mere re-production of meaning. Despite the fact that Gadamer relies heavily on the language of Plato, which is to say the language of $\mu\nu\eta\mu o\sigma\acute{\upsilon}\nu\eta$ and $\acute{\alpha}\nu\acute{\alpha}\mu\nu\eta\sigma\iota\varsigma$, the event of understanding is not a simple reiteration of an original.[34]

A dynamic repetition, then, can be displayed in all the dimensions of hermeneutic experience. A dynamic repetition is what defines the character of the presentation (*Darstellung*) in aesthetic understanding in which there is an "accretion of reality" (*Zuwachs an Sein*). A dynamic repetition is what defines the character of historical understanding where the tradition speaks again, speaks in a *new* voice. A dynamic repetition also identifies the basic trait of linguistic understanding insofar as our finite discourse "brings a totality of meaning into play, without being able to express it totally" (TM 458/GW1 462). In all these instances, it is never a question of willing repetition as it is for Kierkegaard. But this difference is understandable in as much as it is not a question of selfhood for hermeneutics. In a sense, the paradox, for which repetition is demanded, shifts. For Gadamer the paradox is not of the eternal in time, but of the selfsame message that, by virtue of tradition, is always understood differently.[35]

§ 3. Heidegger's Hermeneutics of Facticity

Within the constraints of the task at hand, namely, of providing the philosophical background for Gadamer's hermeneutics, the significance of Heidegger's project for Gadamer's own work cannot be worked out in full detail. For that a separate work is required. Even within the scope of this book, it remains to be seen how the work of the later Heidegger serves to guide Gadamer's own path of thought. The more economical account provided here focuses on two considerations in Heidegger's hermeneutic phenomenology, in which one must include Heidegger's hermeneutics of facticity (1919–23),[36] that are most germane to Gadamer's own work. The first consideration is determined by the scope of the philosophical background as it has been presented thus far. We need to see how hermeneutics is incorporated into the phenomenological movement such that phenomenology is itself transformed. Additionally, because the historicity of understanding plays such a crucial role in the development of a philosophical hermeneutics in *Truth and Method*, a second consideration must be given to Heidegger's analysis of the historicity of existence.

The incorporation of hermeneutics into phenomenology is guided by the very project that gave rise to phenomenology in the first place, namely, the movement beyond the theoretical attitude of Neo-Kantianism. Through the lecture courses that are now being published in the collected edition of Heidegger's works, we now know that Heidegger's philosophical project was already taking shape early on in the 1920s.[37] At this time, Heidegger was attempting to bring together his philosophical concern for the question of being, which was shaped by his reading of historical and theological sources, with the insights of Husserlian phenomenology.[38] From the work of his dissertation and his immersion in the scholastic philosophy of realism,

Heidegger understood the order of being to be simply "whatever can be experienced and lived, in the absolute sense whatever stands over against consciousness, the 'robust' reality which irresistibly forces itself upon consciousness and can never nor again be put aside and eliminated."[39] This meant for Heidegger that the analysis of being must pass through what comes to be the central concept throughout the lecture courses during this time, namely, the concept of factical life. Here the question of being is not yet explicitly formulated as such, at least not in the way it comes to be expressed in *Being and Time*, but is simply the question of being in the historical situatedness of factical life.

Gadamer has pointed out that this word "facticity" was initially used by Rothe and other theologians of the post-Hegelian generation as a word in the dispute over faith in the Resurrection. When this word was taken over by Heidegger it remained fused with the concept of life. "Facticity means the fact [*Faktum*] in its being a fact [*Faktum-sein*], that is, that behind which and back of which one cannot go" (GW3 422). Facticity is, in a sense, the particularity of life that is inescapable, designating the "character of our own Dasein," Dasein in its "there."[40] This notion of factical life we also find in Dilthey (and also in Nietzsche, Bergson, and Natorp, according to Gadamer), but when Heidegger speaks of a "*hermeneutics of* facticity" there is no doubt that it is Kierkegaard (the "how" of existence) and Aristotle (life understood as self-movement) who echo most decisively in the understanding of this notion.[41] A hermeneutics of facticity pertains to the way in which this factical life is accessed and explicated,[42] which is to say it designates the manner of the self-interpretation of factical life: factical life lays itself out (*auslegen*). It does this, not by bringing concepts to bear on it, but as itself "a kind of conceptual speaking that wants to hold onto its origin, and with that its own life's breath [*Lebensatem*], when it becomes translated into the form of a theoretical statement" (GW3 422). Just as for Kierkegaard the Hegelian logic cannot explain the movement of life, so too for Heidegger life cannot be grasped in theoretical reflection but only in its enactment (*Vollzug*). Hermeneutics (of facticity) is thus neither exegesis in its traditional sense, nor a theory of interpretation as in Dilthey, but the manner by which existence is awakened to itself.

How, though, does this hermeneutics of facticity, constitute a movement beyond Neo-Kantianism? In these early lectures, and especially in the "Aristotle-Introduction" that was sent to Marburg, Heidegger maintains that philosophy itself must be understood in terms of factical life. Philosophy must take its departure from factical life experience and always turn back into factical life experience. All philosophical research, in other words, takes its orientation from the lived situation out of which and for the sake of which one is inquiring. As a consequence of this determination of philosophy, philosophical research is from now on hermeneutical, as the manner of grasping something concretely in act. In Heidegger's words: "philosophical research is the explicit actualization [*Vollzug*] of a basic movement of factical life and maintains itself always within factical life."[43] The hermeneutics of facticity, in effect, names the very operation of philosophy.

The significance of this new approach cannot be overstated. In Gadamer's essays, in which he gives an account of this period of transformation in phenomenology, he remarks about the impact that Heidegger had on him and others in showing the way out of the "circle of reflection." He recalls specifically how in his lectures Heidegger had pointed out the significance of the scholastic distinction between *actus signatus* and *actus exercitus*. As Gadamer explains it:

> There is a difference between saying "I see something" and "I am saying that I see something." But the signification "I am saying that . . ." is not the first awareness of the act. The act originally taking place is already such an act, which is to say it is already something in which my own operation is vitally present to me. (PH 123/GW4 17)[44]

There is meaning "in the exercise," in the doing, before it becomes the property of a theoretical consciousness. A hermeneutics of facticity, soon to become a hermeneutic phenomenology, wants to provide that description of the 'here I am' within the act of existing. Accordingly, "knowing" is a matter of interpreting that in which and from which I already am. It is a knowing that takes place "in the exercise," and as such it is first an event of being before it is our own doing.

In the 1921–22 winter semester course, "Phenomenological Interpretations to Aristotle," Heidegger described this "hermeneutical situation" in terms of the sense of having (*Haben*).[45] That there is first factical life, that life makes its claim upon me, means that my questioning is determined in advance by the way in which I *have* things. This having is not to be understood as possession, but as the simple apprehension and determination of an object. The hermeneutic situation is thus one in which the object is held and already grasped, and philosophy is understood accordingly as the knowing comportment with respect to this holding. Philosophical research differs sharply from scientific research, as we find expressed by Neo-Kantianism, because scientific research proceeds in abstraction from the full concretization of factical life. If philosophical research remains bound to the impulses of science, a claim that in retrospect Heidegger himself makes against this early formulation of his project, it can only be understood as a non-theoretical science, at least in the traditional understanding of the theoretical.

In the 1922 summer semester course on Aristotle, Heidegger again set out to reinterpret the basis and essential character of the theoretical, this time drawing from the first book of Aristotle's *Metaphysics*.[46] The opening line of that book, which we usually translate as "all men by nature desire to know," becomes under Heidegger's guidance "the urge to live in seeing, the absorption in the visible, is constitutive of how the human being is."[47] The most obvious difference in Heidegger's reformulation of this classic statement is the interpretation of knowing ($\epsilon i\delta\acute{\epsilon}\nu\alpha\iota$) as a continuous progression of seeing. More important for us is his interpretation of the starting point of this progression in what Aristotle calls experience ($\acute{\epsilon}\mu\pi\epsilon\iota\varrho\acute{\iota}\alpha$). According to Heidegger, experience includes the double character of getting around (*Umgehen*) and know-how (*Auskennen*). If all the other stages of life are to be understood as a development of this starting point, which is never left behind, then the character of research in general pertains to *an interpretive moving about and making one's way in the business of life.*

But in what particular way is philosophy this interpretive moving about in the business of life? According to Aristotle, philosophy begins in wonder, first at difficulties close at hand, then at difficulties about greater matters. In response to these difficulties one pursues knowledge in order to understand, that is, philosophy is done for its own sake. For Aristotle this is borne out by the actual course of events, and then he adds that philosophy takes place in the space of leisure: "for it was when almost all the necessities of life were supplied, both for rest [$\varrho\alpha\sigma\tau\acute{\omega}\nu\eta$] and tarrying [$\delta\iota\alpha\gamma\omega\gamma\acute{\eta}$], that such thinking [$\phi\varrho\acute{o}\nu\eta\sigma\iota\varsigma$] began to be sought."[48] Despite the word that Aristotle uses to designate thinking here, we know that what Aristotle is after in this context is authentic understanding ($\sigma o\phi\acute{\iota}\alpha$). Here, then, our question becomes intensified: How is philosophy an interpretive moving about within this halt in the pressing business of life? According to Heidegger, the tarrying, which is the tarrying of $\theta\epsilon\omega\varrho\epsilon\hat{\iota}\nu$, "bestows a different tempo to life, which proves to be the very essence of life, life at its fullest."[49] The theoretical life is a movement of life, a way of going along with the world, but in a different tempo. It is, to use the language from his "Aristotle-Introduction" written later in the same year, a way of making one's way in life by "taking-a-pause."[50] In tarrying we are drawn back to the questions of life as a whole, but not life in the abstract; rather, with respect to δια-γωγη, we are drawn into the passing of life, how it is carried through to its fullness (*voll-zogen*), and so takes (its) place. In the halt in the pressing busyness of life, there is the opportunity to discover life because life is given its autonomy, at least for a while. In this reading, then, θεωρία, as the pure beholding of authentic understanding, is the way to be in which life has first and last autonomy. "In this original movement we discover the true sense of life as life, in which the ultimate sense of its movement is fulfilled."[51]

But in saying this we have to see, at the same time, how Heidegger has not strayed far from Kierkegaard. We should recall that for Kierkegaard as for Heidegger the task is to awaken life to itself, a task that is accomplished for Kierkegaard in repetition. Repetition is the movement of life whereby life comes to itself. Heidegger's hermeneutics of facticity wants to say the same thing; it too is about repetition. Heidegger appears to use the word *repetition* for the first time in the 1921/22 lecture course on Aristotle when he comments on a passage by Rickert in which Rickert uses the word in his criticism of philosophies of life. In the quoted passage Rickert says that one should give up seeing in philosophies of life a mere repetition (*Wiederholen*) of life. Philosophy means to create and the insight into the distance that separates the created from life must leave life and philosophy content.[52] Immediately following the quoted passage Heidegger responds: "everything depends on the meaning of repetition. Philosophy is a fundamental how of life itself, such that it fetches it back [*wieder-holt*] properly, seizes it back from falling away [from itself]. This seizing itself back, as radical research, is life."[53] Against Rickert's separation of knowing from life, Heidegger claims that knowing is not in the concept but in life. And insofar as there is a duality between object and knowledge for phenomenology, phenomenology too stands under this conviction.[54]

All this is carried over into the announced project in *Being and Time*, where, in an explicit hermeneutic phenomenology, factical life is now Dasein and the determination of the Being of Dasein becomes the issue for the sake of the ultimate question concerning the meaning of Being.[55] The existential analytic of Dasein that comprises the first part of *Being and Time* will not be a deduction from the "emptiest of concepts" but precisely that description of the experience of being-here (Dasein). Such a description is not to be confused with a philosophy of life (Dilthey) or philosophy of existence (Jaspers), for the descriptive analysis of Dasein is to be an analysis of the ontological structure of human reality. At the same time, Heidegger's ontological analysis shares with these "philosophies" the view that being here, existence, is always prior to the reflective ego. In taking over Dilthey's claim that "we cannot go behind life," Heidegger, in his own way, wants to point to the habitual experience of circumspective concern from which reflective experience is derived. Quite pointedly, in *Being and Time* the theoretical attitude emerges as a secondary phenomenon to the pre-reflective basis of our cognition. Hermeneutic phenomenology is an articulation of this experience that precedes the "theoretical" encounter with the world.

Heidegger's articulation of the distinctive character of hermeneutic phenomenology is for the most part well known, the formal expression of which is found in section 7. Heidegger traces the concept of phenomenology to its Greek roots: φαινόμενον and λόγος. The Greek expression φαινόμενον is derived from the verb φαίνεσθαι which means to show itself. Φαίνω means that which shows itself, the manifest. The φα is related to the Greek φῶς as that wherein something can be manifest, brought to light. Phenomenon thus signifies that which shows itself in itself. This is what the Greeks identified with *ta onta*, the things that are. Λόγος, which gets translated as "reason," "judgment," "concept," "definition," "ground," or "relationship," pertains fundamentally to discourse or speech. But speech itself must be interpreted. Aristotle understood the function of discourse as ἀποφαίνεσθαι. What is conveyed in discourse is also a letting something be seen. In genuine discourse, what is said is drawn from what the talk is about; that is, genuine discourse lets us see something from the very thing which the discourse is about. Taken together, "'phenomenology' means ἀποφαίνεσθαι τὰ φαινόμενα—to let that which shows itself be seen from itself in the very way in which it shows itself from itself'" (SZ 34). This formal meaning of the term expresses, for Heidegger, the real sense of Husserl's maxim "To the things themselves!"

Beyond this formal meaning of phenomenology, Heidegger then indicates the hermeneutical character of the investigation:

> Our investigation itself will show that the meaning of phenomenological description as a method lies in *interpretation*. The λογος of the phenomenology of Dasein has the character of ἑρμηνεύειν, through which the authentic meaning of Being, and also those basic structures of Being which Dasein itself possesses, are *made known*

to Dasein's understanding of Being. The phenomenology of Dasein
is a *hermeneutic* in the primordial signification of this word, where
it designates the business of interpreting. (SZ 37)

Interpretation as phenomenological description is required precisely because
the Being of Dasein is not seen; it is not fully in sight, but is for the most
part concealed. The self-showing of the phenomenon—Dasein's making
itself known to itself—is complicated. But its concealment is not oblivion.
The laying out of that which it is and how it is can proceed on the basis
of the way in which Dasein is available to itself already. A hermeneutic
phenomenology proceeds at the outset as a reflective recovery of the vague
average understanding of being. The hermeneutics of *Being and Time* is
accordingly, a hermeneutics of retrieval (*Wiederholung*), of laying out by
fetching back again Dasein's understanding of its Being. The transformation
of phenomenology to a hermeneutic phenomenology rests on Heidegger's
paradoxical emphasis on the hiddenness, the un-givenness, rather than the
givenness, of the phenomenon.

That Heidegger is now far removed from the Neo-Kantianism of his
day is strikingly evident by the way in which the method of *Being and Time*
is itself grounded in the subject matter. The method of hermeneutic phenomenology mirrors the way to be of the being at issue; or, in different
words, the interpretative effort that marks the procedure of the treatise
follows from the anticipatory projection of the Being of Dasein. This interpretive structure at the very core of existence—the ontological basis of
understanding—is articulated by Heidegger in a consideration of how the
Da of Dasein, Dasein's openness to the world, is constituted (§29–34).

Again, Heidegger's analysis here is for the most part well known, but
deserves repeating for the sake of the ultimate clarity it can bring to
Gadamer's own position. To be brief and to limit ourselves to only part
of Heidegger's analysis here, in §29 Heidegger characterizes this openness
first of all in terms of its ontological disposition of *Befindlichkeit*. The
existential structure of *Befindlichkeit* means that Dasein is always already
placed. In effect, it expresses the factum of our existence. Dasein is always
already affected and thus disposed in its Being. Heidegger characterizes
this disposition as being in a mood (*Stimmung*), being attuned to the world
in some fashion. Significantly, this original disposition is, according to
Heidegger, disclosive of Dasein's Being; it informs it about its position
in the midst of things in the world (SZ 134). Mood reveals to Dasein the
pure "that it is," and not the "whence" and "whither." In being aware of

its own Being, of the fact that it is, Dasein's Being appears to itself as thrown (*Geworfenheit*). Dasein finds itself thrown into life, it finds itself "there," the result of which Dasein is aware not only "that it is," but "that it has to be."

Not only is Dasein's way to be that of being already disposed, Dasein's Being is determined equiprimordially by understanding (*Verstehen*). Understanding is not a concrete mode of knowing and even less is it to be considered an operation of a psychological faculty. As a mode of Being of Dasein, understanding is a "being able to." Dasein, in others words, is not something present-at-hand, but is primarily being-possible; it stretches out, projecting itself into a world of everyday concerns and projecting itself into its own possibilities of Being. In this structure of a project (*Entwurf*), in this pressing forward into possibilities, Dasein "understands" its world and itself. Echoing Heidegger's description of research in his 1922 summer semester course on Aristotle, we can say that Dasein throws itself forward upon possibilities within which Dasein must make its way about. Of course, Dasein's possibilities are not logical possibilities as if Dasein can be whatever it wants; Dasein's possibilities are in terms of its ability to be in a world that it is already delivered over to. Thrownness qualifies the character of Dasein's projection. For Gadamer, in his re-appropriation of Heidegger, this qualification of Dasein's understanding (especially as it pertains to historical existence) is decisive. "The Dasein which is projected towards its future 'potentiality-for-being' is a being which here and now *has been*, so that all of its unrestrained posturing comes up against and is halted in the face of the facticity of its own being" (PHC 27). And yet, as Gadamer points out for us, "the unilluminable obscurity of our facticity sustains and does not merely set limits to the projective character of Dasein" (RAS 41). For Gadamer, it is precisely this paradoxical situation of the hermeneutics of facticity, which is set against transcendental phenomenology, that inspires him.

At the beginning of §32 Heidegger introduces the concept of interpretation as the way in which understanding elaborates itself:

> The projecting of the understanding has its own possibility—that of developing itself. This development of the understanding we call "interpretation" [*Auslegung*]. In it the understanding appropriates understandingly that which is understood by it. In interpretation, understanding does not become something different. it becomes itself. Such interpretation is grounded in that understanding; the latter does not arise form the former. (SZ 148)

Interpretation is an exposition, laying out that which has been projected by understanding. The direction in the identification of interpretation and understanding is significant. The identification is not one in which there is first interpretation and on the basis of this understanding always follows.[56] It is the reverse that is the case: interpretations are the working-out (*Ausarbeitung*) of the possibilities which are projected in understanding. Heidegger then proceeds to show us exactly what this working-out entails. At the pre-predicative level of experience that occurs in our everyday concernful dealings with things, we are guided first by a certain kind of understanding, a circumspective concern, in which things are interpreted. The carpenter, for example, in a circumspective concern, is aware of the what-for of the tool he or she encounters. The interpretation of the tool in a circumspective concern occurs when the tool is lifted out of its vague meaningfulness and is made explicit as something "in order to" (the hammering of the hammer). In its serviceability the tool is taken as something. This filling in of understanding by taking something as something, the rendering explicit of the hammer, is interpretation.

Then to emphasize the circularity of this movement of understanding—that is, it is not the case that when we interpret we "throw a signification over some naked thing which is present-at-hand," but that "the ready-to-hand is always understood in terms of a totality of comportments" (SZ 150)—Heidegger lays out the fore-structure (*Vorstruktur*) of understanding that constitutes his version of the hermeneutic circle. Every interpretation depends on a fore-having (*Vorhabe*) or prepossession, a fore-sight (*Vorsicht*) or preview, and a fore-conception (*Vorgriff*) or preconception. More specifically, every interpretation is grounded in something we *have* in advance in the sense that the interpretation has already a totality of involvements which is already understood. Furthermore, every interpretation is grounded in something we *see* in advance in the sense that there is a point of view with respect to what is understood. And finally, every interpretation is grounded in something we *grasp* in advance in the sense that there is a conceptual scheme, drawn either from the entity itself or from something outside it, that guides the interpretation. Here we have Heidegger's explicit account of the hermeneutic situation in *Being and Time*. This circle of understanding, in which what is understood is drawn from anticipatory projections which are themselves worked out in terms of the things themselves, declares that interpretation is never a presuppositionless apprehension of an object. In the appeal to get at what "stands there" in the text, for example, one finds nothing other than the undiscussed assumption

(*Vormeinung*) of the person who does the interpreting; something has been taken for granted in the interpretation as such. What has been taken for granted is that which is presented in the fore-having, fore-sight, and fore-conception. But we should not be misled by the above example into thinking that the pre-understanding is a matter of simply having our own prior view of the matter. If such were the case it would be difficult to understand Heidegger's assertion that in the circle is to be found a positive possibility of the most primordial kind of knowing. Moreover, the issue of a vicious circle, the intrusion of the logical on the ontological, only obscures what is at issue in the circle. Heidegger is quite emphatic in insisting that the fore-structures are to be worked out in terms of the things themselves. According to Heidegger: "we genuinely take hold of this possibility [of the most primordial kind of knowing] only when, in our interpretation, we have understood that our first, last, and constant task is never to allow our fore-having, fore-sight, and fore-conception to be presented to us by fancies and popular opinions, but rather to make the scientific theme secure by working out these fore-structures in terms of the things themselves" (SZ 153).

§ 4. Hermeneutics and Historical Existence

What remains to be seen, as we look ahead to the issue of understanding historical tradition, is precisely how, given the outcome of Heidegger's analytic of Dasein, Dasein's historicity is understood. The question of historical existence is taken up in *Being and Time* in division 2 in the discussion of Dasein's temporality. Prior to the actual discussion of historicity (*Geschichtlichkeit*) Heidegger established that temporality constitutes the horizon for understanding the Being of Dasein. The meaning of Being found in care is itself grounded in temporality. But Heidegger sees that at this point the question of Dasein's wholeness may not have been thoroughly dealt with. Dasein's being-unto-death is simply one of the ends by which Dasein's wholeness is enclosed. There is also birth. Dasein exists in the continuity of life (*Zusammenhangs des Lebens*) stretching between birth and death. This continuity of life is not a sequence of experiences in time, but, considered from Dasein's temporal constitution, is the movement of existence that Heidegger calls the "coming to pass or historizing of Dasein" (*Geschehen des Daseins*).[57]

According to Heidegger, the condition for the possibility of Dasein's historizing, its stretching along between birth and death, is found in the existential-ontological constitution of historicity, which is rooted in temporality. But this phenomenon has been covered over by the way Dasein's history is ordinarily interpreted. Heidegger begins, then, by distinguishing the various ways that history and historical (*Geschichte und geschichtlich*) have been used. *Geschichte*, historical reality, refers first of all to something past; but it also refers to the past that still has an effect as "we cannot get away from history." In another sense, history is not so much the past but a context of events running through past, present, and future. In a third sense, history refers to that which is distinguished from nature; it refers to an existence determined by spirit and culture. Finally, history refers to that which is handed down by tradition (SZ 378–79).

In all four meanings history is seen to be that specific historizing of Dasein which comes to pass in time. Together, the meanings relate to man as the subject of events, but the question remains unanswered as to how the historizing character of such events is determined. Is the historizing a sequence of processes? In what way does the historizing of history belong to Dasein? Is Dasein something present-at-hand that on occasion can get into a history? Or is it that the being of Dasein is constituted first of all through the historizing because Dasein is historical in its being? The upshot of these questions is to point out that Dasein does not simply have a history but is historical in its very being, and it is so because temporality constitutes the being of Dasein (SZ 379).

How, then, are we to understand Dasein's historicity? Heidegger introduces three terms: heritage (*Erbe*), fate (*Schicksals*), and destiny (*Geschick*), which are thought in terms of Dasein's authentic temporality. As a thrown project, Dasein is delivered over to itself, it has been submitted to a world in which it exists factically with others. In resoluteness, Dasein comes back to itself; that is to say, resoluteness "discloses current factical possibilities of authentic existing, and discloses them in terms of the heritage which that resoluteness, as thrown, takes over" (SZ 383). At the same time, in grasping the finitude of its existence, which Dasein does in its anticipatory grasping of death, Dasein is brought into an awareness of the "simplicity of its fate." Fate is not a predeterminism but the recognition of limited possibilities and the significance of one's decisions in view of these possibilities. Fate, Dasein's authentic resoluteness in which it "hands itself down to itself, free for death, in a possibility which it has inherited and yet has chosen," is Dasein's primordial historizing (SZ 384). At the same time, Dasein's fate is inseparable from community: our fate is always guided in advance in being with one another in the same world. This co-historizing is Dasein's destiny. "Dasein's fateful destiny in and with its 'generation' goes to make up the full authentic historizing of Dasein" (SZ 385).

The condition of the possibility of fate, authentic historicity, Heidegger now says is care, that is, temporality:

> Only an entity which, in its being, is essential futural so that it is free for its death and can let itself be thrown back upon its factical "there" by shattering itself against death—that is to say, only an entity, which as futural, is equiprimordially in the process of *having-been*, can, by handing down to itself the possibility it has inherited, take over its own thrownness and be *in the* moment of vision for "its time." Only authentic temporality which is at the same time finite, makes possible something like fate—that is to say, authentic historicity. (SZ 385)

In identifying the finitude of temporality as the hidden ground of historicity, we have come back to the hermeneutical situation, for repetition is what characterizes the "mode by which Dasein exists explicitly as fate." We take over our fate, our personal destiny as well as our collective destiny, in the act of repetition. Repetition, in other words, is the explicit handing down (*ausdruckliche Überlieferung*), the going back into the possibilities of the Dasein that has-been-there. One hears the echoes of Kierkegaardian repetition when Heidegger goes on to say that the repetition does not "bring again [*Wiederbringen*] something that is past." The repetition cannot be understood as a mechanical or literal repetition; it is rather the retrieval or reclaiming of possibilities (of an existence which has been). The movement here is essentially futural, just as the future has priority in the ecstatic character of time. This means "that history has its essential importance neither in what is past nor in the 'today' and its 'connection' with what is past, but in that authentic historizing of existence which arises from Dasein's future" (SZ 386).

It is only after the historicity of existence has been clarified that the question of a science of history can be addressed. Since a science of history is always a science of Dasein's history, the historical (*historische*) disclosure of history (*Geschichte*), whether it is factically accomplished or not, is, in accordance with its ontological structure, rooted in the historicity (*Geschichtlichkeit*) of Dasein. The thematization of historical reality carried out by historical research presupposes that the past as such should already be disclosed and the access to the past be open. This is precisely what is made possible by the historicity of Dasein's being. Once it is recognized that historical research is rooted in historicity, Heidegger thinks we are able to determine what it is that is thematized in such research. It is a theme that must be in conformity with the character of authentic historicity, that is, in conformity with repetition as the disclosure of what has-been-there. "The 'birth' of historical research from authentic historicity therefore signifies that in taking as our primary theme the object of historical research we are projecting the Dasein which has-been-there upon its ownmost possibility of existence" (SZ 395). History is not the study of facts, for what has been is nothing other than the "existentiell possibility" in which fate, destiny, and world-history have been determined. Historical research will disclose the "silent power of the possible." In this sense history is neither the study of universal laws nor particular events (what has happened only once).

Heidegger concludes his analysis with an opening for further analysis. It is an opening that is taken up initially by Dilthey, but in point of fact, it is an opening that is ultimately carried though by Gadamer. Heidegger writes:

> The historical thematization has its main point in the cultivation of the hermeneutical situation which . . . opens itself to the repetitive disclosure of what has-been-there. The possibility and the structure of historical [*historischen*] truth are to be expounded from the authentic disclosedness ("truth") of historical [*geschlichtlichen*] existence. But since the basic concepts of the historical sciences . . . are concepts of existence, the theory of the human sciences presupposes a thematic existential interpretation of the historicity of Dasein. (SZ 397)

The statement with which the above passage concludes could serve, at the same time, as the point of departure for Gadamer's hermeneutics of the humanities. Commenting on his own point of departure in "The Philosophical Foundations of the Twentieth Century," Gadamer writes:

> Heidegger was no longer concerned with conceiving of the essence of finitude as the limit at which our desire to be infinite founders. He sought instead to understand finitude positively as the real constitution of Dasein. Finitude means temporality and thus the "essence" of Dasein is its historicity. These well-known theses of Heidegger's were meant to serve him in asking the question of being. The "understanding" that Heidegger described as the

basic dynamic of Dasein is not an "act" of subjectivity, but a mode of being. By proceeding form the special case of the understanding of tradition, I have myself shown that understanding is always an event. The issue here is not simply that a nonobjectifying consciousness always accompanies the process of understanding, but rather that understanding is not suitably conceived at all as the consciousness of something, since the whole process of understanding itself enters into an event, is brought about by it, and is permeated by it. The freedom of reflection, this presumed being-with-itself, does not occur at all in understanding, so much is understanding conditioned at every moment by the historicity of existence. (PH 125/GW4 18–19)

Ultimately, all of Gadamer's analyses are in one way or another an expression of the event character of understanding. Philosophically, the task of hermeneutics consists in asking the question about a form of understanding that stands within the historicity of existence.

CHAPTER TWO

History and the Voice of Tradition

Our historical consciousness is always filled with a variety of voices in which the echo of the past is heard. Only in the multifariousness of such voices is it there. This constitutes the nature of the tradition in which we want to share and have a part. Modern historical research itself is not only research, but the mediation of tradition.

—Hans-Georg Gadamer, *Truth and Method*

§ 5. *Hermeneutics in the Historical Sciences*

In *Truth and Method* the problematic of understanding at first appears to be synonymous with the question of *historical* understanding. When Gadamer lays out the elements of a theory of hermeneutic experience, in which he defines for the first time the central concepts of philosophical hermeneutics, he does so in the context of the determination of the historical human sciences. For this Gadamer does indeed take over the assumptions of Heidegger's hermeneutics of facticity, and we now know precisely what this entails, that is, in relation to our own being, we cannot get behind it as if it were something at our disposal. "Everything that makes possible and limits Dasein's projection ineluctably precedes it" (TM 264/GW1 269). This general structure of understanding, of Dasein as a *thrown* project, will be concretized in historical understanding "in that the concrete bonds of custom and tradition and the corresponding possibilities of one's own future become effective in understanding itself" (TM 264/GW1 268).

But we also know that Gadamer's project is not simply about historical experience. Strictly speaking, the question of the book is about the experience of truth that would correspond to the whole of our hermeneutic experience. Accordingly, just as there is an experience of truth in art that goes beyond methodical knowledge, so too in historical experience: the reality of historical experience is distorted when viewed under the mastery of historical method. But this is to say that Gadamer is concerned with the way "truth comes to speech" in the historical tradition, and it is precisely this, the coming to *speech* (of truth) in historical tradition that directs Gadamer in his analysis of the historical human sciences (TM xxiii/GW1 3). In this chapter, then, we want to see how, as the title of part 2 of *Truth and Method* indicates, Gadamer extends the "question of truth to understanding in the human sciences."

The focus of Gadamer's remarks at outset of this part of *Truth and Method* is Dilthey (1833–1911) and the romantic hermeneutics of the nineteenth century. Stated in the most general terms, as Gadamer presents it, Dilthey, despite the fact that he recognized an intimate relation between historical reality and historical understanding, nevertheless subjects historical reality to the mastery of historical method. In doing so he fails to do justice to what is in fact going on in historical tradition. That is to say, for Dilthey the task of historical understanding, as methodological research, is to reconstruct the historical reality in order to be able to experience it in its original meaning. But for Gadamer, historical tradition enters into any attempt at reconstruction such that historical understanding is integration rather than reconstruction. The development of this position is what we must attend to first.

Gadamer begins his analysis with a claim that is only understandable in the context of the difference between integration and reconstruction:[1] "If we are to follow Hegel rather than Schleiermacher, the history of hermeneutics must place its emphases quite differently. Its culmination will not longer consist in historical understanding being liberated from all dogmatic bias, and we will no longer be able to view the rise of hermeneutics as Dilthey, following Schleiermacher, presented it" (TM 173/GW1 177). The question of historical understanding is posed in the context of displacing a heretofore accepted history, a history oriented from its origins in Schleiermacher (1768–1834) that regards hermeneutics as reconstruction. Dilthey sets Schleiermacher's hermeneutics, a hermeneutics he credits with being the first to present a general theory of hermeneutics outside the content of what was to be understood, against the background of Kant's transcendental philosophy. Schleiermacher's hermeneutics undertakes a critique, not of pure reason, but of hermeneutic reason, of reason in the connection between thinking, speaking, and understanding. His starting point is the experience of misunderstanding, of the alienation of meaning as the first fact, and the task of hermeneutics is posed accordingly as "the art of avoiding misunderstanding." This is accomplished by following grammatical and psychological rules of interpretation. Whereas grammatical interpretation draws from the system of language that is common to a culture, psychological interpretation concerns the singularity of author's intentions. Psychological interpretation, which was given greater emphasis in his later writings, attempts to transform oneself into the other person through which one arrives at a "felt" understanding of the author's expression. This "divinatory" method of interpretation is a reconstruction of the experience of the author. When successful, the reconstruction allows us to "understand the text at first as well as and then even better than its author."[2]

Dilthey, following the work of Schleiermacher, goes beyond this general methodological hermeneutics of texts by broadening the scope of herme-neutics to include all disciplines in which interpretation is necessary. Hermeneutics is to be a general theory of interpretation relative to the whole sphere of cultural life. As such, hermeneutics is to provide the metho-dological foundation for the human studies (*Geisteswissenschaften*). Since cultural life is synonymous with historical life, the task of providing a foundation for the *Geisteswissenschaften* is identified with a critique of historical reason.[3]

The fact that Dilthey sought to carry out a critique of historical reason is not to suggest that Dilthey regarded himself as a Kantian.[4] The issue of a critique of historical reason pertains principally to the way in which Dilthey situated himself in the opposition between the historical school and Hegelians over the understanding of history.[5] The German historical school, represented by Ranke and Droysen, was founded in order to oppose the "philosophical school" of orthodox Hegelians, who viewed history as a rational construction in the science of spirit. The historical school claimed that this speculative philosophy of history is dogmatic in its claim not only that historical process is teleological, but also that there is progress in history relative to a value in the goal of history. The historical school cannot see how "idea," "essence," and "freedom" can have a complete or sufficient expression in historical reality.

Ranke, in particular, wanted to challenge the very idea of a "philosophy of history," insisting on their separation: whereas philosophy proceeds by way of conceptual reflection on reality, history proceeds by investigating particulars.[6] Ranke's concern is that if history is viewed as a representation of the idea, one must renounce history as an independent way of truth. History is a living reality and rational theory cannot account for the dynamic nature and concreteness of the phenomenon. To the extent there is continuity in history, it has no fixed goal that can be discovered outside it, but is established by the success of placing events into a meaningful whole; it has an effect (*Wirkung*) that lends itself to continuing historical significance (TM 203/GW1 207). History, in other words, is teleological without a *telos*. The whole of history is but these fleeting moments of the present, these "scenes of freedom" of world-historical deeds. This view of history as a living reality has a decisive religious and aesthetic tone. As Gadamer relates it, "if [the historical school] was not to understand its own disposition to think of itself as progressive research, it had to relate its own finite and limited knowledge to a divine spirit, to which things are known in their perfection" (TM 210/GW1 214). In the power and movement of history are the "thoughts of God," which the historian, analogously as priest, must think in the manner of the artist: the telling of the tale of world history is the telling of the epic poet from on high, detached from the very events of which he speaks. Ironically, Ranke never really departs from Hegel entirely; the historian seems to belong to the form of absolute spirit that Hegel called *Kunstsreligion*.

While Dilthey is drawn to this view of history as a living reality because of its congruency with assumptions in his philosophy of life, he had strong reservations about its lack of scientific (i.e., conceptual) rigor. In this respect Dilthey was closer to Droysen, who, writing after Ranke, likens the understanding of history to an immediate intuition, but does not think that this ensnares the concept of understanding in the indefiniteness of "aesthetic communion" as Ranke portrays it. Understanding is the understanding of expression in which an inner essence is immediately present. In its utterances the individual ego belongs to the world of the intelligible. This historical reality is more than the intentions and plans of the persons engaged in history. For Droysen the person's will is never fully realized in the particular situation. The historian then does not penetrate the mysteries of individual people, but attempts to see these individuals as elements in the movement of moral power. Through this approach to historical reality Droysen can provide a basis for Ranke's vague reflections on freedom and necessity. Droysen would not speak of mere "scenes of freedom," "for freedom is the fundamental pulse of historical life and does not exist only in exceptional cases" (TM 214/GW1 218). The movement of history is itself the movement of the moral powers in which freedom in related to necessity as the unconditional will to the unconditional moral imperative. The continuity of historical progress consists in the overcoming of what is on the basis of what ought to be. The historian here is not to be drawn into self-extinction in the manner of the great epic poet, ignoring the concrete conditions of his own historical existence. Droysen's historian is "limited by belonging to particular moral spheres: his native land, and his political and religious persuasions." Accordingly, he must set himself the task of being fair in understanding through research. This research is nothing less than infinite, a "ceaseless research into the tradition" by which the study of history moves progressively toward the "idea" (TM 215/GW1 219). In contrast to the experimental method of natural science, Droysen recognized that historical research must consult a tradition that is always becoming new. And yet, understanding of that tradition is always possible. This "infinite mediation of tradition," though, retains a quality of immediacy, the expressions of historical life are "congenial to us." The historian understands historical life in the same immediate way the hearer understands the speaker: understanding here as with Schleiermacher is the understanding of expression. History, as the acts of freedom, is as intelligible and meaningful as a text. The model for this understanding is the same as it is for Schleiermacher: the detail (part) is understood from the whole and the whole from the detail. The hermeneutics of history for Droysen amounts to a reconstruction of the great text (of history).

But Dilthey considered even Droysen's romantic hermeneutics of history to be inadequate. In his eyes, he saw that the historical school uncritically combined its epistemological postulates with those of German Idealism. Dilthey wanted to radically sever any connection with speculative idealism, yet at the same time, he did not want to align himself with the Neo-Kantians, who in their own fashion let logical categories intrude into the flow of life that constitutes history. For Dilthey the issue of history is the issue of an adequate account of historical experience. The Neo-Kantians took the historical world to be based on facts taken from experience, which then acquire a value relation. The Neo-Kantians, in other words, make the mistake of failing to distinguish historical experience from the experience of nature. They want to derive the categories of historical experience from the categorical structure found in the investigation of nature. Dilthey considers such derivation groundless, and maintained that historical experience should be based "on the inner historicity [*Geschichtlichkeit*] that belongs to experience itself" (TM 221/GW1 225). The construction of the historical world must be seen as a living historical process, that "strange fusion of memory and expectation" into a whole that we name experience and that we acquire through experiences. The human sciences simply advance the thought already resident in the experience of life.

Dilthey's divergence from Neo-Kantianism has a direct consequence on the starting-point of historical research. At the outset there is no question of the proper coordination between subject and object, between our ideas and the external world, since the historical world is always a world constructed and formed by the human mind. In this assumption Dilthey echoes Vico's claim against the position of Descartes; for Vico the historical (experiential) world has epistemological primacy over the world of the abstract ego. It also explains why Dilthey does not see the Kantian question of experience—"How are synthetic apriori judgments (of history) possible?"—as a problem. There are not two things (thought and intuition) that need to be united through a third. The categories of historical experience are to drawn from life itself, and, as Dilthey remarks, behind life one cannot go.[7] In Dilthey's mind, this starting-point suffices to overcome the limitations in Ranke and Droysen's methodological reflections.

But Gadamer thinks that this starting-point simply presents the real epistemological problem of history. There is no question that from the outset Dilthey's efforts were directed at separating the relationships of the historical world from the causal relationships of the natural order, and the key to this is the systematic relation between life, expression, and understanding. The expressions of life (*Lebensausserung*) emerge from lived experience (*Erlebnis*), from a pre-reflective immediate experience. These expressions, which are always individual, are referential to other aspects of culture and life. Natural science, on the other hand, proceeds on the basis of an abstraction from lived experience where it takes an outer sensory experience (*aussere Erfahrung*) as its object. This external experience can be observed and tested so that causal laws of nature can be formulated. Inner experience, on the other hand, is grasped within its context of interrelationship with experience as a whole. On the basis of this distinction, Dilthey draws the distinction between explanation and understanding: "we explain [*erklaren*] nature but understand [*verstehen*] the expressions of life."[8]

The question, though, is how the experience of the individual comes to be historical experience, since history is not concerned "with the coherent wholes that are experienced as such by the individual or are re-experienced as such by others" (TM 222/GW1 226). For Gadamer, this question is really the problem of the transition from the structure of coherence in an individual's experience to historical coherence, which is not experienced by the individual. It is the problem of the transition from the "psychological" to the "hermeneutical" grounding of the human sciences.[9] The solution to the problem rests on the concept of structure. The structure of this structure is the hermeneutic circle: the continuity of life is determined by the relation between whole and part. But by itself the hermeneutical circle simply tells us what is common to both individual and historical experience. The transition from the structure of continuity in the experience of an individual life to historical continuity is made by replacing real subjects with logical subjects (TM 224/GW1 228). Gadamer thinks that Dilthey saw the difficulty in this move, but thought it justifiable nonetheless; the historian makes statements about this kind of subject whenever he speaks about the deeds and destinies of peoples. The issue of historical understanding, then, depends upon the epistemological justification of such statements.

For this justification Dilthey is indebted to Husserl's work in the *Logical Investigations*.[10] According to Gadamer, "Dilthey's concept of the structural quality of the life of spirit [*Seelenlebens*] corresponds to the theory of the intentionality of consciousness in that structure is not merely a psychological fact but the phenomenological description of an essential quality of consciousness" (TM 225/GW1 229). Dilthey recognized that Husserl's notion of ideal significance, obtained in the analysis of the intentionality of consciousness, allowed him to account for the continuity of life without having it depend on the elements on which it is based. Dilthey, however, did not take the notion of significance as Husserl did, namely, as a logical concept, but understood it as an expression of life. With this Gadamer feels the problem is solved:

> Life itself, flowing temporality, is ordered towards the formation of enduring units of significance. Life interprets itself. Life itself has a hermeneutical structure. Thus life constitutes the real ground of the human sciences. Hermeneutics is not a romantic heritage in Dilthey's thinking, but follows from the fact that philosophy is grounded in "life." (TM 226/GW1 230)

But the solution to one problem can easily lead to another problem, which seems to be the case with Dilthey. Gadamer now asks whether it can be said that Dilthey completely breaks with speculative idealism. Not only does Dilthey increasing use "spirit" (*Geist*) in place of "life" (*Leben*), but the concept of "objective spirit," borrowed from Hegel, is given a central place. The study of life by the human sciences is now the study of objective spirit, which he defines as the manifold forms in which what individuals hold in common have objectified themselves in the world of the senses. In this objective mind the past is a permanently enduring present for us. Its realm extends from the style of life and the forms of social intercourse to the system of purposes which society has created for itself and to custom, law, state, religion, art, science, and philosophy.[11]

It would be misleading to make too much of the reemergence of the language and thought of speculative idealism. Dilthey would still oppose the abstract construction of the Hegelian account of objective spirit. What is most remarkable about Dilthey's definition is its inclusion of those elements that fall under Hegel's category of absolute spirit. This inclusion can be read as part of Dilthey's continual effort to replace metaphysics with historical consciousness: art, religion, and philosophy are brought back to the sphere of human culture. Gadamer thinks that the only real difference between Dilthey and Hegel is found in the rethinking of the forms of absolute spirit. For Hegel the return of spirit to itself takes place in the philosophical concept, whereas, for Dilthey "the philosophical concept is significant not as knowledge but as expression" (TM 229/GW1 233). For Dilthey there is still a notion of absolute spirit, but only for historical consciousness not speculative philosophy; spirit's knowledge of itself occurs in historical consciousness, not in the speculative knowledge of the concept. Historical spirit is in all things.

The question then is not really whether Dilthey escapes speculative idealism but whether Dilthey's notion of historical consciousness adequately fills the void that occurs with the removal of Hegel's concept of absolute knowledge. For Gadamer, this is fundamentally an epistemological issue, and he concludes the first section of the chapter on Dilthey's entanglement in the difficulties of historicism with a series of unanswered questions:

> Is not the fact that consciousness is historically conditioned inevitably an insuperable barrier to its reaching perfect fulfillment in historical knowledge? Hegel could regard this barrier as overcome by virtue of history's being superseded by absolute knowledge. But if life is the inexhaustible, creative reality that Dilthey thinks it, then must not the constant alteration of historical context preclude any knowledge from attaining to objectivity? Is it not the case, then, that historical consciousness is ultimately an utopian ideal, containing an internal contradiction? (TM 231/GW1 235)

§ 6. Dilthey's Ambiguity

Gadamer's questions are meant to reveal the conflict between the demand for objective science and the assumptions of life-philosophy found in Dilthey's analysis of historical understanding. On the one hand Dilthey recognized that the one who studies history also makes history, that the knower is historically conditioned. On the other hand Dilthey did not want to give up the ideal of objectivity in historical understanding; his analysis of historical understanding attempts to legitimate as the achievement of objective science the knowledge that is historically conditioned. Dilthey, in other words, thought he could gain objectivity in historical research and thus escape the problem of historicism without giving up historicism.[12] Dilthey sees in historicism only a kind of liberation.

> The historical consciousness of the finitude of every historical phenomenon, every human or social state, of the relativity of every sort of belief, is the last step towards the liberation of man. With it, man attains the sovereignty to wring from every experience its content, to surrender wholly to it, without prepossession. . . . Every beauty, every sanctity, every sacrifice, re-lived and interpreted, opens up perspectives which disclose a reality. . . . And, in contrast with the relativity, the continuity of the creative force makes itself felt as the central historical fact.[13]

But this effort at resolving the conflict by embracing historicism is precisely the problem for Gadamer. Again, Dilthey seems to insist that being finite and historical does not place any fundamental restriction on the possibility of knowledge in the human studies. Historical consciousness can rise above its own situatedness. But exactly how can this be justified without turning historical research into a philosophy of absolute idealism, where a concept of philosophical knowledge is posited beyond all historical consciousness? Gadamer does not think we find an explicit answer in Dilthey. Implicitly, though, Gadamer thinks that Dilthey recognizes that historical consciousness can take a reflective posture in which, relative to its indissoluble immersion in historical life, it "can still understand historically its own capacity to take up a historical orientation. . . . It understands itself in terms of its own history. *Historical consciousness is a mode of self-knowledge*" (TM 235/GW1 239). The question then is how, in terms of life, self-knowledge gives birth to scientific consciousness. Undoubtedly, life is oriented towards reflection when it objectifies itself, for example, in great works of art. There is for Dilthey a fundamental connection between life and knowledge, but this connection is such that "it does not try to base the one possible philosophy on the unity of a speculative principle, but continues along the path of historical self-reflection" (TM 236/GW1 241).

In following this path, however, Dilthey displays the inner disunity of his thought. In his later writings most notably, Dilthey calls for a philo-sophical foundation that would extend to every area in which "consciousness has shaken off authority and is trying to attain valid knowledge through reflection and doubt."[14] Dilthey maintains an unresolved Cartesianism in which it is not simply philosophical prejudice that is to be overcome, but the tradition itself—that knowledge that life has of itself.[15] The standpoint of reflection is incompatible with the life philosophy. Dilthey's demand for an objective science proved to be so strong that "the historicity of historical experience is never truly integrated in his thought" (TM 241/GW1 246).

Dilthey's hermeneutics of the human sciences, Gadamer argues, is thus ultimately tied to the Enlightenment project. Everything is to be made intelligible, but this means for Gadamer that, in Dilthey's hermeneutics, hermeneutical inquiry is deciphering and not self-consistently historical experience (*Erfahrung*). For Dilthey, understanding is understanding the expressions of life. These expressions are not only signs and symbols but the manifestations of psychic content that are themselves "deep" and not simply surface. We can understand an author better than the author under-stands him or herself because the expressions contain more than is present in the consciousness of the artist. For Dilthey, understanding may not be a simple reconstruction of psychic life, but it is a reconstruction nonetheless. Understanding must re-experience (*Nacherleben*) in the manner of a transposition backwards; understanding must project itself into a given expression as a means of reliving that expression.

> In a lyrical poem we can follow the pattern of experiences in the sequence of lines, not the real one which inspired the poet, but the one, which, on the basis of this inspiration, he places in the mouth of an ideal person. . . . The narrative of the novelist or historian, which follows the historical course of events, makes us re-experience it. It is the triumph of re-experiencing that it sup-plements the fragments of a course of events in such a way that we believe ourselves to be confronted by continuity.[16]

Historical understanding as re-experiencing is objective in the same way that an interpretation of a text is objective. Its objectivity is measured by the criterion of immanence in which the historical object is understood out of the whole in which it is contained. But its objectivity is also measured, for Dilthey, by the criterion of totality in which the historical event is measured in relation to universal history. Dilthey's hermeneutic circle entails the continual building up of enduring units of significance in part-whole fashion into a knowledge of universal history. When Gadamer says that "for Dilthey the awareness of finitude did not mean that consciousness was made finite or limited in any way; rather that awareness bears witness to the capacity of life to rise in energy and activity above all limitations" (TM 232/GW1 236), we must understand these remarks in the context of Dilthey's criteria for objectivity. In the criterion of totality Dilthey at least posits the possibility that in historical reason the infinite is realized.

§ 7. Historical Understanding: Tradition

Dilthey's ambiguity—that the historicity of life, of historical experience, is never truly integrated in his thought because he wants to capture at the same time the ideality of this historical experience (the Cartesianism residing within his project)—is what must be overcome for a truly consistent hermeneutics of the human sciences. For Dilthey, in other words, a reflective moment prevails over historical consciousness, whereas for Gadamer "history does not belong to us; we belong to it" (TM 276/GW1 281). The overcoming of this ambiguity in Dilthey means that Gadamer must challenge the assumption of distance (*Verfremdung*) that displaces the fundamental belonging (*Zugehörigkeit*) to the historical as such. As a consequence of this replacement of historical understanding back into its element, the character of historical understanding ultimately undergoes a fundamental shift from the reproduction of meaning to the production of (new) meaning.

This movement beyond Dilthey begins by passing through the insights of phenomenological research. In this Gadamer turns formally to Husserl but more substantially to Heidegger, who Gadamer regards as the first to truly liberate Dilthey's philosophical intention. Husserl, in the end, remains too close to Dilthey with respect to the operative assumptions in their respective projects: whereas Dilthey wants to "derive the structure of the historical world from the reflexivity inherent in life," Husserl wants to "derive the constitution of the historical world from conscious life" (TM 250/GW1 254). What is common to both is not only the epistemological schema in which the concept of life is articulated, but also—and here Gadamer points in the direction of his own contribution to this analysis— the omission of the "Thou" within the schema of the experience of life. With Heidegger of course the concept of life, as we have seen in the previous chapter, is broken free of its "theoretical," that is, epistemological frame- work. "Life understands itself from out of itself" is a statement about the being of life in its self-interpretation. This means for Heidegger that "under- standing is not a resigned ideal of human experience adopted in the old age of the spirit, as with Dilthey; nor is it, as with Husserl, a last metho- dological ideal of philosophy in contrast to the naiveté of unreflecting life" (TM 259/GW1 264), but is the original form of realization of Dasein. Gadamer thus places the problematic of understanding in the historical human sciences against the background of the existential analytic of Dasein, where understanding is no longer considered to be a methodological concept (as in Droysen), or (as in Dilthey) a hermeneutical basis for the human sciences, "an operation of life that traces backward life's tendency toward ideality" (TM 259/GW1 264).[17] Rather, understanding is first of all a movement of transcendence in existence, and as such it is to be considered ontologically (universally), rather than epistemologically (methodologically).

Given the analysis of understanding from the existential analytic of Dasein in *Being and Time*, then, the question for Gadamer is how this analysis can contribute to the construction of historical hermeneutics. But this question does not exhaust the scope of Gadamer's analysis. That is to say, at this point where Gadamer is about to describe the elements of a theory of hermeneutic experience within the question of truth in the human sciences, Gadamer does indeed make much of Heidegger's contribution to the question of historical hermeneutics. But in this he is not simply taking over Heidegger's insights and applying them back into the problem of historical understanding in Dilthey. We already have a hint as to how Gadamer will differ from Heidegger when he says, in reference to his critique of Husserl and Dilthey, for example, that the speculative import of the concept of life is undeveloped. For this Gadamer needs not only the insights of Heidegger, he also needs the insights of Hegel. The immediate concern here, though, is to see precisely how the general structure of understanding as given by Heidegger is concretized in historical understanding.

In what has seemingly become the most familiar aspect of Gadamer's hermeneutics, the focal point of his application of Heidegger's hermeneutics to the problem of historical understanding is the hermeneutic circle, and more specifically, the insight that issues from it, namely, that all understanding involves a prior understanding, a pre-understanding that gives the hermeneutic problem its real thrust. There is no zero-point from which meaning is first encountered. The reader of a text, for example,[18] always projects a meaning for the text in advance; the reader comes to the text, in other words, with particular expectations, anticipations, of meaning. These initial anticipations of meaning that direct the reader into the text give way to a meaning for the text as a whole, a meaning that is constantly revised in terms of what emerges (what the texts comes to say). The movement of understanding is this working out of the fore-projections, which are constantly being revised in terms of the emergence of (new) meaning.[19] But always, Gadamer insists, what guides the revision within the movement of understanding is an attentiveness to understanding what is *there*. Gadamer reminds us that in Heidegger's formulation of the circle of understanding, the pre-understanding is always worked out in terms of the things themselves. The question of objectivity, which naturally arises in the interpretation of texts, is decided within this movement of understanding. Objectivity, in this case, is the confirmation of an anticipation of meaning, while the erroneousness of inappropriate anticipations of meaning is found when they come to nothing in the working out of the meaning of the text as a whole.

But is it not possible to break the spell of our anticipations of meaning, to step outside of the circle? And in fact is this not desirable since, in being guided by our anticipations of meaning, there appears to be nothing to contradict our misunderstandings, nothing that obviously provides for a principle of verification or even falsifiability of our expectations of meaning? The answer is of course "no"; that is, irrespective of its desirability, neutrality is not possible. But this is precisely the point for Gadamer: one does not have to be neutral to be sensitive to the text's quality of newness in which the text is able to tell the reader something. If one is attentive to the fact that, in attempting to understand a text, one is always projecting, then one will not be resigned to one's initial fore-meanings but is prepared to let the text speak. The important thing for Gadamer is to be aware of this initial bias "so that the text can present itself in all its otherness and thus assert its own truth against one's own fore-meanings" (TM 269/GW1 274). To let the text present itself is precisely what it means, following Heidegger, to place the emphasis on the things themselves: "when Heidegger disclosed the fore-structure of understanding in what is considered merely 'reading what is there'," he also indicated the task arising from this, namely, making the anticipations conscious "so as to check them and thus acquire right understanding from the things themselves [*Sache*]" (TM 269/GW1 274).

Now, the fulfillment of this same task is required of every historical, hermeneutical consciousness. For historical understanding, this means that "it is not a matter of securing ourselves against the tradition that speaks out of the text then, but, on the contrary, of excluding everything that could hinder us from understanding it in terms of the subject matter [*Sache*]" (TM 269–70/GW1 269). What primarily hinders us in understanding the tradition that speaks out of the text is the tyranny of hidden prejudices (*Vorurteile*). In effect, this is "error" of nineteenth-century historicism:

> historicism, despite its critique of rationalism and of natural law philosophy, is based on the modern Enlightenment and unwittingly shares its prejudices. And there is one prejudice of the Enlightenment that defines its essence: the fundamental prejudice of the Enlightenment is the prejudice against prejudice itself, which denies tradition its power. (TM 270/GW1 275)

In the Enlightenment the concept of prejudice is given its negative connotation as an unfounded judgment and comes down to us as a blind belief that closes itself off from the domain of reason. But for Gadamer prejudice need not be taken in its pejorative sense as a one-sided distortion of the truth, but is simply that condition in which we at first experience something. Gadamer will use this term, pointedly drawn from the humanist tradition, to refer to the judgment that is given before all the elements that determine a situation have been fully examined. The Latin *praejudicium* meaning "disadvantage" is derivative. "The negative consequence depends precisely on the positive validity, the value of the provisional decision as a prejudgment, like that of any precedent" (TM 270/GW1 275). That prejudice has a positive value, and more so that there are legitimate prejudices, is the basis on which Gadamer will rehabilitate prejudice, authority and tradition against the claims for the autonomous power of reason that emerges in the Enlightenment.

In Kant's dictum "dare to know" we have the motto of the Enlightenment. The motto demands that we do not accept authority without question but must decide everything before the court of reason. What is written down, Scripture, like any other historical document, cannot claim absolute validity. As a corrective to the authority of tradition which asserts itself in dogmatic interpretation, the Enlightenment wants to understand tradition correctly, that is, to understand it reasonably and without prejudice. It regards authority, then, as a source of prejudice and accordingly wants to free itself from the prejudices of the past. Its own standpoint becomes that of a radical new beginning, at least so it seems. Gadamer maintains that the distinction between authority and reason is legitimate if the prestige of authority takes the place of one's own judgment. Authority in this sense is in fact a source of prejudice, and this is the deformed view of authority that is held by the Enlightenment. But is authority really a matter of blind obedience? According to Gadamer:

> Admittedly, it is primarily persons that have authority; but the authority of persons is ultimately based not on the subjection [*Unterwerfung*] and abdication of reason, but on an act of acknowledgement and recognition [*Anerkennung und der Erkenntnis*]— the recognition, namely, that the other is superior to oneself in judgment and insight and that for this reason his judgment takes precedence—i.e., it has priority over one's own. This is connected with the fact that authority cannot actually be bestowed but is earned, and must be earned if someone is to lay claim to it. It rests on acknowledgement and hence on an act of reason itself which, aware of its own limitations, trusts to the better insight of others. Authority in this sense, properly understood, has nothing to do with blind obedience to commands. Indeed, authority has to do not with obedience but rather with recognition. (TM 279/GW1 284)

Undoubtedly, in this passage we can see the basic structure that comes to define Gadamer's explicit hermeneutic theory, namely, that within tradition it is the voice of the other that is to be heard, heard not in terms of the demands of subjectivity, but from its own freeing in the trust—good will—that this other is right. The point here is that the Enlightenment thinks too abstractly about authority and reason. Not only is the correlation between authority and blind obedience questioned by Gadamer, he also questions the notion of reason freed from authority. Reason, Gadamer insists, is dependent upon the given circumstances in which it operates, and in this sense is essentially a "practical" reason.[20] The acceptance of authority is tied to the performance of reason, which is engaged in critique by definition.

But it is not just that the Enlightenment thinks too abstractly about authority and reason, it conceives one particular form of authority, tradition, abstractly as well. This is the form of authority defended by Romanticism against the Enlightenment. It is the authority of what has been handed down (*Über-lieferung*), the authority that has been sanctioned by custom (and thus not necessarily clearly grounded), the authority that has always had power over our behavior. This notion of authority is in effect present in the practical philosophy of Aristotle where the character of moral life depends on the condition of one's education and citizenship. The development of oneself in moral life does not occur free from tradition; on the contrary, the force of morals is based on tradition. From the standpoint of tradition, moral values are freely taken over but by no means are they created by a free insight. This is not to suggest that tradition is that before which reason remains silent. It is not, as conceived by Romanticism, "the antithesis to the freedom of reason," regarding it "as something historically given, like nature" (TM 281/GW1 285–86). This too is a "prejudiced" view. According to Gadamer, in tradition there is always an element of freedom and history itself.

Gadamer's analysis of the Enlightenment thus reveals that it exhibits its own prejudice in concealing from itself the fact that its standard of reason is itself a historical one. The Enlightenment, in other words, failed to realize that its rejection of all prejudice was itself a prejudice concerning its own concealed historical roots. By removing this prejudice against the overcoming of all prejudice, the way is open, according to Gadamer, "to an appropriate understanding of the finitude which dominates . . . our historical consciousness" (TM 276/GW1 280). Historical consciousness is inescapably situated within traditions. It is in this context that Gadamer's claim "history does not belong to us; we belong to it" is to be understood. It is also in this context that Gadamer can say that "the prejudices [*Vorurteile*] of the individual, far more than his judgments [*Urteile*], constitute the historical reality of his being" (TM 276–77/GW1 281).

Accordingly, if tradition is not opposed to reason, and if tradition holds within it the element of freedom and of history itself, the question becomes one of how to give tradition its full value in the hermeneutics of the human sciences. The understanding in the human sciences cannot escape the fact that it is itself addressed by tradition such that there is no antithesis between tradition and historical research, between history and the knowledge of it. The task now is "to recognize the element of tradition in historical research and inquire into its hermeneutic productivity" (TM 283/GW1 287).

This defense of tradition is an essential point, and often a misunderstood point, in Gadamer's hermeneutics of the humanities. The issue is only exacerbated by Gadamer's insistence that it is not just that the movement of tradition is at work in the human sciences, but that tradition is something to be preserved.

Even the most genuine and pure tradition does not persist because of inertia of what once existed. It needs to be affirmed, embraced, cultivated. It is, essentially, preservation [*Bewahrung*], and it is active in all historical change. But preservation is an act of reason, though an inconspicuous one. For this reason, only innovation and planning appear to be the result of reason. But this is an illusion. Even where life changes violently, as in ages of revolution, far more of the old is preserved in the supposed transformation of everything than anyone knows, and it combines with the new to create a new value. At any rate, preservation is as much a freely chosen action as are revolution and renewal. That is why both the Enlightenment's critique of tradition and the romantic rehabilitation of it lag behind their true historical being. (TM 281–82/GW1 285)

Is it the case that Gadamer's position here takes a conservative turn, as his critics maintain? Is it the case, as John Caputo claims, that Gadamer is fundamentally looking backward, concerned with how truth gets passed down and never putting that truth in question, that is, "the deep unity of tradition is always safe"?[21] Is it the case, in yet one other formulation, this one by Terry Eagleton, that Gadamer presents us with a "grossly complacent theory of history" in which history is not a place of struggle but almost a club of the like-minded"?[22]

To be sure, tradition for Gadamer, is certainly not a collective subject in the manner of Hegel's *Geist*, that is, Gadamer has not simply substituted the word "tradition" for Hegel's "objective Geist." Gadamer himself says that there is no support in *Truth and Method* for this kind of construction.[23] And insofar as tradition is not a collective subject the continuity of tradition is not a familiar common history that is nothing more than the accumulation of customs. The continuity of tradition is simply its "continuing-ness," its "unsurpassability," which effects historical consciousness. Nowhere does Gadamer make an argument for a political position that wants to adopt the "mainstream" tradition. Rather, tradition "is simply the collective name for each individual text (text in the widest sense, which would include a picture, an architectural work, even a natural event)" (DD 111/GW2 370). In this sense what is of tradition is not only high German culture, it is Gunther Grass, Bauhaus, Karl Marx, Eldridge Cleaver, whoever and whatever.

In this more focused context, there are several senses of the word that can be distinguished.[24] Tradition refers first of all to traditionality, to a style of interconnecting historical succession. This style of succession is rooted in the dynamic of historical experience in which there is a tension "between the efficacity of the past that we undergo and the reception of the past that we bring about."[25] Tradition is literally a trans-mission (*Über-lieferung*) caught up in a chain of interpretations. When Gadamer speaks later of a fusion of horizons, we can understand it in the context of this use of the word *tradition*. Tradition is used in a second sense to indicate not the formal concept of traditionality but the material concept of the contents of tradition. Tradition is traditions; it signifies being in a tradition: we are never "absolute innovators, but always first of all in the situation of being heirs."[26] When Gadamer says that tradition is essentially linguistic we should understand tradition in this sense. Language always precedes are speaking as that in which we have already taken hold of a world.[27] Through tradition we understand the things already said. Following this use of *tradition*, when Gadamer says of hermeneutic understanding that it is a matter of letting the text speak, we can understand this to mean that the past questions us before we question it.

Tradition is used in a third sense as "tradition" in the singular, and *can* be taken as an anti-argumentative authority.[28] This use of tradition, tradition linked to authority is what Gadamer defends in his critique of the Enlightenment prejudice against prejudice. In effect, we are always confronted with the voices of the past as *voices of the other* that make a claim upon us.[29] The claim that these voices make upon us is a claim to truth (what we receive from the past is that which is held to be true in the sense that the voices of the past make a claim to be truly articulating their deep experience of the way things are). This is why the voice of tradition that does indeed speak "truly" can be tied to authority for in the best sense authority is not blind obedience but the recognition of superiority. This idea carries over into Gadamer's analysis of language and the character of speaking in language. What is at stake in speaking is "speaking truly," that minimally pertains to the *strength* rather than the weakness of words. In conversation the point is not to attack the words of the other for the sake of sophistical persuasion, but to make the words of the other within dialogical exchange so strong such that the truth of what one says becomes evident. But this very gesture is the gesture that breaks self-identity![30] Of course, Gadamer is aware that the strength of words is inseparable from its intrinsic corruption. To say the least, idle talk (*Gerede*) infects conversation at every turn, as do the interests of power. There is indeed always the possibility of the failure of communication.

When Gadamer speaks of preserving tradition it must be interpreted in this same context of recognizing the strength of words. Preservation is not to be confused with conservation of a natural reality, as one would undertake to preserve, for example, for ecological reasons our nation's wetlands. Preservation has to do primarily with holding open.[31] In this case what is held open are the possibilities for hearing the extinguished voices of the past! Habermas's criticism of Gadamer, as well as ironically the post-modern criticism of Gadamer—loosely stated here as the criticism that by virtue of the emphasis on the continuity of tradition, one only hears the same voice—fails to see that Gadamer's defense of tradition is done for the sake of an openness to that which has been excluded.[32] Again, if historical understanding, by virtue of the historical as such *finds itself* in tradition, then "objective" historical research always finds itself standing within tradition as well. The distinction between tradition and historical research, between history and knowledge, is an abstract antithesis that must be discarded. But the consequence for the hermeneutics of the human sciences of this element of tradition in historical research is yet to be seen.

§ 8. Historical Understanding: The Principle of Wirkungsgeschichte

The analysis of historical understanding proceeds to answer three questions: (1) What follows for understanding from the hermeneutic condition of belonging to tradition? (2) What distinguishes legitimate prejudices from those that obstruct understanding? (3) What happens when historical understanding takes account of its own historicity?

Regarding the first question, what follows for understanding is that the hermeneutic circle is understood differently. As it was initially conceived, the hermeneutic circle produced understanding in the referential operation between whole and part. For nineteenth-century hermeneutics, this circular movement between whole and part could be described generally as a movement from expression to its context and from context to expression, just as a word is understood in light of the entire sentence and the sentence, in turn, takes its meaning from the individual words. In principle, this movement would ultimately dissolve all "foreign" elements in an achievement of perfect understanding.

Following Heidegger's reformulation of this circle, Gadamer maintains, as we have seen, that the understanding of a text remains permanently determined by the anticipatory movement of pre-understanding. His version of this insight is that it is not so much our judgments but our prejudices that constitute our being. To be prejudiced means that we have already taken up the world in some way, and for historical consciousness this means that we always find ourselves in tradition. Consequently, for Gadamer the circle is neither a formal relation between whole and part, nor a methodological principle for textual or cultural interpretation, but is conceived ontologically as the relation between a living tradition and its interpretation.

> The circle . . . describes understanding as the interplay of the movement of tradition and the movement of the interpreter. The anticipation of meaning that governs our understanding of a text is not an act of subjectivity, but proceeds from the communality [*Gemeinsamkeit*] that binds us to tradition. But this commonality is constantly being formed in our relation to the tradition. Tradition is not simply a permanent precondition; rather, we produce it ourselves inasmuch as we understand, participate in the happening of tradition [*Überlieferungsgeschehen*], and hence further determine it ourselves. Thus the circle of understanding is not a "methodological" circle, but describes an element of the ontological structure of understanding. (TM 293/GW1 298–99)

The fact that understanding is not an action of subjectivity but an entering into—a participation in—an event of transmission is perhaps the central insight of Gadamer's philosophical hermeneutics. In it we find the decisive turn away from Dilthey and romantic hermeneutics, which is to say that in it we find precisely what it means, as Gadamer continually insists, to take finitude seriously.

From this definition of the circle, though, we see how Gadamer tends to confuse the operation of the circle in his description of it. The very talk of a circle (and tacitly of whole and part) suggests that Gadamer is simply giving us a variation of the hermeneutic circle as described in nineteenth-century hermeneutics, or else—and this gives further credence to a conservative reading of Gadamer—he is giving us a variation of the hermeneutic circle as described in *Being and Time*, a description that Heidegger eventually comes to distance himself from.

This confusion is most apparent in his description of the "further hermeneutic implication" of the circle that he identifies as the fore-conception of completeness (*Vorgriff der Vollkommenheit*). The fore-conception of completeness is a formal condition of all understanding that amounts to a necessary but not a sufficient condition for understanding. For the sake of understanding the reader of a text assumes that the text is complete, that is, an intelligible whole, and does so in a double sense. The content of the text is regarded initially as neither incoherent within (itself ("immanent unity of meaning") nor inconsistent with what is true concerning the subject matter ("transcendent expectations of meaning that proceed from the relation to the truth of what is being said"). Naturally a text could be otherwise, but if a text is not regarded as having a completed unity of meaning there would be nothing to call into question the prejudices guiding the interpretation. A text would say whatever the reader wanted it to say. The completed unity of meaning thus enables the text to stand as a self-presenting and authoritative *whole*. From the point of view of the reader, the negative experience which causes the fore-conception of completion in a text to fail is simply the change that would not allow the text to speak any longer "be it that we find it boring, empty or ridiculous, sentimental, imitative or simply not working."[33] A text thus cannot say anything it wants to and at the same time Gadamer eschews a methodology of a correspondence theory of meaning. The fore-conception of completion is regulative rather than constitutive of understanding; nevertheless it appears that the movement of understanding is still fundamentally a whole-part relation.

In point of fact, though, Gadamer's hermeneutic circle is more accurately described alone the lines of the later Heidegger. The key to understanding this is the way Gadamer understands the interplay of tradition. For Gadamer this is not a movement of making the implicit explicit, nor is this a new version of whole and part. The hermeneutic circle is constituted as a relation of belonging in the same way that Heidegger speaks of the belonging together of Being and Dasein as the more proper hermeneutic dimension of the Being question. Toward the end of *Truth and Method* where Gadamer extends his remarks on the linguistic nature of hermeneutic experience, he asks again about the state of affairs that follows from the fact that there is a dialogue between tradition and its interpreter. The state of affairs is such that something happens (*etwas geschieht*); in this the subject is not in a position of mastery over some object, nor is the knowledge reached in this encounter progressive such that one could posit an infinite intellect in which the whole of tradition comes to be held. That something happens is made possible "only because the word that has come down to us as tradition and to which we are to listen really encounters us and does so as it is addresses us and is concerned with us" (TM 461/GW1 465). The encounter with tradition, then, transpires in the particular dialectic in hearing (*hören*) as the form of relatedness (*Zugehörigkeit*) between interpreter and the tradition. Gadamer says that the one who hears is not just the one who is addressed, but the one who cannot not hear, in contrast to the one who sees who can look away from what is seen. In this way of encountering tradition, the concept of belonging (*Zugehörigkeit*) "is brought about by tradition's addressing us." In effect, the modern schema of subject-object, as the polarity of distance in which the historical world is encountered is displaced by Gadamer's version of the hermeneutic circle. In beginning with distance, historical understanding regards the past as that which is foreign and stands over against the knower. For Gadamer, insofar as tradition is the "fact" of existence, it is the element of continuity, not strangeness, that constitutes the schema for hermeneutic understanding. In the continuity is the commonality that binds us to tradition, a commonality, Gadamer insists, that is constantly being formed. This formation, by virtue of the belongingness, is thus not a reconstruction, but the producing of meaning. More specifically, historical understanding happens as a mediation of past and present, not a taking hold of the past as it really was. This is not to suggest that the continuity so dominates that there is nothing but "the unbroken stream of a tradition." The hermeneutic consciousness is always related to the object in a dialectic of strange/familiar,[34] otherwise there is nothing to understand. The traditionary text cannot speak—that is its strangeness, and the effort to understand is to bring the text to speak again. The true locus of hermeneutics is in between a historically intended, distanciated object and the belongingness to tradition (TM 295/GW1 300).

Now, because of the belongingness to tradition, the one who wishes to understand cannot separate *in advance* the prejudices that make understanding possible form those that obstruct understanding. This separation can take place only within the event of understanding itself, that is, since prejudices cannot be put aside the task is to work them out interpretively. The issue of this separation, this working out, is the issue of the second question that Gadamer answers in terms of the temporal distance in historical understanding. For nineteenth-century hermeneutics, temporal distance was regarded as something to be overcome in the achievement of historical understanding. The task of the historian was to place him or herself within the spirit of the age that was to be understood, and to think within its thought as a means of gaining historical objectivity. Gadamer insists, however, contrary to the assumption of historicism, that one cannot overcome temporal distance in this way. Temporal distance, too, must be understood from the direction given it by Heidegger's ontological project in which Dasein's mode of Being is interpreted in terms of time. This means that "time is no longer primarily a gulf to be bridged, because it separates; it is actually the supportive ground of the course of events in which the present is rooted" (TM 297/GW1 302). Temporal distance actually enables understanding because it is filled with the continuity of custom and tradition "in which everything handed down presents itself to us."

More often than not, for the historical event (and even, as Gadamer illustrates, for the case of judging the significance of a contemporary work of art) the determination of meaning depends on unverifiable prejudices "that have too great an influence over us to know about them." Our immediate prejudices are actually no different than hidden prejudices. Through temporal distance, the prejudices that are of a particular and limited nature die away. This is not simply a matter where our own interest in the object fades away, and now objectivity is possible; but rather, that a "truer" meaning of the object emerges. The emergence of meaning is of course an infinite process: fresh sources of error are excluded and new sources of understanding are continually emerging. Accordingly, temporal distance serves as a filter for distinguishing legitimate prejudices from those that obstruct understanding.

In this function temporal distance provides for the critique necessary for historical understanding.[35] The matter of distinguishing prejudices requires isolating a prejudice, suspending its validity, so that it can be valued on its own. The isolation can not occur while the prejudice is "constantly operating unnoticed, but only when it is, so to speak, stirred up" (GW2 64). But what is capable of stirring up the prejudice is precisely the movement with the tradition in which something addresses us, asserting itself in its separate validity, which in turn requires the suspension of our own prejudice. Such suspension has logically the structure of a question, and it is in this context that Gadamer says "the hermeneutical task becomes of itself a questioning of things" and as such it places the hermeneutical work on a firm basis (TM 269/GW1 273). Questioning opens up possibilities and places our own prejudices at risk.[36]

Let us turn then to the final question: What happens when historical understanding takes account of its own historicity? Gadamer's response to this question introduces the notion of historically effected (*wirkungsgeschichtlicher*) event.

> The true historical object is not an object at all, but the unity of the one and the other, a relationship that constitutes both the reality of history and the reality of historical understanding. A herme-

neutics adequate to the subject matter would have to demonstrate the reality and efficacy of history within understanding itself. I shall refer to this as "history of effect" [*Wirkungsgeschichte*]. (TM 299–300/GW1 305)

To see what Gadamer means by the efficacy of history within understanding we should recall the issue in overcoming Dilthey's ambiguity: historical understanding cannot be regarded as an action of subjectivity in which it extricates itself from historical becoming through a methodological procedure that would allow it to claim historical objectivity. Every such attempt to claim objectivity, as in Mommsen's *History of Rome*, cannot ignore the prejudices that guide the work: "we know who alone could have written it, that is, we can identify the political situation in which this historian organized the voices of the past in a meaningful way" (PH 6/GW2 222). Historical objectivism, in appealing to its critical method does not recognize the presuppositions, which are by no means arbitrary, that govern the understanding of the historical object. In contrast to this ideal of understanding in which the knower would appear to be effaced from the situation of history, Gadamer insists that the actual situation is one in which historical consciousness is always operative in the situation of history. The prejudices that condition understanding emerge from a particular historical horizon. And, most importantly, this is not a negative situation to be overcome, or for that matter can be overcome. At the same time, the historicity of the knower does not prohibit critical scholarship; in fact, the analysis of temporal distance was shown to have its own critical component.

Given this situation, Gadamer proceeds to state its implications. Historical consciousness must recognize that every historical investigation, that is, research in which historical distance embraces the historical phenomenon, is such that it is always already effected by history (*Wirkungen der Wirkungsgeschichte*). To assume that one can reach historical objectivity through a critical method simply "conceals the fact that historical consciousness is itself situated in the web of historical effects" (TM 300/GW1 306). The power of effective history does not depend on its being recognized, for it prevails even where "faith in method leads one to deny one's own historicity" (TM 301/GW1 306). But in recognizing that the efficacy of history is at work in historical understanding, historical consciousness does not, by virtue of the recognition, overcome it. Historically effected consciousness expresses the true meaning of finitude. A reflection on the prejudgments that enter into historical understanding brings historical consciousness before something that otherwise happens "behind one's back" (PH 38). A consciousness of being affected by history (*wirkungsgeschichtliches Bewußtsein*)[37] is primarily consciousness of the hermeneutic situation, that is, the situation in which we *find* ourselves, the thrownness of our (historical) "there." The fact that we cannot overcome the efficacy of history is not a deficiency of reflection but an indication of the historical being that we are. In this sense Gadamer can say that "effective historical consciousness is more being than being consciousness" (GW2 496). Effective historical consciousness describes for hermeneutic understanding precisely what is entailed in the claim of a hermeneutics of facticity that life interprets itself from itself. Hermeneutic understanding is an understanding in act, in the exercise where what is encountered cannot be extricated from the experiencing activity. In "The Continuity of History and the Existential Moment" Gadamer is most direct in his description of effective historical consciousness:

> What I wish to express through this somewhat ambiguous expression is primarily that we cannot raise ourselves above the course of events and as it were confront it in such a way that the past turns into an object. To think this way would be to miss catching even a glimpse of the authentic experience of history. We are always already in the middle of history. Not only are we links in a forward-rolling chain, to use Herder's expression, but at every moment we are in the possibility of understanding what comes to us and is handed over to us from the past. I call it consciousness of being affected by history because on the one hand I want to say that our consciousness is historically [*wirkungsgeschichtlich*] determined, that is, it is determined by real events [*wirkliches Geschehen*] rather than left on its own to float free over against the past. On the other hand I want to say that it is important to produce within ourselves always again a consciousness of this being effected [*ein Bewußtsein dieses Bewirktseins*]—just as the past which comes to us to experience forces us to deal with it, and in a certain respect to take its truth upon ourselves. (GW2 142–43)[38]

Wirkungsgeschichtliches Bewußtsein is thus both a consciousness effected *by* history and a consciousness *of* history's effects.

Finally, it remains to be seen precisely how the efficacy of history is at work in historical consciousness. That is to say, if it is the case that a consciousness of being affected by history is situated, the question arises as to how understanding is possible from this situatedness. Gadamer accounts for this understanding through the further notion of the fusion of horizons (*Horizontverschmelzung*). Every finite present naturally has its limitations, and being in a situation simply means that one never has full vision; a situation represents a standpoint. An essential part of the concept of situation is thus the concept of horizon as the range of vision that includes everything that can be seen from a particular vantage point. But the concept of horizon also implies that in it one knows the relative significance of everything within it. Analogously Gadamer insists that "working out the hermeneutical situation means acquiring the right horizon of inquiry for the questions evoked by the encounter with tradition" (TM 302/GW1 308).

Historical understanding in particular must acquire an appropriate historical horizon. But this is precisely the question romantic hermeneutics faced, how to transpose ourselves into the historical horizon from which the traditionary text speaks since without it we misunderstand what the text has to say to us. The real question though is whether placing ourselves into the situation of the other is ever adequate (or to that extent really possible). To highlight the difficulty, Gadamer compares historical understanding as a transposition into the horizon of the other to a certain kind of conversation between two people. It is more or less simply a conversation one has simply to get to know the other person, but it is not a conversation in which we seek agreement on a subject matter. Similarly, the person who thinks historically "comes to understand the meaning of what has been handed down, without necessarily agreeing with it, or seeing himself in it" (TM 303/GW1 308). But in this Gadamer thinks we give up the claim to find in the past any truth that is intelligible for ourselves. "Acknowledging the otherness of the other in this way, making him the object of objective knowledge, involves the fundamental suspension of his claim to truth" (TM 304/ GW1 309).

But again, the question is whether we can place ourselves into the situation of the other, or to say it now in the way that Gadamer wants to rephrase the question, whether there are really two different horizons. Is there really something like a closed horizon, a horizon bounded in such a way that the question of entry can be posed at all? The past does not stand behind us as something isolated from the horizon out of which we speak. The horizon of the past, existing in the form of tradition, is always in motion. We should recall that the hermeneutic circle is between a living tradition and its interpretation. This means that the historical movement of human life is "never absolutely bound to any one standpoint, and hence can never have a truly closed horizon" (TM 304/GW1 309). If horizons are not closed, but open, then "when our historical consciousness transposes itself into historical horizons, this does not entail passing into alien worlds unconnected in any way with our own; instead, they together constitute the one great horizon that moves from within and that, beyond the frontiers of the present, embraces the historical depths of our self-consciousness" (TM 304/GW1 309).

The fusion of horizons then is not that there are two horizons that meet, namely the horizon of the past and the horizon of the present. The horizon of the present cannot itself be formed without the past, as evident by the fact that we test our prejudices. "There is no more an isolated horizon of the present in itself than there are historical horizons which have to be acquired" (TM 306/GW1 311). Historical understanding is nevertheless a fusion of these horizons *"supposedly existing for themselves."* But if there are not two horizons, why speak about a fusion of horizons and not simply the formation of one horizon? The answer to this question, which Gadamer himself poses, is found in what was said earlier about hermeneutic consciousness. In describing the hermeneutic circle, it was pointed out that hermeneutic consciousness does not find itself in an unbroken stream of tradition but stands intermediate between an "historically intended separate objectivity" and the belongingness to tradition. The encounter with the tradition involves the experience of the tension between the (historical) text and the present. This tension is not to be assimilated—the continuity of tradition is not simply the unity of discourse. Accordingly there is a need to project a historical horizon that is different from the horizon of the present. Of course in historical understanding a new unity is formed in acquiring the historical horizon. Thus the historical horizon is not "solidified into the self-alienation of a past consciousness, but is overtaken by our own present horizon of understanding" (TM 307/GW1 312). In what sounds clearly Hegelian—although unequivocally the mediation in historical understanding is not to be confused with the Hegelian mediation of Geist[39]— Gadamer concludes by saying that in the taking over of the historical horizon there is indeed "a real fusing of horizons," and that bringing about this fusing is the problem of application (*Anwendung*).

In the fusion of horizons, then, the present no longer has a privileged status, and yet it remains productive and disclosive of what is said in tradition. The understanding of tradition is an event of repetitive disclosure, and as such, understanding is real experience. But this is precisely what remains to be seen.

CHAPTER THREE

Hermeneutic Experience

Hermeneutic philosophy understands itself . . . not as an absolute
position, but as a way of experience.
　　　　　　　—Hans-Georg Gadamer, "Selbstdarstellung"

§ 9. Philosophical Hermeneutics as Experience

In historical understanding (and also in aesthetic experience) Gadamer insists
that there is a strong affinity between the structure of understanding and
the structure of experience (*Erfahrung*). With respect to the experience of
art this affinity is most intriguing because the question of truth, which
remains unaddressed, is at least given a direction by being turned into the
question of experience. At the end of the section "Retrieving the Question
of Artistic Truth" Gadamer indicates that knowledge in art, which is at
once the claim to truth in the experience of art, cannot be recognized if
"one measures the truth of knowledge [*Erkenntnis*] by the scientific concept
of knowledge and the scientific concept of reality" (TM 98/GW1 103).
Rather than proceeding to a further consideration of scientific knowledge,
Gadamer simply proposes that it is now necessary to take the concept of
experience (*Erfahrung*) more broadly than Kant did, "so that the experience
of the work of art can be understood as experience" (TM 98/GW1 103).

But this analysis of experience does not occur immediately after it is
proposed, and when it does occur later on it is not highlighted in any special
way. Given the centrality that Gadamer himself attributes to the analysis
of experience, perhaps it should have been. What happens in between is
of course the analysis of historical understanding in which the concept of
experience as *Erlebnis* plays a central role in Dilthey's account of historical

understanding. Actually, Gadamer had already discussed the concept of *Erlebnis* in the analysis of aesthetic experience because, historically considered, the concept was already being used in connection with the experience of art. According to Gadamer the noun *Erlebnis* first came into prominent use in the 1870s with Dilthey's essay on Goethe (1877). This work was an example of the genre of biographical literature in which the works of artists and poets are understood from their life. Dilthey's use of *Erlebnis* in this connection captured the double meaning found in the verb *erleben*: what is experienced is what one has experienced oneself (the immediacy that offers a starting point for interpretation), but at the same time what is experienced yields a permanent content (the result of experience).

With Dilthey of course this word is eventually conceptualized to indicate the field of research in the human sciences. What is given for research in the human sciences is not sensation (as claimed in Neo-Kantianism) but a unit of consciousness that Dilthey calls *Erlebnis*, lived experience. That is to say, what is given for research is life, but life manifests itself in experience. When Dilthey claims that life carries in itself reflection, he means by that that life objectifies itself in structures of meaning, and the task is to translate these objectifications of life *back* into the spiritual life (*geistige Lebendigkeit*) from which it came. In this the concept of lived experience forms "the epistemological basis for all knowing of the objective" (TM 66/GW1 71).

Dilthey's claim that life manifests itself in experience is not, however, without its difficulties. Not only Dilthey, but Natorp and Bergson as well, get caught up in the problem of the inner relation of life to experience. In looking more closely at this matter Gadamer contends that we cannot understand the relationship of life to experience as that of universal to particular. "Rather, the unity of experience as determined by its intentional content stands in an immediate relationship to the whole, to the totality of life" (TM 68/GW1 74). Gadamer points out that it is principally through the work of Georg Simmel that this "organic" relationship of whole and part is developed further. For Simmel life is such "that it always reaches out beyond itself."[1] In this particular understanding of life the concept of *Erlebnis* is effectively transformed. According to Simmel, in the momentary *Erlebnis* is a presentation of the whole of the life process. As such every *Erlebnis* has something of an *adventure* about it that is not to be confused with an episode of life. Whereas an episode has no permanent significance because its succession of details has no inner coherence, an adventure, which interrupts the customary courses of events, is related to the context that it interrupts. As an undergoing and return, an adventure "lets life be felt as a whole, in its breadth and in its strength." In fact every *Erlebnis* is something like this.

> Every experience is taken out of the continuity of life and at the same time related to the whole of one's life. It is not simply that an experience remains vital only as long as it has not been fully integrated into the context of one's life consciousness, but the very way it is "preserved and dissolved" (*aufgehoben*) by being worked into the whole of life consciousness goes far beyond any "significance" it might be thought to have. Because it is itself within the whole of life, the whole of life is present in it too. (TM 69/GW1 75)

But for certain good reasons Gadamer does not use the term *Erlebnis* but the broader term *Erfahrung* in his analysis of experience.

The concept of experience as *Erfahrung*, which is the word in play in Gadamer's hermeneutic experience, explicitly connotes this sense of venturing out (*fahren*). *Erfahrung* is of course the word for experience used by Hegel in the *Phenomenology of Spirit*, and pertains primarily to the sense that something is undergone and through it one changes.[2] Thus, unlike *Erlebnis* where the venturing out is a return to the order of life, an order in which one is now enriched, *Erfahrung* essentially entails a transformation of that life. Equally important, Gadamer's desire to link understanding to experience as *Erfahrung* is tied directly to the way in which this experience is itself learning, is itself knowing.

In this chapter then we want to follow Gadamer in his analysis of experience, and then to analyze the related thematics that indeed take us to the core of hermeneutic experience. Accordingly, we want to, first of all, see how this concept of experience itself is understood and how it is related to the account of philosophical hermeneutics given up to this point (§9). Then secondly, insofar as experience has within it the element of recognition, we are led to a further analysis of the knowing peculiar to hermeneutic experience (§10). But this account of knowing is not unrelated to Aristotle's notion of $\phi\rho\acute{o}\nu\eta\sigma\iota\varsigma$, which Gadamer takes as a model for the problems of hermeneutics (§11). Finally, the analysis of $\phi\rho\acute{o}\nu\eta\sigma\iota\varsigma$ directs us to a further analysis of the sense in which hermeneutics can be understood as practical philosophy (§12).

The Concept of Experience

Historically effected consciousness has the structure of experience. But it is not immediately apparent how this is so since the concept of experience, according to Gadamer, has been obscured by the attitude of modern science. On the whole modern science regards experience teleologically, by the degree to which it ends in knowledge and ignores the element of knowing *within* experience, where knowledge is to be thought in terms of experience. This scientific concept of experience is what we find in a theory of induction where experiences are built up to form a generalization. The building up is such that experience is valid only if it is confirmed; that is to say, under the demand for objectivity, scientific inquiry wants to secure the general repeatability of experience (and experiment). Validation, as the test of objectivity in science, is predicated upon the element of self-sameness that is found within the interlocking chain of experiences (and experiments) where a first one confirms the next one and so on. In this Gadamer sees that experience is stripped of its historical element, its historicity, its dynamic character of unfolding and undergoing.

This procedure owes much to Francis Bacon, to what he called the experimental method in which we can rise "above the irregular and accidental way daily experience occurs and certainly above its dialectical use" (TM 348/GW1 354). Bacon wanted to guard against the weakness inherent in a "natural interpretation" of nature and the only way to do this was, not to leave the mind to its own devices, but to proceed through methodically conducted experiments. In doing so one achieves the "true and tenable universals, the simple forms of nature" (TM 348/GW1 354).

For Gadamer, there is certainly an element of truth in the perspective of modern science that views experience as valid so long as it is not contradicted by new experience. This is a feature of the general nature of experience that holds true not only for scientific procedure, but also for our experience of daily life. This feature of experience is also in accord with the analysis of the concept of induction in Aristotle. But in Aristotle we can see a difference between the process of induction in science and the process of induction in the experience of daily life. In science, there comes a point in the accumulation of experience at which an abstraction is made to form a general concept for the accumulated experiences. In the concept, there is no longer a need to refer back to the accumulated experiences and to have additional experiences for it. In this way the τέλος of experience is knowledge as the knowledge of the concept. In Aristotle's account of how the unity of experience occurs such that we arrive at the universal (*Allgemeinheit*) of experience—that is, the one that corresponds to the many (τοῦ ἑνὸς παρὰ τὰ πολλά)—it is not the case that this universality of experience is identical to the universal of the concept. According to Aristotle:

> As soon as one individual percept has come to a halt in the soul, this is the first beginning of the presence there of a universal [χαθόλου] (because although it is the particular that we perceive, the act of perception involves the universal, e.g., "man," not "a man, Callias"). Then other "halts" occur among these <proximate> universals, until the indivisible genera or <ultimate> universals are established. E.g., a particular species of animal leads to the genus "animal," and so on. Clearly then it must be by induction that we acquire knowledge of the first things [τὰ πρῶτα], because this is also the way in which general concepts are conveyed by sense perception.[3]

What interests Gadamer here is this first universality of experience and in particular he wants to know how it evolves "into the new universality of the logos." That is to say, he wants to know how one is able to move from the universality of experience ("these <proximate> universals") to the universality of science ("the indivisible or <ultimate> universals"). Following Aristotle, it appears that only after the universality in experience is attained that we can look to the reason and thus begin a scientific inquiry. Gadamer gives the following example: "If experience shows us that a particular remedy has a particular effect, this means that something common has been noticed in a number of observations, and it is clear the actual medical question, the scientific question—i.e., the question about the logos—is possible only on the basis of this kind of observation" (TM 350/GW1 356).

The movement seems to require a shift in the very structure of unity. In the case of the unity of science, there is in place a unity based on "the undifferentiated commonality of many single observations" (on the basis of which predication then becomes possible). In contrast to this, not only is the unity of experience affected by the element of memory,[4] the unity itself is only present in individual observation. Gadamer finds Aristotle's image of the fleeing army an apt description of how this unity of experience is formed. The many observations we make is similar to a retreat that occurs in battle. If one man makes a stand and then another, and still another, a position of strength is reached, the retreat is halted, and the battle is turned.[5] The image illustrates the "curious opening in which experience is acquired": something beyond one's control, always subject to the contingency of a particular observation (an unpredictability and yet not without preparation), and valid from then on until there is a new experience.

In Aristotle's example the movement from the unity of experience to that of science is not problematic because he has simplified the process. He remains guided by a theory of science. His concern about experience is with resect to the formation of concepts, and in the example he "presupposes that what persists in the flight of observations and emerges as a universal is, in fact, something common to them: for him the universality of the concept is ontologically prior" (TM 353/GW1 358). Nevertheless, Aristotle does allow us to see an element of experience that is covered over in the emphasis on repetition and validation, that is to say, insofar as experience is not in one's control, one's expectations are not always confirmed. In effect there is always an element of surprise in experience.[6] The generation of generalizations from experience "takes place as false generalizations are continually refuted by experience and what was regarded as typical is shown not to be so" (TM 353/GW1 359). But the disappointment of expectations in experience does not have the same results as the disappointment in methodological procedure (the falsification of a hypothesis), for in the situation of experience the disappointment leads to a more comprehensive knowledge.

Thus, when we attend to the process of experience itself, we see that it entails not only an openness to new experience, but also a fundamental negativity. This negative element, Gadamer argues, is essentially a positive phenomenon, as Hegel rightly saw. In the introduction to the *Phenomenology of Spirit*, Hegel describes experience as the "dialectical movement which consciousness exercises on itself—on its knowledge as well as its object—such that the new true object emerges from it."[7] Gadamer understands this dialectical character of experience as a "skepticism in action" where the experiencing consciousness gives *voice* to an otherness in experience as it (the otherness) confronts the experiencing consciousness about its initially fixed determination of the actuality of its experience.

> Natural consciousness with show itself to be only the concept [*Begriff*] of knowledge, or in other words, not to be real knowledge. But since it immediately takes itself to be real knowledge, this path [of experience] has a negative significance for it; what is in

fact the realization of the concept, counts for it rather as the loss of its own self, for it loses its truth on this path. This way can be viewed as the pathway of doubt, or more properly as the pathway of despair.[8]

What Hegel means here seems unduly complicated, but it is so only if one takes too simplistic a view of experience in the first place. Our "English" way of regarding experience is a case in point. For the most part, it equates experience with awareness as such, where awareness is simply a passive reception of sensation somewhat analogous to the opening of a lens on a camera. One takes in experience and becomes experienced by virtue of the amount of experiences. Although under this interpretation one is able to account for the possibility of new experiences (the lens can always be opened), it cannot account for the transformation that occurs in the one who experiences. But this is precisely Hegel's point. Real experience is an undergoing that in its effectiveness involves a reversal (*Umkehrung*) in the experiencing consciousness. Consciousness, in other words, always undergoes a double experiencing, an experiencing of both the world and itself; and in fact, one can say that undergoing an experience lies precisely in this doubling: consciousness returns from the encounter with the unexpected phenomenon to the framework in which it initially grasped the phenomenon and transforms itself as a result of the encounter. In this negative experience consciousness has become aware that its object has changed and that it has changed as well. Such transformation can be described as a "reversal" whereby the experiencing conscious, in finding its expectations disappointed, turns back on itself and acquires a new horizon for future experience.

This reversal of consciousness constitutes the experiencing consciousness's education (*Bildung*), in the conversion to new experience the experiencing consciousness has learned something. As such the pathway of despair is a pathway to insight: in the dialectical movement of experience an initial unity is dissolved when confronted by something other, and in the insight into error discloses another truth. As dialectical, in the disclosing of another truth, the experiencing consciousness eventually moves to a higher level of insight. But this is not to say that Hegel interprets experience dialectically; on the contrary, the very character of dialectic is drawn from the nature of experience.[9] Moreover, in the reversal of consciousness, in the education of the experiencing consciousness, we are able to see at least the general character of the knowing that occurs *within* experience, namely, the insight achieved by the experiencing consciousness is recognition. The precise character of this recognition, however, remains to be seen.

But here too, as with Aristotle, we are faced with something in the thought of the thinker from which Gadamer recoils. In Hegel's case, Gadamer wants to reject any account of experience that has its foundation in a self-conscious spirit whose reshaping of itself ends with completion (absolute knowing), or for that matter that there is necessary advancement. For hermeneutic consciousness, experience itself can never be science (*Wissenschaft*), and in this sense, experience will always stand in opposition to knowing (*wissen*).[10] For Gadamer, "the dialectic of experience has its proper fulfillment not in definitive knowledge but in the openness to experience that is made possible [*freigespielt*] by experience itself" (TM 355/GW1 361). The person who is called experienced has become so not only through experiences, but also in the very openness to new experiences. This openness has little to do with being open-minded, as compared to someone who is prejudiced (in the narrow sense of this term). The openness is the exposure to what confronts us as other. Moreover, the openness to experience does not admit of closure for the end keeps on delaying its arrival in the sense that the openness is an openness to *more* experience.[11] If, for Gadamer, there is the dialectical element of reversal in experience, there is not at the same time any dialectical progression. What is delayed is not only absolute knowing, but also greater knowing. Thus, the experienced person, as it turns out, is not necessarily someone who simply has a vast storehouse of knowledge, but rather is someone who, drawing from the many experiences encountered, is now equipped to have new experiences and to learn from them.

Gadamer would consequently have us add a "qualitatively new element" to the concept of experience beyond the fact that it is a event over which no one has control (Aristotle) and that it is essentially always negative (Hegel). This new element is derived from the fact that experience, from which none are exempt, is constantly being acquired. But notice how it is, following Hegel, that experience is acquired. Within experience we are continually faced with the inevitable disappointments of our expectations, with the shattering of our accustomed way of life. Acquiring experience is essentially painful,[12] but this itself engenders insight in accord with the historical nature of the human: experience engenders the insight into contingency, the insight that we are not masters of our own fate. According to Gadamer:

Insight is more than the knowledge of this or that situation. It always involves an escape from something that had deceived us and held us captive. Thus insight always involves an element of self-knowledge and constitutes a necessary side of what we called experience in the proper sense. Insight is something we come to. It too is ultimately part of the vocation [*Bestimmung*] of man, i.e., to be discerning and insightful. (TM 356/GW1 362)

The negativity that emerges in the relation between experience and insight, was also witnessed, according to Gadamer, by Aeschylus. We learn, as Aeschylus says, through suffering ($\pi \acute{\alpha} \theta \epsilon \iota \ \mu \acute{\alpha} \theta o s$). This means not only that we learn from our mistakes and acquire a better knowledge of things through this disappointment. It also means why this is so: what we learn through suffering is the insight into the limitations of humanity, the religious insight into the boundary that separates the human from the divine. What we learn is the uncertainty of all predictions and the folly of attempting to master the future.[13] Experience is the experience of human finitude, and "genuine [*eigentliche*] experience is that whereby the human becomes aware of its finitude" (TM 357/GW1 363).

Thus, in the end, one could say that in the name of philosophical hermeneutics Gadamer is giving a renewed account of Socratic humility. Genuine experience, like Socratic wisdom, asks us to recover the space that separates the human from the divine in the attempt not only to recognize that space, but also to preserve it. And this means that in the openness to new experience dogmatism reaches its "absolute boundary."[14]

In undergoing experience we discover the limits of the power and the self-knowledge of our planning reason. The idea that everything can be reversed, that there is always time for everything and that everything somehow returns, proves to be an illusion. Rather, the person who is situated and acts in history continually experiences the fact that nothing returns. To acknowledge what is does not just mean to recognize what is at this moment here, but to have insight into the limited degree to which the future is still open to expectation and planning or, even more fundamentally, to have the insight that all the expectation and planning of finite beings is finite and limited. Genuine experience is experience of one's own historicity. (TM 357/GW1 363)

Philosophical Hermeneutics as Experience

The question remains for Gadamer how historically effected consciousness as a genuine form of experience reflects the general structure of experience. In what is perhaps the most curious transition in the whole of *Truth and Method*, Gadamer does not proceed directly to show how the elements of experience just discussed are in fact elements in hermeneutic experience. Rather, he restates in the broadest terms what has already been established about hermeneutic experience, and then proceeds to introduce the way in which the voice of the other is structured in hermeneutic experience. Hermeneutic experience, he tells us, is concerned with tradition. And tradition, as we have seen, is the transmission of meaning within the historicity of understanding. This is what is conveyed when Gadamer states without any explanation that tradition "is language—i.e., it expresses itself like a Thou [*Du*]" (TM 358/GW1 364).

Drawing on Buber's distinction between an I-It relation and an I-Thou relation without explicitly identifying it as such, Gadamer wants to press the point here that our involvement in tradition is a participatory relation, even more so, a dialogical participatory relation. For Buber the distinction between an I-It relation and an I-Thou relation is one between a relation (that is not actually a relation at all) characterized by distance, detachment, and instrumentality (I-It), and a relation characterized by directness, involvement, openness, mutuality, and presentness (I-Thou). Accordingly, the "Thou" is not an object (an "it"), but is in relationship with the I: the I-Thou is a true relation as a subject-to-subject relation. In Gadamer's hands, the I-Thou is not a subject-to-subject relation as a "mysterious communion of souls," but simply a participating, a sharing in meaning. This sharing is a sharing in tradition. This is why Gadamer says that "tradition is a genuine partner in dialogue, and we belong to it, as does the I with a Thou" (TM 258/GW1 364).

Although the I-Thou relation is overtly Buberian, one sees in the way this comes to be described by Gadamer that he has Hegel in mind as well.[15] That the I-Thou on its initial and even second level, as described by Gadamer, is not yet real, and that the I-Thou on the third level is something like mutual recognition, suggests that Gadamer's analysis is following the same pattern as the master-slave dialectic in Hegel's *Phenomenology*.

In looking at Gadamer's text, then, the meaning of experience implicit in the I-Thou relation unfolds on three levels, and for the kind of experience occurring on each level Gadamer is able to relate a corresponding notion of hermeneutic experience. It is only at the third level, however, that we can talk about genuine hermeneutic experience as such. First, there is the kind of experience of the Thou "that tries to discover typical behavior in one's fellowmen and can make predications about others on the basis of experience" (TM 358/GW1 364). The corresponding hermeneutic experience is characterized by a naive faith in scientific method that "flattens out the nature of hermeneutic experience" as we saw in the case of induction. Here tradition is turned into an object, confronting the interpreter in a free and uninvolved way. But this view of tradition, not unlike what we found in Neo-Kantianism, conceals the attempt to dominate tradition.

A second way of experiencing the Thou is to acknowledge the Thou as a person but still remain within a form of self-relatedness wherein the Thou loses the immediacy with which it makes its claim. This level is similar to the inauthentic dialectical relationship in the quest for mutual recognition that characterizes the master-slave relationship in Hegel's *Phenomenology*. That is to say, it is a level that lacks the genuine reciprocity of mutual recognition. The corresponding hermeneutic experience has traditionally been termed historical consciousness: "Historical consciousness knows about the otherness of the other, about the past in its otherness, just as the understanding of the Thou knows the Thou as a *person*" (TM 360/GW1 366). At this level there is a "false dialectical appearance" since it sees its task as one of mastering the past. The past is posited as a closed matter rather than being allowed to come forth in its own truth. Such a position fails to notice that the interpreter is influenced by historical circumstances; the interpreter reflects himself or herself out of the mutuality of the relation. The written (historical) text is questioned, but the interpreter is not!

The third, and genuine, form of experience of the Thou is this recognition of the other in a fundamental openness.

> In human relations the important thing is, as we have seen, to experience the Thou truly as a Thou—i.e., not to overlook his claim but to let him really say something to us. Here is where openness belongs. But ultimately this openness does not exist only for the person who speaks; rather, anyone who listens is fundamentally open. Without such openness to one another there is no genuine human bond. Belonging together always also means being able to listen to one another. . . . Openness to the other, then, involves recognizing that I myself must accept some things that are against me, even though no one else forces me to do so. (TM 361/GW1 367)

Thus in the genuine experience of the Thou there is the possibility of being corrected by the other. The corresponding hermeneutic experience is the recognition of the truth-claim that tradition presents. Here I acknowledge that tradition has something to say to me which calls for a fundamental openness. But openness, in view of its characterization in the analysis of experience, means something other than a liberal-mindedness. The openness to experience itself is an openness to what is alien and other. It is to face what refuses my framework. Thus Gadamer concludes: "The hermeneutical consciousness culminates not in methodological sureness of itself, but in the same readiness for experience that distinguishes the experienced individual from the individual captivated by dogma. As we can now say more exactly in terms of the concept of experience, this readiness is what distinguishes historically effected consciousness" (TM 362/GWl 368).

In view of this third and genuine form of hermeneutic experience we have all the more reason to say that hermeneutic experience is the encounter with the voice of the other. And the openness to experience, as the willingness to listen, means accordingly not to consume and assimilate the other but to suffer what is beyond oneself. But there is no waiting to be addressed, one is always already addressed by the voice of the other, even if it happens behind my back. Such is the event character, the happening, of experience.

§ 10. Experience and Memory

To be sure, Gadamer's analysis of experience is guided primarily by the way this concept is understood by Hegel. For Hegel, as we have seen, the concept of experience is such that knowing takes place within experience, as the experience of the real (*wirklich*). This knowing is consistent with the inner historicity of experience that even Dilthey ignores in his orientation toward science. We have also seen that Hegel describes this knowing commensurate with this condition of experience as recognition. Gadamer too speaks of recognition in conjunction with (hermeneutic) experience. The issue here is to say something more about this knowing peculiar to hermeneutic experience.

In "The Universality of the Hermeneutical Problem," an essay that summarizes the project of *Truth and Method*, Gadamer tells us that the human experience of life presents itself as historically effected consciousness, which has its fulfillment in what is linguistic. To this he then adds that as such historically effected consciousness provides an initial schematization for all our possibilities of knowing. This schematization is described through an illustration of how a child learns to speak:

> In his first apperception, a sensuously equipped being finds himself in a surging sea of stimuli, and finally one day he begins, as we say, to know something. Clearly we do not mean that he was previously blind. Rather, when we say "to know" [*erkenen*] we mean "to recognize" [*Wiedererkennen*], that is, to pick something out [*herauserkennen*] of the stream of images flowing past as being identical. What is picked out in this fashion is clearly retained. But how? When does a child know its mother for the first time? When it sees her for the first time? No. Then when? How does it take place? Can we really say at all that there is a single event in which a first knowing extricates the child from the darkness of not knowing? It seems obvious to me that we cannot. (PH 14/GW2 229)

This illustration, which is identical in structure with Aristotle's image of the fleeing army, underscores the sense in which a first knowing is precluded from within the process of experience, and yet there is knowing. The knowing appropriate to this condition is re-cognition, a knowing again, a knowing that secures the identity of what was encountered once before.

This notion of recognition in its most general form has been present from the outset in as much as the hermeneutic "circle" is a configuration of repetition and recognition. The hermeneutic "circle" acquires its movement on the basis of an always prior interpretation, such that, in one form at least, interpretation is simply a matter of making explicit, of laying out (*Auslegung*), what we already implicitly understand.[16] Moreover, this knowing which excludes inaugural acts is, at once, always beyond self-contained consciousness. We are always already given over to the world in some way. For Gadamer, what we are given over to is not a set of ideas but tradition, where tradition designates the giving over itself as *trans-dure*. In tradition there is the element of belongingness (*Zugehörigkeit*) as such. And this too we have encountered before, namely, in the preceding analysis of the experience of the Thou as the form of hermeneutic experience. Belongingness, which demands listening (*Hören*) as the ability to be fundamentally open, means that every event of understanding "dissolves" into a new familiarity "in which tradition belongs to us and we to it." And so, by virtue of this element of "being given over," of finding oneself in an already constituted framework of interpretation, hermeneutic experience can be nothing less than a re-cognizing as a gathering-together-again. The knowing appropriate to hermeneutic experience can thus be said to be a form of recollection. But this means that hermeneutic experience, like Socratic knowing caught between knowing and not knowing, endures in the element of memory.[17]

How, though, are we to understand this element of memory? In the context of a discussion of the nature of *Bildung*, one of the guiding concepts of humanism, Gadamer remarks how Helmholz speaks of the concept of memory, but in a way that is insufficient to explain what is at issue. From what has already said about hermeneutic experience, it is apparent that memory cannot be regarded here as merely a general talent or capacity, that is, as a psychological faculty in which remembering functions as an operation of retrieval of stored facts (TM 15/GW1 21). And it has even less to do with a theory of innate ideas as a remembering of what the mind already knows. The question of memory is one of understanding memory as an element of our finite historical being. A direction for this question can be found in the phenomenon of forgetting as the condition for the possibility of remembering, in any form. That is to say, there is a need to remember only because something has been forgotten.

This direction is provided by Gadamer himself, but surprisingly, he gives us only the direction. "Forgetting," he tells us, "is closely related to keeping in mind [*Behalten*] and remembering [*Sich-Erinnern*] in a way that has long been insufficiently noticed; forgetting is not merely an absence and a lack, but as Nietzsche pointed out, a condition of the life of the mind" (TM 16/GW1 21). What Gadamer means is easy enough to see. In its ordinary use, forgetting is thought of as an omission, absence pure and simple, of a presence. The businesswoman forgets her appointment, the actor forgets his lines, the schoolgirl forgets to do her homework. In each case the omission is an absence of a prior presence. A similar notion of forgetting is found in the phenomenon of habit. The habitual, by its very nature, omits the inaugural event that provides the condition for the habit. For example, a relationship between two people that is merely habitual omits, by covering over, original promises, intentions, and insights. But it not is just the origin that is omitted; the merely habitual omits, again by covering over, the new through the routine that pervades the merely habitual.

And yet, upon further consideration the phenomenon of habit shows itself to be a complex phenomenon, and as such points to the dynamic sense of forgetting suggested in Gadamer's remark. If in one sense the merely habitual omits the new, in another sense, the habitual makes the new possible. The practicing of a musical instrument is illustrative here. Through practice we cover over originality; the form of repetition of practicing is by its design that of self-sameness. And yet, through this very habit originality is made possible. On the basis of the habitual the accomplished musician is able to explode the piece of music from the inside so that it is never the same. In such a situation forgetting, as the covering over of original presence, is not at all a mere absence but more like a latent possibility for originality. The forgetting of the habitual gives the event its future.

In similar fashion we can understand the reference to Nietzsche, which is in fact a reference to Nietzsche's notion of an "active forgetfulness." In "On the Advantage and Disadvantage of History for Life," Nietzsche's second of four *Untimely Meditations* (*Unzeitgemässe Betrachtungen*), the dynamics of remembering and forgetting are taken up in conjunction with the issue of the way in which the human species lives historically. Authentic life, by virtue of temporality, must be lived in history. But the burden of the past, its intractability, continues to thwart this authenticity. For Nietzsche, the problem is one not of denying the past, but of learning to forget it, to clear a space for thought.[18] But such forgetting is simultaneously a remembering, as an act of the will, of choosing to remember in one particular way or another. Thus Nietzsche too recognizes that memory is not a mere retrieval of a past event. The individual's remembrance of the past, which serves to define the present—and *a fortiori* the future—will manifest the individual's creative or destructive tendencies toward life. Accordingly, countering the self-destructiveness in our capacity to remember, Nietzsche calls for a creative forgetfulness to turn historical consciousness toward an empowering of life itself.

In *On the Genealogy of Morals*, we once again encounter this notion of active forgetfulness. And here too, as in the earlier work, Nietzsche describes memory as a form of willfulness which displaces the creative individual by binding individuals to a fixed past and thus to a specific future. What is new here is the way in which morality, and the notion of obligation in particular, is now understood in this context. A promise taken and remembered imposes a kind of order on human life. Conscience, by chaining the will to a prior condition, is itself a form of memory that binds us to a fixed past and to a specific future. But unlike conscience, as the remembering of a promise which imposes a fixed order on human life, forgetting works in the opposite direction. Nietzsche writes:

> To close the doors and windows of consciousness for a time; to
> remain undisturbed by the noise and struggle of our underworld
> of utility organs working with and against one another; a little
> quietness, a little *tabula rasa* of the consciousness, to make room
> for new things, above all for the premeditation (for our organ is
> an oligarchy)—that is the purpose of active forgetfulness, which
> is like a doorkeeper, a preserver of psychic order, repose, and
> etiquette: so that it will be immediately obvious how there could
> be no happiness, no cheerfulness, no hope, no pride, no *present*,
> without forgetfulness.[19]

In forgetfulness we make room for new things. In active forgetfulness we
are, as paradoxical as it sounds, remembering what is one's ownmost
possibility, that is, one's will.

It is somewhat curious that Gadamer would make his brief remark
on forgetting by a reference to Nietzsche and not to Heidegger; after all,
Nietzsche does not make any attempt to place the notion of forgetting within
the context of recollection as does Heidegger. What we learn from Heidegger
actually serves to unlock the whole problem as it pertains to hermeneutic
experience. In *Kant and the Problem of Metaphysics* Heidegger remarks
that "the finitude of Dasein—the understanding of Being—lies in forgetfulness [*Vergessenheit*]."[20] As a dimension of finitude, forgetfulness is not
at all accidental or temporary, but is constantly and necessarily renewed.
Heidegger continues: "All fundamental-ontological constructions which take
aim at the unveiling of the inner possibility of the understanding of Being
must, in projecting, wrest the forgetfulness away from what is apprehended
in the projection. The basic fundamental-ontological act of the Metaphysics
of Dasein as the laying of the ground for metaphysics is hence a 'remembering again' [*Wiedererinnerung*]."[21] The hermeneutics of fundamental
ontology is enacted as a recovery from forgetfulness, from oblivion.[22]

We know, following Heidegger along his path of thinking, that the
character of this ontological forgetfulness, as with everything that is
"essential" for Heidegger, takes its bearing from the Greeks, and in particular, from the Greek word ἀλήθεια. In the letter to William Richardson,
written in 1962, Heidegger tells us that forgetting must be thought in Greek
fashion as withdrawal into concealment (λήθη).[23] How then does it stand
with remembering? Here too Heidegger would have us give it a "genuinely
Greek interpretation," naturally enough, as attaining to unconcealment.
Heidegger remarks without elaboration that "Plato's ἀνάμνησις of Ideas

implies: catching-sight-once-again [*wieder-zu-Gesicht-Bekommen*], the revealing of beings."[24] The hermeneutics of the Being-question holds within it something of the character of recollection that we find in Plato.

Perhaps the best evidence for this is found in Heidegger's description of thinking in *What is Called Thinking*. Here Heidegger says that thinking is a remembering, but the memory of remembering does not signify the "capacity to retain things that are in the past." Memory as retention is derivative of a more primordial sense of memory, just as thinking as logical-rational representations is a reduction from a more primordial sense of the word. The fundamental sense of thinking and memory in their interconnectedness can be traced to the Old English word for thought, *"thanc"* (*Gedanc*).[25] What is said in the originary word is that thinking is in need of memory. According to Heidegger, "originally, memory means as much as devotion: a constant concentrated abiding with something—not just with something that has passed, but in the same way with what is present and with what may come."[26] As abiding with something, memory is imbued with the quality of recalling but equally so with the quality of unrelenting retention. Retention refers as much to past as what is present and to come. Ultimately, retention is limited to what is past because the past slips away "and in a way no longer affords a lasting hold." This kind of retention, the recovery of what is past, is re-calling memory. *"Thanc"* is memory in this original sense of the "gathering of the constant intention of everything that the heart holds in present being." *"Thanc"* means the heart's core; it is the gathering of all that concerns us. This is memory: "the gathering of thinking back into what must be thought." Such gathering-together is never an "after-the-fact collection of what basically exists, but the tidings that overtake all our doings."[27]

The essential belonging together of thought to the matter of thought unfolds as a recollecting—a gathering-together-again. It is this recollecting that unites and at the same time divides the hermeneutics of Gadamer and Heidegger. For Gadamer too all our attempts at philosophizing are attempts at the remembrance of Being as a recovery from forgetfulness.

> Remembrance [*Erinnerung*] is always what comes to one, what comes over one, so that a bringing-to-mind-again [*Wiedervergegenwärtiges*] offers a brief respite from passing away and forgetting. Remembrance of being however is besides not remembrance of something formerly known and now brought to mind, but remembrance of a former questioning, remembrance of a missing

[*verschollene*] question. But then any question that is posed as a question is no longer remembered. As the remembrance of what was once asked, it is the now asked. (GW2 503)

For Gadamer the remembrance of Being is nothing more than "that of 'the spirit that would like to unite us'—we who are a conversation" (DD 110/GW2 369). This means, against Heidegger, that the remembrance of Being is not about the remembrance of the *history* of Being. Remembrance has no history for Gadamer.[28]

But precisely how is hermeneutic recollection understood in philosophical hermeneutics? We should recall that from the perspective of historical understanding the task of the human sciences as a whole is one of letting the tradition speak. And, in the effort to do this—to overcome the fundamental distantiation of the past—we must bring it near so that it speaks in a new voice.[29] The analysis of experience reveals the same structure. Experience, by virtue of its undergoing, is an openness to new experience. This element of newness, through which the voice of hermeneutic understanding becomes a voice of difference, means that hermeneutic recollection is never a mere making-present-again of a past actuality, but a making-present-again as a gathering-together-anew. Hermeneutic recollection is not the recovering of something lost (prior presence) but discovery.[30]

Earlier on in *Truth and Method* Gadamer had actually linked the sense of this discovery to the function of imitation in art. Imitation is a reproduction of the real in an image. But as Gadamer understands this, such reproduction is not a copying of an original but a presentation (*Darstellung*) such that what is is *there*. The performance of a theatrical play for example is to be understood as a (re)production that does not make-present-again a past actuality, but, in the transformation of the play of art into figurative structure (*Gebilde*), produces a present (new) meaning. Even in something so simple as the imitation present in the child playing at "dressing-up," the presentation is such that only what is presented should exist. The child does not want to be discovered behind the disguise, but wants to be discovered as the disguise, and that is also what the spectator to this little game is to see. The cognitive import of imitation, the making-present-again, lies in recognition. And in recognition it is not so much that the familiar is known again as it is that more becomes known than is already known (TM 114/GW1 119).

Gadamer is not at all hesitant to suggest that this way of viewing recollection as recognition is actually quite close to the description of recollection given by Plato.

In recognition what we know emerges, as if illuminated, from all the contingent and variable circumstances that condition it; it is grasped in its essence. It is known as something.

This is the central motif of Platonism. In his theory of anamnesis Plato combined the mythical idea of remembrance [*Wiedererinnerung*] with his dialectic, which sought the truth of being in the *logoi*, i.e., the ideality of language. In fact this kind of idealism of being is already suggested in the phenomenon of recognition. (TM 114/GW1 119)

Insofar as Plato's theory of recollection is not taken in its traditional metaphysical way, the interpretation that Gadamer presents here is indeed plausible. In interpreting the myth of the cycle of souls in the *Phaedrus*, Socrates equates recollection, as a gathering-together, with the philosophic life. Such gathering-together is what for Plato renews the vision of true Being: "for a human being must understand a general conception formed by collecting into a unity by means of reason the many perceptions of the senses."[31] Recollection is simply the way in which human knowing "gives an account"; it is the particular form of human *logos*: to recollect is to gather together in the sense of both collecting and preserving in its collectedness.

Certainly for Gadamer the historicity of understanding argues against the assertion that hermeneutic recollection aims at the achievement of the "the timeless target of all learning." But, of course, the same argument could be made, for different reasons, for Socratic recollection. In view of this, one could say that recollection, whether Socratic or hermeneutic, is the event of continual reacquisition that has the character of "present enactment,"[32] the gathering together that leaves behind what is unessential in speaking. Such recollection is in accord with the repetition in the transmission of tradition. Gadamer insists that tradition should speak not only in a new voice—in which case hermeneutic recollection can only be a recollecting forward[33]—but in a clearer voice.

The sense of present enactment is decisive for philosophical hermeneutics. As enactment, the recollective recognition is identified as an event of meaning that takes place in the doing, in the exercise, in the performing. This is most obvious in the case of art that for Gadamer has its being only in the performance (*Vollzug*) (GW2 391). But it is also true of the event of understanding in its most actualized form as a linguistic communicative event. The communicative event is the *Vollzug* of language. The character of the enactment as a *present* enactment, though, is given expression even before part 3 of *Truth and Method*; it is precisely what is at issue in Gadamer's model for the problems of hermeneutic understanding, namely, φρόνσις, which includes the specific hermeneutic problem of application (*Anwendung*).

It is not without reason that Gadamer's first consideration under "The Recovery of the Fundamental Hermeneutic Problem" in *Truth and Method* is the problem of application. Here Gadamer points out how it was the Romantic tradition of nineteenth-century hermeneutic theory that separated application from understanding and interpretation. In the earlier tradition of hermeneutics, in the Pietism of J. J. Rambach for example, one still finds a threefold distinction within the act of understanding between *subtilitas intelligendi* (understanding), *subtilitas explicandi* (interpretation), and *subtilitas applicandi* (application). Strictly speaking, Gadamer does not want to return to the threefold distinction, since understanding, interpretation, and application are in this context three separate "subtleties." Rather, he sees the three elements comprising one unified process. Application is to be regarded as an integral part of the event of understanding. For Gadamer "understanding is always already application" (TM 309/GW1 314). Meaningful interpretation requires adaption to the actual situation. This, Gadamer claims, has always been the task of hermeneutics. The ancient Greeks had to interpret (read: translate, apply) the message of the Delphic oracle to the concrete situation to which it was speaking.

This does not mean, of course, that the issue of application is how understanding can be properly applied, as if it were a matter of a practical activity of taking a prior understanding (through concepts) and applying this to a situation, as if it were a matter of a simple application of the general to the particular. We have already seen in the context of the analysis of experience how this model is insufficient to account for the knowing that takes place in process.

Equally misleading is the confusion of application with appropriation.[34] Although it is true that for Gadamer all understanding is self-understanding and consequently appropriation (which conveys the idea of making one's own) could be seen as integral to hermeneutic experience, it is not a sufficient rendering of *Anwendung*, which conveys the Latin applicatio. This confusion can be traced to the failure to adequately separate the hermeneutic projects of Gadamer and Ricoeur.[35] It is Ricoeur who specifically argues that the mediation of meaning that takes place in any "objectifying study of a text" occurs as appropriation, which is his translation of the German term *Aneignung*. As Ricoeur understands it:

According to the intention of the word, the aim of all hermeneutics is to struggle against cultural distance and historical alienation. Interpretation brings together, equalizes, renders contemporary and similar. This goal is attained only insofar as interpretation actualizes the meaning of the text for the present reader.[36]

Ricoeur even goes so far to say that, as appropriation, interpretation is an event. It all sounds like Gadamer, but Gadamer does not privilege sameness—the rendering similar, the reduction of the other to the same, that appropriation seeks—in the way Ricoeur does, and in fact has to for the sake of the correspondence required in any methodological orientation. Gadamer does not really see hermeneutics as a subject's struggle against cultural distance, but asks about the possibility of hearing voices that are culturally distanced. Gadamer does not say that every interpretation is an *Aneignung*; he says it is an *Anwendung*: the concretization of meaning that defines the present enactment. In speaking about the practice of understanding, Gadamer writes: "In the end it was the great theme of the concretization of the universal that I learned to think of as the basic experience of hermeneutics" (RAS 49).[37] This experience is such that the universal is in need of application, and that for the application of rules there exists no rule (being in the thick of things of experience). *Anwendung* is a form of practice.

To see precisely what Gadamer means one has only to look at his own examples from theological and legal hermeneutics. There has always been an "art" of interpretation with respect to the Holy Scripture. But, as Gadamer tells it, this art served more as guidelines "for making the Holy Scripture useful to the dogmatic tradition of the Church" and was not intended "to supply a way of interpreting Holy Scripture for the sake of mediating correct doctrine" (RAS 127). But the Reformation's return to the Scripture itself changed all this. The Reformation had the effect of setting the Christian message in the foreground such that the interpretation of Scripture in the sermon became more prominent in the worship service. Accordingly, theological hermeneutics serves, not a scientific understanding of Scripture, but "the practice of proclamation by which the good news is supposed to reach the simple person in such a way that he realizes that he is addressed and intended" (RAS 128–29). The sermon of the preacher is the application of Scripture to the particular situation of the congregation; in this sense application is at the core of understanding itself.

A similar situation holds for legal hermeneutics.[38] The judge, in interpreting the law, is performing a practical task, but it is not an arbitrary reinterpretation of the law that he or she performs. What takes place in hermeneutic experience in general would also be true of the judge in interpreting the law: "to understand and to interpret means to *discover* and *recognize* a valid meaning" (emphasis added; TM 328/GW1 333). The judge, in adapting the law to the needs of the present, seeks to discover the "legal idea" of a law by linking it with the present, which cannot be done in a methodological or formal way. For if such were the case the meaning of the law would be present before the application to the concrete situation. But, in fact, the law is *there* only in its application to the concrete situation. The hermeneutic circle of whole and part, expressed here in the relation between the universality of the law and the particular case, acquires its movement with the inception of application. And here, as legal hermeneutics makes us so acutely aware, one is constantly confronted with the "indissoluble problematic" that the universal, as something of which we are aware, is subject to in its application.

> [T]he task of finding the law and coming up with a verdict contains an inexorable tension that Aristotle has already thematized clearly: the tension between the universality of the valid legal framework, whether codified or uncodified, and the individual concrete case. That a concrete passing of judgment in a legal question is no theoretical statement but an instance of "doing things with words" is almost too obvious to bear mentioning. (RAS 125–26).

This dynamic procedure of passing judgment describes the work of concretization.

What legal hermeneutics demonstrates—and this would pertain to theological hermeneutics as well—is that application, as a form of practice, is this "present enactment." The application of the law is at once the *recognition* of what is meant in this particular present case. But how does the recognition of meaning pertain to new meaning, to the accretion of reality that happens in dynamic repetition? To the extent that the application of a law and the interpretation of a law go hand in hand, "each application of a law goes beyond the mere understanding of its legal sense and fashions a new reality" (RAS 126).[39] The interpretation of a law, analogous to task of the hermeneut of bringing the voice of tradition to speak again in a clearer voice, clarifies further the meaning of a given law.

If it is the case then that *Anwendung* is a form of praxis, what remains to be seen is how the event of understanding is linked to the notion of practical reasoning in Aristotle and ultimately how philosophical hermeneutics is understood as practical philosophy. What cannot be overlooked is that it is φϱόνησις that exhibits hermeneutic recollection: from within one's education and citizenship, there is application, the gathering-together-again, of the vague ideals of virtue to the concrete demand of the situation.

§ 11. Φϱόνησις *as a Paradigm for Hermeneutic Experience*

Thus far it has been established that experience is more than a process in service to the objective order of scientific knowledge. But this does not mean that experience is consequently relegated to a subjective order. The issue is rather that genuine experience precedes the methodical process that produces scientific knowledge. Furthermore, the account of experience has shown itself to hold within itself a conception of knowledge that is likewise independent of the methodological procedure of modern science. The concept of experience for which this knowing is appropriate emerges from practical life. This is what was suggested at the end of the previous section where the issue of application in hermeneutic experience was said to lead to a consideration of Aristotle's practical philosophy.

Actually, the analysis of practical reasoning fulfills a double intention, the fulfillment of which clearly demonstrates the centrality of the analysis for the project of philosophical hermeneutics. In *Truth and Method*, under the section "The hermeneutic relevance of Aristotle," Gadamer intends to show how Aristotle's analysis of φϱόνησις "is in fact a kind of model of the problems of hermeneutics" (TM 324/GW1 329). This intention completes the analysis that was anticipated at the end of the previous section. The problem of application in interpretation is similar to the problem of application in Aristotle's account of ethical action. Applying ethical norms to the conduct of our life, to the concrete demands of the situation, is the model for interpreting the text for the one who wishes to understand.

But at the same time Gadamer wants to claim that philosophical hermeneutics is the successor subject to the classical tradition of practical philosophy. Philosophical hermeneutics provides an orientation, which is present in Aristotle's practical philosophy, "for a scientific and critical effort which shares the modern ideal of method and yet does not lose the condition of solidarity with and justification of our practical living."[40] This means that philosophical hermeneutics is to be viewed as an authentic description of the conditions of our practical life. More to the point, philosophical hermeneutics speaks to the conditions of our moral and social practice in such a way that it is to be seen as a corrective to the inappropriate extension of modern methodological science to the conditions of social life.

Let us consider, first, how Aristotle's practical reasoning is a model for hermeneutic experience. According to Gadamer, the fact that Aristotle sought to make a distinction between theoretical and non-theoretical sciences—based on the methodological principle that method must always be directed toward its object—is a decisive step beyond the Platonic identification of virtue and knowledge.[41] Aristotle recognized that human civilization differs from nature insofar as human behavior derives its character from what one has become. Accordingly, ἔθος differs from φύσις "in being a sphere in which the laws of nature do not operate, yet not a sphere of lawlessness but of human institutions and human modes of behavior which are mutable and like rules only to a limited degree" (TM 312/GW1 318). A unique kind of legitimation is called for then in the realization that the good in human life lacks a certain specificity. But even though, as Aristotle tells us, we can attribute only as much precision in any science as the subject matter allows, it is not just a question of a lesser degree of certainty on the part of non-theoretical sciences. Since we encounter the good in the concrete situations which we find ourselves in, the task of practical reasoning (φρόνησις) is to see in that concrete situation what is asked for, and this is of a different order of knowing. Φρόνησις differs from ἐπιστήμη, which not only aims at verifying what is always the case but also demands a sense of detachment from the observed situation.[42]

With respect to this other kind of knowledge, the knowledge not of eternal things, but of what is variable—a knowledge with respect to activity—there is a most important distinction drawn by Aristotle. That is to say, φρόνησις not only differs from ἐπιστήμη, it also differs from a knowledge similar to itself, namely, τέχνη. Both φρόνησις and τέχνη involve the application of knowledge to the particular task, but practical (ethical) know-how is not the same as practical (technical) know-how. We do not make a human life, a making with respect to φρόνησις, in the same way we employ a technical skill to make a specific thing, a making with respect to τέχνη. Following Aristotle, Gadamer points to three ways in which φρόνησις and τέχνη differ.

First, as we have just indicated, although in both cases knowledge is acquired through practice, the manner of this practice is different for each. In technical knowing the knowledge does not change in any fundamental way; the skills of the carpenter are acquired and the carpenter gains proficiency in the repetition of the skill. Such a skill can be learned, but for that matter it can also be forgotten. Ethical knowing, on the other hand, is such that knowing how to act with respect to a certain moral virtue may indeed change. Moreover, ethical reasoning is not something we can choose to utilize or not; rather, we find ourselves (always already) in an acting situation and have to apply ethical knowledge to the exigencies of this concrete situation. This determination of ethical knowing only serves to heighten the problem of the difference between φϱόνησιs and τέχνη inasmuch as application is itself problematic. It would appear that we can only apply what we already possess, yet the situation of our ethical life is that we are not in possession of ethical knowledge prior to the action itself; the particular situation will affect the knowledge of what the virtue is. The application is not simply a matter of following a procedure as one follows a recipe in cooking, but is a matter of perceiving what is at stake in the situation. In Gadamer's view, the full scope of the problem can be seen in Aristotle's analysis of natural law.

In Book 5 of the *Ethics* Aristotle distinguishes natural law from convention in order to oppose the strict framework of legal positivism. The distinction, though, is not simply one between an unchangeable natural law and a changeable positive law, for, by Aristotle's account, unchangeable natural law would seem to be limited to the gods. Among men "all rules of justice are variable."[43] The issue then is to see how change is compatible with natural law. Gadamer interprets Aristotle to be saying the following: "some laws are entirely a matter of mere agreement (e.g., traffic regulations), but there are also things that do not admit of regulation simply by mere human convention, because the 'nature of the thing' constantly asserts itself. Thus it is quite legitimate to call such things 'natural law'" (TM 319/GW1 324). So, insofar as natural law has a certain free-play within it, it can admit of change. Aristotle gives us several examples of what is meant here: (1) the right hand is naturally stronger than the left, although it is possible to become ambidextrous; (2) wine measures are not equal everywhere with respect to buying and selling and thus there seems to be a free-play within set limits; (3) the best state is everywhere the same but not in the same way that fire burns everywhere the same whether in Greece or in Persia.[44] According to Gadamer, natural law has only a critical function; in deciding what is equitable we appeal to natural law when there is a conflict between one law and another or when we need to correct the one-sidedness of any law.

But what does this say about the problem of application? Gadamer is arguing here that what Aristotle says about natural law is true of all the ideas that we have of what we ought to be. Despite the variety of ethical ideas, there is still in this sphere something like "the nature of the thing." But the nature of the thing is not some kind of fixed yardstick that we first recognize and then apply it; the norm itself is at stake in ethical life. And, if it is true that we are always already involved in a moral and political commitment—and again, for Aristotle the ethical man does begin with his citizenship and education and from this he is asked to make claims about the good—then we can only acquire the nature of the thing from this standpoint. Can it be otherwise than to say that our guiding principles have the validity of schemata which is to say that "they are concretized only in the concrete situation of the person acting"? (TM 320/GW1 326). But this means that everything depends on *seeing* the situation, a seeing that is not theoretical, which affects the guiding principles.[45]

Second, ethical knowledge differs from technical knowledge in the conceptual relation between means and ends. Here the distinction is more straightforward. At the level of technique the end is a particular thing or product, and technical skill is a knowledge of the means; it is a calculation of the means for producing it. At the level of ethical knowledge the end is the good life, "right living in general," which is not so determined as the product of technical skill. More important, though, Gadamer tells us that with respect to the means "technical activity does not demand that the means which allow it to arrive at an end be weighted anew on each occasion and personally by the subject who is the practitioner" (PHC 36). But such is the case for ethical knowing; thus unique to it is self-deliberation, which only reinforces the idea that ethical knowledge is never something known in advance in the manner of a technique. In connection with this difference, it must also be noted that the determination of means in ethical knowing affects the determination of the end whereby ethical knowledge entails a reciprocal (or perhaps circular) relation between means and ends. Again, for ethical knowledge there can be no anterior certainty concerning what the good life is directed toward as a whole, for the ends themselves are at stake in deliberating about the means appropriate to *this* situation.[46]

Third, the "knowledge-for-the-sake-of-oneself" of ethical judgment, unlike τέχνη, has a unique relation to itself. This can be seen most clearly in the notion of understanding (σύνεσις) in practical matters. This "modification" of the virtue of ethical judgment is directed, not at oneself, but toward the other person as the ability to judge statements made by another person about matters that belong to the realm of practical wisdom. Gadamer thinks that this notion of placing oneself in the concrete situation in which the other person has to act points, once again, to the fact that ethical knowledge is not a generalized knowledge but always a specification at a particular moment that can't be determined in advance. This kind of productive knowledge cannot be understood as technical knowledge: "Understanding another as a unique phenomenon is not simply the technical knowledge of the psychologist, nor the equivalent everyday experience possessed by the 'wily' [*malin*] or 'resourceful' [*debrouillard*] man" (PHC 36).

Gadamer recognizes that Aristotle employs a narrow designation of σύνεσις when it stands for a kind of intellectual virtue; Aristotle wants to make a distinction between understanding and practical wisdom in order to say that we ourselves do not have to be morally excellent in order to recognize moral excellence in others. Nevertheless, the more neutral sense of the word that is encountered in the context of the phenomenon of learning and stands in close proximity to μάθησις is also used by Aristotle. In this sense, one would say that the person with understanding—"being habitually understanding toward others"—does not judge as one who stands apart and unaffected. But this projecting oneself into the situation of the other implies for Gadamer much more than a mere understanding of something said. Rather, it involves

> a kind of communality in virtue of which reciprocal taking counsel, the giving and taking advice, is at all meaningful in the first place. Only friends and persons with an attitude of friendliness can give advice. In fact this points right to the center of the questions connected with the idea of practical philosophy, for moral implications are entailed by this counterpart to moral reasonableness (*phronesis*). What he analyzes here in his *Ethics* are virtues, normative notions that always stand under the presupposition of their normative validity. The virtue of practical reason is not to be thought of as a neutral capacity for finding the practical means for correct purposes or ends, but it is inseparably bound up with what Aristotle calls *ethos*. *Ethos* for him is the *arche*, the "that" from which all practical-political enlightenment has to set out. (RAS 133)[47]

In what way, then—if it is not already apparent—can we say that Aristotle's description of ethical reasoning is a model for hermeneutic experience? The interpreter who seeks to understand the text, or what this piece of tradition says, or for that matter, another person, cannot disregard him or herself and his or her particular hermeneutical situation. This deep connection between that which is to be understood and the one who seeks to understand is what characterizes the virtue of practical reasoning with respect to ethical knowledge. To possess the virtue of practical reasoning is to be aware of the normative viewpoints one follows and to know "how to make them effective in the concrete decisions demanded by the practical situation." The best word for φρόνησις in English is in fact "judgment"; it is the determination of the good that cannot be done by rules. Certainly the situational character of ethical judgment makes philosophical ethics a "methodologically difficult problem," but then again, this is precisely the problematic that motivates the whole discussion of "truth and method." Hermeneutics is not a *Kunstlehre*, a doctrine for a technique, but a practice requiring moral wisdom, engagement, and practical application in relation to oneself.

§ 12. The Primacy of Practice

At the outset of the previous section we indicated that as a result of the recovery of the hermeneutic problem in the analysis of φρόνησις, Gadamer can claim that philosophical hermeneutics is the successor subject to the classical tradition of practical philosophy. This succession goes decisively beyond what our previous section asserted—that hermeneutics is not simply a theory or even the mechanical application of a set of rules but a practice involving judgment. The succession entails also that the hermeneutic problem in the humanities and social sciences concerned with understanding human life is inseparable from the hermeneutic problem in our human practical life, in what Gadamer calls "our communicatively unfolded orientations in the world." In this latter context Gadamer understands the problem to be one of the distortion in the notion of practice in contemporary life that has occurred as a result of a certain forgetfulness about the nature of science in relation to practical life.

In order to see this distortion in the notion of practice, let us recall the distinction in science made by Aristotle: the realm of "rigorous" science (θεωρία) is distinguished from the realm of human action (πρᾶξις). In the former, demonstration yields certainty and knowledge for its own sake (ἐπιστήμη); in the latter, demonstration occurs in the form of practical reasonableness (φρόνησις). In the previous section the principal concern was with the distinction between φρόνησις and τέχνη; that is, with the difference in knowing occurring in the realms of πρᾶξις and ποίησις, the artificial production for which τέχνη is appropriate. These distinctions underscore the point for Aristotle that the realm of $\pi\rho\hat{\alpha}\xi\iota\varsigma$ does not stand outside the activity of knowing, nor is $\pi\rho\hat{\alpha}\xi\iota\varsigma$ something ancillary to the realm of $\theta\epsilon\omega\rho\iota\alpha$. Yet this is how it is interpreted in modern science. In Gadamer's judgment modern science has become a hybrid of $\dot{\epsilon}\pi\iota\sigma\tau\dot{\eta}\mu\eta$ and $\tau\dot{\epsilon}\chi\nu\eta$, and in this union distorts practice by transforming it into the application of science to technical tasks.

Historically, the intrusion of $\tau\dot{\epsilon}\chi\nu\eta$ into science occurs with Galileo's mechanics. Here science will renounce the primarily experienceable and familiar totality of our world in its subjection of nature to mathematical construction. This new notion of science makes possible, in an encompassing way for the first time, the ability to see the world in terms of abstract relations. Theoretical knowing becomes a "calculus of quantification" where the anticipation of objectified results guides the procedure. Modern experimental science thus makes possible an "ideal of construction," "the ideal of a nature artificially produced in accord with an idea" (RAS 70). In these terms modern science is essentially monological—making no real distinction in methodology between the natural and human sciences.

More to the point, science's subjection of nature expresses the overall pattern of science as an advancing into unmastered realms, an advancing that does not halt.[48] In the last two centuries this framework of science has entered the social sphere in an encompassing way. But this is to say at once that $\tau\dot{\epsilon}\chi\nu\eta$ has entered the sphere of $\pi\rho\hat{\alpha}\xi\iota\varsigma$ resulting in a distortion of $\pi\rho\hat{\alpha}\xi\iota\varsigma$. Contemporary life is determined to a large extent by its technical production in which the technical expertise from the mastery of the forces of nature has been transferred to social life. We look to science for guidance in overcoming the problems of social reality and in the guise of intentional planning there emerges the expectation of a mastery of society by scientific reason.[49] From scientific market analysis to scientific rearing of children, the application of science to all fields of social life gives expertise a commanding position in economy and society. But it is precisely here that we begin to see the distortion in the notion of practice; for the expert, which the scientist becomes because of his or her superior knowledge, has been invested with an exaggerated authority. The expert is the one we look to for giving us true directives for acting, that is, "for the discharging of the practical, political, and economic decisions one needs to make," instead of relying on our own practical and political experience. The discontinuity between the technical expert, as the master of applied scientific knowledge and the fact of his or her own membership in society is troublesome for Gadamer. Gadamer does not doubt that the expert is a reliable investigator and even acknowledges that the expert is perhaps aware that the results of his or her investigation have a limited relevance, but the expert cannot substitute for genuine practical and political reason and act in the name of everyone else. The expert, and a society that relies on the expert, remains essentially rootless without practical (hermeneutical) reason, which one employs to guide and illuminate life situations.[50]

In a somewhat different form, this same problem of social reason appears in the technologizing of the formation of public opinion. Who can deny that "the opinions which form the patterns of social life and constitute the normative conditions for solidarity are today dominated to a great extent by the technical and economic organizations within our civilization"?[51] What is at stake here for Gadamer is not simply the distortion of social reason; public organization also has a correlation to the condition of existential alienation. What is at stake is the loss of identity. In what sounds very much like Kierkegaard's description of the present age in which the individual is stripped of responsibility by the anonymous presence of the public, Gadamer writes:

> The real political activity of a citizen has become more or less restricted to his participation in elections, and exactly on this account the formation of public opinion has become the central political task. In the old days it was the personal participation of the citizens in the administrative work which controlled and neutralized the impact of special interest groups and public affairs on the common welfare. Today it is much more difficult to control and neutralize the organization of powerful economic interests.[52]

In light of this situation Gadamer wants to ask once more, "What is practice?". Again, what we learn from Aristotle is that practice is "the actuation of life (*energeia*) of anything alive, to which corresponds a life, a way of life, a life that is led in a certain way (bios)" (RAS 90). This way of life of human beings, in distinction from animals, is not fixed by nature, but involves προαίρεσις, knowingly preferring one thing to another and choosing among possible alternatives.[53] But as previously noted, what really delimits the notion of practice is its difference from technical skill. This means that practice, properly understood, is the form of human life that goes beyond the technical "choice" of the best means for a pre-given end. Practical reasoning in the actuality of life preeminently pertains to what is each individual's due as a citizen, and no technique can spare us from this deliberation and decision, for which there are no determinate rules. What constitutes the practical knowledge of action only arises from practice itself. Thus, properly understood, practice vindicates the noblest task of the citizen—decision-making according to one's own responsibility. In "The Limitation of the Expert," Gadamer suggests that we should follow Kant in this matter.

> [Kant] distinguished between the conditional imperative of prudence, where in fact purpose rationality alone rules, and the unconditional imperative of the morally commanded. This unconditional categorical imperative states that there is something which I can never discharge to the knowledge of another. That exactly defines the concept of responsibility and, in a certain sense, also the concept of conscience. One who could have known better or could have acquired a better understanding knows himself to be responsible for the results of his decisions. Without a doubt, this is contained in the concept of practical reason which the Greeks developed. (EPH 189)

Gadamer goes on to insist that one does Kant an injustice if the distinction between the hypothetical imperatives of prudence and the categorical imperative of morality is taken to imply a separation of the imperatives. His point is that in the realm of praxis, where the ends themselves are at stake, we are still guided by the general end of solidarity, of authentic community. For the individual in modern society, "whose needs and goals have become complex and even contradictory, there is a need for enlightened choice, just deliberation, and right subordination under common ends" (RAS 76). Our practical reason in the realm of practice is not concerned simply with the reflection upon the attainability of ends, but must take up the aims themselves in and through our practices. Global technical rationality today confronts us with the need to posit human solidarity as an end that helps us to know ourselves in our humanity. In contrast to Heidegger, who sees the dark night of technical domination as the most current configuration of the sending (*Geschick*) of being in which human life is in danger of being assimilated to a "constant standing reserve" (*Bestand*) and to which one responds by engaging in a new form of thinking, Gadamer immediately situates the response to technical domination in a renewed from of humanism. "Practice," Gadamer writes, "is conducting oneself and acting in solidarity. Solidarity, however, is the decisive condition and basis of all social reason" (RAS 87).

Accordingly, the issue that is at stake in contemporary life is, for Gadamer, the primacy of practice. His renewed humanism demands that we bring everything knowable by the sciences "into the context of mutual agreement in which we ourselves exist." Of course, we cannot fail to notice that implicit in this demand is the Socratic and "existential" element of Gadamer's hermeneutics, namely, the participatory, and ultimately dialogical character of hermeneutic experience. It is interesting to see here how Gadamer is able to include this existential element in his understanding of theory and practice. Although for Aristotle there is a difference within knowing between θεωρία and πρᾶξις, Gadamer insists that the opposition of πρᾶξις to θεωρία is not so determinative here, for even Aristotle will say that θεωρία itself is a practice.[54] This relation of theory to practice has always been part of the Greek notion of rationality. The Greeks understood all too well how, in being human, we succeed in knowing the world only in finite measures, and that within this fate we are still capable of pure contemplation of the world. But this look at the world, this θεωρία, is not a matter of construction whereby, on the basis of self-consciousness, one is able to take distance from beings and subject them to anonymous domination. For the Greeks, the proper distance that should be taken is, paradoxically, one of proximity and affinity. In Gadamer's words: "The primitive meaning of *theoria* is participation in the delegation sent to a festival for the sake of honoring the gods. The viewing of the divine proceedings is no participationless establishing of some neutral state of affairs or observation of some splendid demonstration or show. Rather it is a genuine sharing in an event, a real being present" (RAS 17–18). Θεωρία is properly a participation, and thus human reason takes its bearing from its participation in the order of being.

Hegel, Gadamer contends, is a witness to this Greek conception of rationality. And interestingly enough, with respect to the appraisal of the contemporary age, there is some justification for suggesting that Gadamer wants to accomplish something similar to what Hegel sought in the nineteenth century. Despite Hegel's insistence that the philosopher can only describe what is the case, Hegel's project can be read as an attempt to restore the power of reason within the articulation of life as a means of overcoming the crisis of the fragmentation of his age.[55] For this project Hegel sought to unite Greek rationality with modern self-consciousness in a new unity. In similar fashion, Gadamer would have us unite a hermeneutically transformed understanding of Greek rationality with the workings and doings of our contemporary life.[56]

It is also interesting to note at this point that what Gadamer does say about contemporary life invites comparison with American pragmatism. In recent writings both Richard Rorty and Richard Bernstein have made much of the link between hermeneutics and pragmatism. In a passage that could have been written by Gadamer, Rorty refers to Dewey and James as two philosophers who

> ask us to liberate our new civilization by giving up the notion of "grounding" our culture, our moral lives . . . upon "philosophical bases." They ask us to give up the neurotic Cartesian quest for certainty which has been one result of Galileo's frightening cosmology, the quest for "enduring spiritual values."[57]

Gadamer's hermeneutics shares with American pragmatism the recognition that philosophy is not a transcendental operation of securing first principles as its way of making sense of the world. The pragmatist and the hermeneut of philosophical hermeneutics do not want to separate reason from the practice of life, and in this sense both are fundamentally Socratic: there is the "willingness to talk, to listen to other people, to weigh the consequences of our actions upon other people."[58]

And here too the end in the ongoing work of life and culture, namely, human solidarity, is invoked. Dewey thinks that the issue of social life is always one of social hope, that is, of giving mankind the opportunity to grow up. In this context the will to truth is transformed into the order of the urge to create.

> Philosophically speaking, this is the great difference involved in the change from knowledge and philosophy as contemplative to operative. The change does not mean the lowering in dignity of philosophy from a lofty plane to one of gross utilitarianism. It signifies that the prime function of philosophy is that of rationalizing the possibilities of experience, especially collective human experience. The scope of this change may be realized by considering how far we are from accomplishing it. In spite of inventions which enable men to use energies of nature for their purposes, we are still far from habitually treating knowledge as the method of active control of nature and of experience. We tend to think of it after the model of a spectator viewing a finished picture rather than after that of the artist producing the painting.[59]

What is at issue in shaping practical life to the goal of human solidarity is a certain production, a production as performance. And, consistent with the makings and doings towards human community, it is a performance for which there are no determinate rules given in advance.

Richard Bernstein, however, suggests that Gadamer should have gone further in providing a solution to the ills of contemporary life. According to Bernstein, Gadamer "not only stops short of facing the issues of what is to be done when the polis is corrupt," but also has failed to adequately account for the domination of technical control in modern societies.[60] Bernstein is by no means unsympathetic to Gadamer's position and even acknowledges that he may be asking more than can be expected of Gadamer. Nevertheless he thinks that the "beginning" that Gadamer makes in shaping the political being can become false unless one confronts the practical task of reshaping one's actual community. But despite his insistence to the contrary, Bernstein does ask too much of Gadamer. To be consistent, the notion of human community, in Kantian language, must remain regulative not constitutive of experience. To ask about what must be done—which to me appears as a Marxian strain in Bernstein's thought derived from his work with Habermas— would be to prescribe the ends in advance, and thus ultimately to be engaged in some form of social engineering. But this is $\tau \acute{\epsilon} \chi \nu \eta$ not $\phi \varrho \acute{o} \nu \eta \sigma \iota \varsigma$. This is no longer the experienced person who is open to new experience. If we fully appreciate what is really at work in participation, it appears unreasonable to expect more. Gadamer observes that "participation" (*Teilnahme*) "is a strange word." Although it literally means "taking part" its dialectic

> consists of the fact that participation is not taking parts, but in a way taking the whole. Everybody who participates in something does not take something away, so that others cannot have it. The opposite is true: by sharing, by our participating in the things in which we are participating, we enrich them; they do not become smaller, but larger. The whole life of tradition consists exactly in this enrichment so that life is our culture and our past: the whole inner store of our lives is always extending by participating.[61]

Participation, like experience, is a dialectical growth. In a way it is simply experience "writ large" as the constant process of transformation of what was previously held valid. This is not to suggest that participation is simply a "going along"; rather, in participation, we become vigilant to the question. The condition of finitude can expect nothing more.

Here more than anywhere else, we see that philosophical hermeneutics is not just a matter of an alternative methodology. Hermeneutics as practical philosophy uncovers (in its theoretical attitude toward the practice of interpretation) the insight that practical rationality is unique to our social life as a natural human capacity.

PART TWO

The Voice of the Text

CHAPTER FOUR

Philosophical Hermeneutics and Finitude

§ 13. The Question of Finitude in Philosophical Hermeneutics

Finitude may be *the* term around which the discourse of philosophical hermeneutics is organized. At the outset of *Truth and Method* hermeneutics is defined as "the basic being-in-motion of Dasein that constitutes its finitude and historicity, and hence embraces the whole of its experience of the world" (TM xxx/GW2 440). Hermeneutics is a hermeneutics of existence as a hermeneutics of finitude. We have already seen some of the consequences that follow from this determination, for example, because of the finitude of our historical existence, the possibility of the one, final, objectively correct interpretation must be deferred. We have also seen how Gadamer carried the notion of finitude forward into the analysis of experience; in the end, experience is the experience of finitude as the condition of essential limitation. When Gadamer goes on to relate language to hermeneutic experience in part 3 of *Truth and Method*, this too is understood in terms of finitude: "Language is the trace [*Spur*] of finitude not because the structure of human language is multifarious but because every language is constantly being formed and developed the more it expresses its experience of the world" (TM 457/GW1 461).

This defining concept of finitude underscores the real indebtedness that Gadamer has to the work of Heidegger, an indebtedness that Gadamer himself has never been hesitant to acknowledge. In "Text and Interpretation" Gadamer speaks explicitly of this indebtedness in order to met the "challenge" to hermeneutics—a challenge concerning his position on the nature of linguisticality—that emerges in his "encounter with the French philosophical scene" (TI 24/GW2 333). Gadamer identifies the indebtedness here as that whereby the ontological determination of understanding, found in the analytic of Dasein, is taken over for his own point of departure in "the critique of the idealism and methodologism in our era dominated by epistemology" (TI 22/GW2 331). In effect the indebtedness becomes the opportunity to further substantiate the hermeneutics of facticity (in which the concept of finitude is rooted). But because the later Heidegger abandoned the concept of hermeneutics, it appears that, in his indebtedness, Gadamer is simply holding fast to the basic framework of the early Heidegger, even though, as Gadamer himself has said, it was the new trajectories in thought opened by the later Heidegger that confirmed his own path of thought.[1] In fact, what Gadamer holds to in the work of Heidegger, whether early or late, is this finitude as such. When Gadamer says in "Text and Interpretation" that, in full accord with Heidegger's critique of the concept of the subject, "he tried to conceive of the original phenomenon of language in dialogue" (TI 23/GW2 332), he means by this that he wanted to hold fast to the inexhaustibilty of the experience of meaning consistent with a philosophy of finitude. In this situation, Gadamer does indeed follow Heidegger into his later writings, especially as they pertain to the question of language, but he does not follow Heidegger in pursuing the language of metaphysics as a way of raising the question of the history of the forgetfulness of Being. The radicalization of the hermeneutic project that turns to the thinking of the withdrawal of Being is a step from which Gadamer step backs. As Gadamer understands himself,

> [M]y own efforts were directed toward not forgetting the limit that is implicit in every hermeneutical experience of meaning. When I wrote the sentence "Being which can be understood is language," what was implied thereby was that that which is can never be completely understood. This is implied insofar as everything that goes under the name of language always refers beyond that which achieves the status of a proposition. That which is to be understood is that which comes into language, but of course it is always that which is taken as something, taken as true. This is the hermeneutical dimension in which Being "manifests itself." In this sense, I retained the experience the "hermeneutics of facticity,"

an expression that signifies a transformation of the meaning of hermeneutics. (TI 25/GW2 334–35)

This step back from the radicality of Heidegger's project, from the radicality that would move hermeneutics closer to the standpoint of deconstruction, has led some critics to accuse Gadamer of failing to escape the trappings of modernist foundationalism in his project of philosophical hermeneutics. In "Gadamer's Closet Essentialism: A Derridean Critique," John Caputo insists that Gadamer has retreated "into the classical idea of *Wesen* as deep essence, *essentia*, albeit with historical embodiment . . . in an unmistakable resistance to Heidegger's attempt to think *Wesen* verbally, as the sheer coming to presence [*An-wesen*] and passing away [*Ab-wesen*] of the epochs of presence."[2] Because of Gadamer's talk of history and change, time and becoming, philosophical hermeneutics may give the appearance of being something other than essentialism, but this talk is simply a front for a "theology of lasting essence." Tradition, for Gadamer, has the goods (the *ousia*), the deep deposits of meaning that the hermeneut must learn how to mine and pass along to the current generation. Philosophical hermeneutics delivers everything that essentialism promises, but wrapped in historical form, and is thus a "closet" essentialism.[3]

Caputo thinks that Gadamer's step back from Heidegger's own radicalization of the hermeneutic project can be attributed to his attachment to Hegel, whose essentialism is likewise historical. For Hegel, essence "must become what it is—through historical hard work—in order to be [*wesen*] what it has been all along [*gewesen*]."[4] Similarly, for Caputo the "inexhaustible depth" that Gadamer constantly refers to in the description of the hermeneutic event is an essentialism of infinite spirit that gradually keeps unfolding over the course of time. As a consequence of this attachment to Hegel Caputo also argues that for Gadamer finitude functions in a profoundly Hegelian manner. For Caputo Gadamer's finitude is actually a cover for a metaphysics of infinity. According to Caputo, the hermeneutic event is not really the isolable (finite) historical entity but a whole history, "a continuity of movement made up of both the original and the history of its effects which follow after it like a comet's tail."[5] The interpreter, situated within a history of wholeness (i.e., infinite), remains too finite to contain the fullness that sweeps over him or her. With Gadamer the Hegelian *Wesen* has a bit more modesty, a bit more of its finitude showing, but all this means is that it is a very liberal version of a fundamentally conservative, traditionalist, essentialist idea.

Gadamer's finitude thus appears to Caputo to be too bound up with its other, with the infinite, to be anything but a variation of Hegel's essentialism. It is a closet theory of essence, ideality, and infinity. Granted, Gadamer himself gives ample evidence for this charge whereby understanding is always seen in relation to the infinity present. In describing the mediation that takes place in linguistic tradition, for example, Gadamer writes: "All human speaking is finite in such a way that there is laid up within it an infinity of meaning to be explicated and laid out" (TM 458/GW1 462). In the end, what Gadamer offers us through this metaphysics of infinity, Caputo insists, is actually a theory of *deep* essence where the metaphor of depth means not only that the essence is deep enough to forbid a final canonical version, but also that beneath the multiplicity of historical formulations there is an underlying, undying truth.[6]

Ironically, seen from a different perspective, Gadamer has also been attacked by the "traditionalist"—the one who insists on foundations in philosophy that would secure a criteria for adjudicating questions of meaning and truth—for not providing the very thing that Caputo thinks Gadamer holds so dear, namely, truth. Hirsch, for example, has argued that when the historicity of understanding is applied to the interpretation of texts, the possibility of correct interpretation, and thereby the question of truth, vanishes.[7] That is to say, without the proper measure of adequation we are no longer in a position to say that any particular interpretation of a text is true or false; the multiplicity of interpretation that philosophical hermeneutics demands simply disseminates the goods of the tradition. If one counters this by saying that in philosophical hermeneutics truth is to be understood differently—that truth has the character of an event, of an occurrence of coming to light, rather than of correctness—this proves to be insufficient for the traditionalist who would argue that this is nothing more than an clever disguise for relativism.

Although these two criticisms (the one about truth, the other about infinity) come from the opposite ends of the spectrum—one accusing Gadamer of a failure to be essentialistic, the other accusing him of remaining essentialistic—they are brought together by their common misunderstanding of the ontological commitments in the philosophy of finitude of philosophical hermeneutics. Both criticisms occur under the sway of a metaphysics of actuality, either by insisting that the question of truth is only possible within a metaphysics of actuality or by falsely accusing philosophical hermeneutics of holding to a metaphysics of actuality (Gadamer's limited Hegelianism). Both critiques fail to see that it is an ontology of the possible, which is ultimately to be traced back to Aristotle, that constitutes hermeneutic experience and *mutatis mutandis* frames the notions of finitude and truth. In the remainder of this chapter I want to attend only to the question of finitude and the implied metaphysics of actuality in philosophical herme-neutics. What is to be shown is precisely how an ontology of the possible, which displays the real depth of Gadamer's indebtedness to Heidegger, structures hermeneutic experience, and thereby supports Gadamer's con-tention that in his own way he does in fact follow Heidegger beyond metaphysics.[8]

§ 14. An Ontology of Living Being

This issue of an ontology of the possible begins to take shape when we see that, in its indebtedness to Heidegger's ontology of understanding, philosophical hermeneutics repeats in its own way an *Existenzphilosophie* wherein possibility stands higher than actuality. This means that one must look to Kierkegaard (who in turn looks to Aristotle) as well as Hegel when one traces the lineage of philosophical hermeneutics. Here, what is decisive for our purposes is precisely what was decisive in Kierkegaard's attack on Hegelianism, namely, the issue of existence itself and the movement (κίνησις) intrinsic to existence that, according to Kierkegaard, was bas-tardized by the system. For Kierkegaard, the κίνησις of existence presents us with an ontology of living being in which possibility stands higher than actuality and will disrupt the system by this very fact.

In chapter 1 we gave a provisional indication of how philosophical hermeneutics embraces the κίνησις of existence by showing that the movement in philosophical hermeneutics is not unlike the structure of Kierkegaardian repetition (of existence). Without explicitly identifying it as such this κίνησις of existence is restated by Gadamer in a number of contexts. The hermeneutics of facticity from which philosophical herme-neutics starts is itself a description of the movement of existence and its explication. When this gets translated into the movement of historical existence in relation to historical research, Gadamer describes the condition of the historically effected consciousness as a consciousness effected by a *living* tradition in which our interpretive efforts are disclosive of possibilities within tradition. When Gadamer eventually turns to the lan-guage, as the medium of the event of understanding, it is always in *living* language—that liveliness of dialogical conversation where questioning opens up possibilities of meaning—where disclosiveness of Being's possibilities is effected. Thus the ontology of a philosophical hermeneutics can also be said to be an ontology of living being.

In this context, it is not enough to say of philosophical hermeneutics, as Gadamer himself has said, that philosophical hermeneutics is a matter of "saving the honor of the 'bad infinity' " (GW2 505).⁹ Taken by itself this statement suggests that the dialectical κίνησις of hermeneutic conversation is simply the mediation of otherness in the absence of a grand teleological construction. What is missing is precisely what is required by an ontology of living being, namely, a reversal in the priority in the relation between possibility and actuality so that possibility stands higher than actuality.

The issue then is to see precisely how the priority of possibility in the ontology of living being, an ontology that, rooted in Aristotle, receives its decisive formulation in Heidegger is in play in philosophical hermeneutics. To proceed to this end let us recall that Kierkegaard's critique of Hegel was motivated by the fact that Hegel could not adequately incorporate an ontology of living being into his onto-logico system. From Kierkegaard's perspective the question of an ontology of living being was simply the question of movement, κίνησις, properly understood, that is, of the transition from possibility to actuality in individual existence. Ironically, Hegel actually thought that the failure of previous philosophy, to which his own philosophy stood as a corrective, was that it did not adequately deal with movement. From Hegel's perspective understanding (*Verstand*) simply separates possibility and actuality leaving the transition between the two concepts unexplained, but reason (*Vernunft*), by virtue of its dialectical character, suffers no such incompleteness. The logic of dialectical reason can claim that actuality is possible, for were it not so it could not be actual, and conversely, the possible is actual in the sense that real possibility, in contrast to formal possibility, is the totality of conditions which is presupposed by a certain actuality. Necessity, as the third movement of the triadic structure, is the truth into which possibility and actuality are absorbed. By virtue of the identity-within-difference of dialectical logic Hegel maintains that this necessity is freedom.¹⁰

Against this production of dialectical necessity, Kierkegaard insists that the transition occurring in human existence is in no way comparable to the transition occurring in dialectical development.¹¹ He argues that the speculative mediation of opposites does not apply to concrete existence, which of its nature gives priority to possibility over actuality. Hegelian movement actually renders becoming as the transition from possibility to actuality illusory by ignoring the temporality of existential becoming. The becoming of human existence is not effected by means of a necessary transition precisely because necessity characterizes purely atemporal relations of logical ideas.[12] Thus in contrast to Hegelian becoming, Kierkegaard argues that the becoming of human existence is marked by a fundamental creative repetition whereby existence which has been now becomes. This means that in the repetition of existence we return to possibilities that have already been there in existence: past possibilities become future possibilities in each moment of decision. All decisive changes in existence, the acts by which we become who we are, are brought about by the projection of imaginative possibilities which are actualized in the concrete. By virtue of the fact that existence is essentially a "qualitative dialectic," a self-projection of the individual toward the openness of the future in the movement from possibility to actuality in temporality, possibility, in this sense, is prior to actuality. The future is the condition for possibility for the freedom of possibility. Thus Kierkegaard would have us reorder the relation between necessity and possibility: the existing self is that which it has been (necessity) and becomes that which it is not yet (possibility qualified by futurity). This is precisely what freedom is for Kierkegaard, the $\kappa\acute{\iota}\nu\eta\sigma\iota\varsigma$ through which the existing self realizes itself.

Of course this structural relation between possibility and actuality is familiar to the student of Aristotle's *Physics*, where movement in general is described as the transition from possibility ($\delta\acute{\upsilon}\nu\alpha\mu\iota\varsigma$) to actuality ($\acute{\epsilon}\nu\acute{\epsilon}\varrho\gamma\epsilon\iota\alpha$), and this fact did not escape Kierkegaard. Kierkegaard was specifically drawn to the transition from possibility to actuality in Aristotle's description of qualitative change since this could be accommodated to historical freedom, to the capacity to act in accordance with a subjectively posited $\tau\acute{\epsilon}\lambda o\varsigma$.[13] But by drawing attention to this connection to Aristotle a question naturally arises whether Kierkegaard completely succeeds in separating his ontology of living being from an essentialist metaphysics in which actuality is always prior to possibility. We can see this in the way that Kierkegaard remains too close to the Hegelianism he wants to reject. From a Hegelian perspective, dialectical thought is certainly compatible with Kierkegaard's emphasis on possibility in so far as the real is initially conceived as contingency and the real contains within itself the negation of its possibility. If it is simply a question of whether there is a law that determines self-development we are simply looking at two sides of the same coin. We should not forget that Hegel also roots his philosophy of movement in Aristotle!

Hegel's reading of movement in Aristotle undoubtedly follows that traditional reading of movement in Aristotle where possibility is recognized as a fundamental mode of οὐσία, and in the interplay with actuality that expresses the inner movement of an essential being, there is always a priority accorded to actuality. For Aristotle, actuality is prior to possibility not only with regard to οὐσία but logically and temporally as well.[14] Moreover, this "ousiology" is inseparable from teleology: the movement to actuality is that for the sake of which a thing becomes, which of itself is a purposive structure. Every δύναμις exists only for the sake of the τέλος which is the ἐνέργεια of a being: "We do not see in order that we may have sight, but we have sight that we may see." In this teleological movement, the priority of actuality demands that the end be connected with its beginning; the movement, in other words, exhibits a circular structure: In the movement towards actualization "what is prefigured comes forth and out into the open in a circular form as the remaining—within-itself of the *telos* as the teleological self-actualization in which the *ousia* returns to its beginning, the *archē*."[15] When ἐνέργεια is translated into Latin as *actus* or *actualitas*, being is determined in such a way that the Being of a being is only insofar as it is actual. Potentiality must be understood in terms of actuality. Hegel, standing at the end of the tradition, does nothing to overturn this formulation, the modality of possibility is oriented towards a kind of essence which appears.

It is only with Heidegger that this formulation comes to be rethought. In the existential analytic of Dasein, which is indebted as much to Kierkegaard as it is to Aristotle, Heidegger shows that Dasein is disclosed not as an actualization of its own potential but as primarily possibility, an ability to be. This existential possibility is to be distinguished from empty logical possibility as well as from the mere contingency of something *Vorhandenheit* (what is not yet actual and what is not at any time necessary). When Heidegger asserts that "higher than actuality stands possibility" (SZ 38), possibility is understood as a mode which simply cannot come to actualization. Dasein is such that it is always "ahead of itself" within possibilities.

What this means is succinctly described by Heidegger in *The Basic Problems of Phenomenology*, the text of a lecture course given in Marburg in the summer of 1927, the same year in which *Being and Time* was published. Here Heidegger claims, in response to the question about how understanding belongs to Dasein's existence, that to exist is essentially to understand. This equivalence occurs because, as existing, Dasein is occupied with its own ability to be, with projecting itself upon possibility, and this is the meaning of the existential concept of understanding. Heidegger explains:

> A can-be, a possibility as possibility, is there only in projection, in projecting oneself upon that can-be. If in contrast I merely reflect on some empty possibility into which I could enter, and, as it were, just gab [*beschwatze*] about it, then this possibility is not there, precisely as possibility; instead for me it is, as we might say, actual. The character of possibility becomes manifest and is manifest only in projection, so long as the possibility is held fast in the projection.[16]

Possibility is what it is only when it is left standing before us as impending and not such that it becomes actualized in the traditional sense. What Heidegger says here sounds very much like Kierkegaard: the projection upon possibility is the way in which I am the possibility and is the way in which Dasein exists freely. Heidegger continues:

> Understanding as the Dasein's self-projection is the Dasein's fundamental mode of happening [*Geschehen*]. As we may also say, it is the authentic meaning of action. It is by understanding that the Dasein's happening is characterized: its historicity [*Geschichtlichkeit*].[17]

The happening of Dasein *is* understanding which is at the same time, with proper qualification, historicity. Possibility as the horizon of transcendence, in other words, makes historicity itself possible.

This attempt by Heidegger to rethink the question of Being beyond the traditional concepts of substance (and subject) as permanent presence in the analytic of Dasein is itself rooted in a creative reading of Aristotle's $\varkappa\acute{\iota}\nu\eta\sigma\iota\varsigma$,[18] and thus ultimately the issue of historicity can be located here as well. According to the reading given by Heidegger, Aristotle always regards experience as the experience of beingness: the condition of being which at once stands in its $\tau\acute{\epsilon}\lambda o\varsigma$ without having fully arrived there—"the state of being which is present in partial appearance, yet absent in relative non-appearance ($\acute{\epsilon}\nu\acute{\epsilon}\varrho\gamma\epsilon\iota\alpha$ $\grave{\alpha}\tau\epsilon\lambda\grave{\eta}\varsigma$)."[19] The relative non-appearance is what Heidegger takes Aristotle to mean by $\delta\acute{\upsilon}\nu\alpha\mu\iota\varsigma$, the possibilizing condition for a moving being's partial and negatived appearance whereby a play of presence and absence is enacted. The play is such that the moving being's possibilizing absence becomes present in a special way. The placing into the appearance—Heidegger's expression for $\varkappa\acute{\iota}\nu\eta\sigma\iota\varsigma$, the change which in itself is the breaking out of something—"always lets something become present in such a way that in the becoming-present a becoming-absent simultaneously becomes present."[20] In a growing natural being such as a flower the relative non-appearance of the source of growth indirectly becomes present in allowing the flower to appear. Thus, in Heidegger's reading of Aristotle, κίνησις is at bottom a play of presence and absence.

More importantly, with respect to living being as a being of movement, its δύναμις must be preserved if it is to remain what it is; it must conserve its δύναμις precisely as possibility. From this claim that living being must constantly go back into its δύναμις as it comes forth into appearance, Heidegger is able to say that there is a formal pattern of retrieve (*Wiederholung*) in κίνησις of becoming what one already is. The plant retrieves (*Wiederholung*) its δύναμις in order to appear. Retrieval names the way in which any laying out (*Auslegung*)—hermeneutics in other words—occurs for Heidegger. Retrieval is thus the essential structure of the analysis of Dasein as well as the structure of the way to be of Dasein itself: "the act of resolve is the self-disclosive retrieval whereby existence accepts and understandingly becomes the most proper possibility it already is, its dying." In the stretching ahead of itself toward death, Dasein opens the realm of sense as such. But it is important to see here that Heidegger's dramatic transformation of κίνησις is not simply an elevated form of biologism or *Lebensphilosophie* based on a notion of organic growth. At one place Heidegger writes: "All origination and genesis in the field of the ontological is not growth and unfolding, but degeneration, since everything arising arises, that is, in a certain way, runs *away*, removes itself from the superior force of the source."[21] What Heidegger later on calls *Ereignis* can be read as an extension of this notion of movement in Aristotle.

But even before this when Heidegger takes the movement that is φύσις and transforms it into the movement of the λόγος of human existence we have the basis for the structure of historicity. Historicity is nothing other than the pattern of retrieve with respect to the temporality of Dasein.

> The resoluteness in which Dasein comes back to itself, discloses current factical possibilities of authentic existing, and discloses them *in terms of the heritage* (*Erbe*) which that resoluteness, as thrown, *takes over*. In one's coming back resolutely to one's thrown-ness, there is hidden a *handing down* (*Sichüberliefern*) to oneself of the possibilities that have come down to one, but not necessarily as having thus come down. (SZ 383)

Historical retrieve does not hand down possibilities so much as it frees up possibilities. The χίνησις of historical retrieve does not cancel its δύναμις and thus is not drawn into full present appearance, but brings δύναμις into presence by leaving it possible.

§ 15. Finitude, Language and Possibility

The question before us is whether Gadamer betrays the subversiveness of Heideggerian facticity such that the finitude of understanding gives way to an Aristotelico-Hegelian metaphysics of infinity, such that every understanding is an actualization of a potential (Aristotle's ousiology) carried out in a Hegelian process of historical unfolding.

Clearly, as Gadamer sees it, the project of philosophical hermeneutics defines itself in opposition to any metaphysics of infinity. At the beginning of part 3 of *Truth and Method* Gadamer is concerned with the problem of the relation between language and world. In this context he points out that philosophical hermeneutics is not to be confused with the essentially theological answer to the problem that appears in Greek thought, and ultimately this means that philosophical hermeneutics is not to be confused with the Hegelian answer to the problem as well.

> In considering the Being of beings, Greek metaphysics regarded it as a being that fulfilled itself in thought. This thought is the thought of *nous*, which is conceived as the highest and most perfect being, gathering within itself the being of all beings. The articulation of the *logos* brings the structure of being into language, and this coming into language is, for Greek thought, nothing other than the presencing [*Gegenwart*] of the being itself, its *aletheia*. Human thought regards the infinity of this presence as its fulfilled potential, its divinity. (TM 456–57/GW1 460–61)

Gadamer is emphatic in saying that he cannot follow this way of thinking, for above all the hermeneutic phenomenon is guided by the finitude of historical experience. The question though is just how decisively finitude sustains the structure of hermeneutic experience. The answer still lies in the analysis of language as λόγος, and in this respect Gadamer does not depart from the Greeks. As Gadamer has emphatically stated, "Being that can be understood is language" (TM 474/GW1 478).[22] But language for Gadamer is expressly the record of finitude! This means that "in language the order and structure of experience itself is originally formed and constantly changed"

(TM 457/GW1 461). In indicating that he cannot follow the λόγος philosophy that unites thought and being Gadamer is not so much rejecting the notion of being able to say the same (ὁμολόγεῖν)—which at least gives the appearance of a project of an unfolding essence—as he is maintaining that language cannot be transcended, in which case one gets caught up in another version of the play of presence and absence.

But precisely how is the phenomenon of language understood by Gadamer? To answer this question, let us first recall our previous analysis of part 2 of *Truth and Method*. In that analysis we noted that tradition is simply the collective name for each individual text, and the task of interpreting tradition is one of bringing the text to speak again. We also noted that the structure of this speaking has within it the element of application, which is understood in terms of Aristotle's model of practical philosophy. The basic structure of this speaking, though, follows the form of experience that for Gadamer holds within it a relation of self to other. In the section immediately following the analysis of experience, which to this point has only been mentioned in passing, Gadamer then turns to the model of Platonic dialectic, in which the logical structure of openness is made explicit through the analysis of the question. The art of asking questions, which is the art of questioning even further, is nothing other than the art of conducting a real dialogue (TM 367/GW1 372). Gadamer brings part 2 of *Truth and Method* to a close then by broaching the turn to language in the dialectic of question and answer in dialogue.

> When we try to examine the hermeneutical phenomenon through the model of conversation between two persons, the chief thing that these apparently so different situations—understanding a text and reaching an understanding in conversation—have in common is that both are concerned with a subject matter that is placed before them. Just as each interlocutor is trying to reach agreement on some subject with his partner, so also the interpreter is trying to understand what the text is saying. This understanding of the subject matter must take the form of language. It is not that the understanding is subsequently put into words; rather, the way understanding occurs—whether in the case of a text or a dialogue with another person who raises the issue with us—is the coming-into-language of the thing itself. (TM 378/GW1 383–84)

From this point on, the problematic of understanding is framed in terms of the dialogical encounter of conversation (*Gespräch*), of the coming to agreement (*Verständigung*) about the subject matter. The task of bringing the traditionary text to speak again is the realization of understanding in dialogical conversation. The defense of this claim, which encompasses a claim to the centrality of language in hermeneutic experience, is the task of part 3 of *Truth and Method*.

At the outset of part 3, Gadamer repeats the claim he made when he linked experience to the experience of the Thou: the essence of tradition is to exist in the medium of language (TM 389/GW1 393). The correlation between tradition and language immediately suggests not only that language is not to be understood as an object at one's disposal (any more than tradition is something at one's disposal), but more specifically, that the element of application in understanding will now entail a *performance* of meaning in language whereby the object comes into words, "and yet is at the same time the interpreter's own language" (TM 389/GW1 392).

Gadamer prepares the ground for this understanding of language in the first two sections of part 3. In the first section, Gadamer describes how language is not only the object of interpretation, but also that through which interpretation takes place. As to the former, since tradition is literally that which is handed down, it is essentially verbal in character and it is this that is to be understood. Written texts, in which one encounters the ideality of the word, simply present the real hermeneutical task of bringing the text into language, that is, bringing it to a condition of speaking again.

As to the latter, Gadamer wants to claim that understanding has a *fundamental* connection with language. Such a claim rests initially on the recognition that all understanding is interpretation. We have seen how Gadamer takes over Heidegger's argument for this in the formulation of the hermeneutic "circle." Interpretation is the explication of understanding such that, in light of the fore-structure of understanding, when we interpret we have already understood the matter in some way and the interpretation is the working out of this understanding. In linking understanding and interpretation in this way Gadamer's hermeneutic theory rejects the separation of understanding from interpretation that can occur in either of two ways. Philosophical hermeneutics rejects the claim that interpretation precedes understanding, as if interpretation were a means to an end (understanding). But philosophical hermeneutics also rejects the claim that interpretation follows understanding. The rejection of this claim, although rooted in the assumption of the circularity of understanding, is ultimately tied to the connection between understanding and language.

In the situation where interpretation follows understanding one is claiming by that that an immediacy of understanding is possible. Someone hearing a musical performance or the therapist who empathetically senses the condition of a client are examples one might give for the immediacy of understanding. But how is this *direct* understanding possible? When it is really a *question* of understanding, Gadamer follows Schleiermacher in that it is not just that understanding involves interpretation, but that this intertwining of understanding and interpretation is expressed through language; it is in finding the words for understanding that understanding occurs. To understand the meaning of a text, that meaning must be translated into one's own language (the element of application), which involves relating it to a whole constellation of possible meaning in which we always find ourselves. The issue here reflects once again Gadamer's critique of nineteenth-century historical understanding where one assumed that the concepts used for historical research were neutral. Gadamer's point is that language affects the very "process" of interpretation. Gadamer thus challenges any romantic claim to immediacy of understanding by arguing that verbal interpretation is the form of all interpretation, and only through this can something be understood. That is to say, when confronted with bringing tradition to speak again, it is always entrusted to some form of linguistic interpretation, even, Gadamer insists, when the text is not verbal in nature. His argument here is subtle:

> We must not let ourselves be confused by forms of interpretation that are not verbal but in fact presuppose language [*Sprachlichkeit*]. It is possible to demonstrate something by means of contrast— e.g., by placing two pictures alongside each other or reading two poems one after the other, so that one is interpreted by the other. In these cases demonstration seems to obviate verbal interpretation. But in fact this kind of demonstration is a modification of verbal interpretation. In such demonstration we have the reflection of interpretation, and the demonstration is used as a visual shortcut. (TM 398/GW1 402)

For philosophical hermeneutics, to be in thought is to be in language. Certainly, Gadamer argues, there are times when we cannot find the words to say what we mean, but this is not itself an argument against the priority of language in understanding.

In the second section of part 3, then, Gadamer constructs a certain reading of the history of philosophy in order to fully understand how understanding is the coming-into-language of the thing itself (*die Sache selbst*). In particular, the reading explores the breaking down and thus the breaking apart of word and thing as it was experienced by the Greeks. This is the question of the *Cratylus*: Whether the word is nothing but a pure sign (*Zeichen*) or has something about it of the image (*Bild*/εἰκών), in which case it is internally related to the thing it names? Such a question only arises for Plato when the unity of word, meaning and thing is called into question. This of course is something that is easily done, for it appears obvious that we have conventionalism in language where a word is only a name and thus it cannot substitute for true being. This position is evident by the fact that we do indeed have things for which a word is *simply* given, as when a new-born child is given a name; and such names can always be changed. On the other hand a similarity theory of language would maintain that we have a thing and a word is found for it, with the implication that we can find the *right* word that would have to be based on an agreement with the thing. The limitation here though is that we must be able to explain the plurality of words and languages.

But in the *Cratylus* the discussion of the problem, whether from a theory of conventionalism or similarity, assumes that the thing is already known and the problem is one of how words can be joined to them. Plato wants to reject both ways of regarding the relation of word and thing in favor of a non-linguistic knowledge of the Forms. By doing so, Plato feels he can counteract the misuse of the power of words in sophistical argumentation. Of course, Plato does not maintain that there is knowledge without words, "but only that it is not the *word* that opens up the way to truth" (TM 407/GW1 411). As Gadamer reads Plato here in the *Cratylus*, Plato covers up the essence of language more completely than the sophist. Plato is caught up in these arguments because he assumes the priority of knowledge to language.[23]

What Gadamer wants to maintain is that the difficulty in the *Cratylus* does not necessitate that we abandon language as a locus of truth in favor of a wordless λόγος. Truth is not in the individual words, and yet it can be said that truth belongs to discourse. Rather than starting from the thing and from this then construct a theory of language as correspondence, Gadamer would have us start from the word. But then the word is here not first a sign, but more like a copy or image (*Abbild*), where the mimetic dimension of the word pertains to the very presentation of the thing.[24] Gadamer does not agree, in other words, that knowledge can be constructed in advance of experience, but coping with experience is precisely what occurs in language: "Experience is not wordless to begin with subsequently becoming an object of reflection by being named, by being subsumed under the universality of the word. Rather, experience of itself seeks and finds words that express it" (TM 417/GW1 421). To find the right word is thus not to copy the thing, but simply to have the thing come into language.

This dynamic of language, of the coming into being of the thing—which obviously cannot be understood literally, but describes the coming into appearance of the intelligibility (λόγος) of what is—is developed in the third and final section of part 3 and serves to bring *Truth and Method* to a close. It is a dynamic that can only be understood as κίνησις, and accordingly language is the particular expression of the ontology of living being for philosophical hermeneutics. Language is always *living* language, which means that language has its being, not in the proposition (that by itself is a unit of meaning abstracted from its experiential expression), but in its speaking, its performance, its lived execution—*actus exercitus*—whereby what is comes forth in the coming to agreement in conversation. And to the extent that this notion of language moves outside the ambit of a philosophy of the subject, where language is secondary to the thought of a subject that is represented in language, it would be most proper to say that language itself produces the movement of sense (*Sinn*): language is a communicative event having "its true being only in dialogue [*Gespräch*], only in the taking place of agreement in understanding [*Ausübung der Verständigung*]" (TM 446/GW1 449).

When Gadamer speaks of infinity in this context of living language it has nothing to do with an actualizing essence, an unfolding actualization, but describes the character of language as a center (*Mitte*), which holds within itself a totality of sense from which every word breaks forth. Here the *totality* is not a presence to be actualized, it is rather that which withholds itself in being held in language. In this sense living language is the "virtuality of speech," the opening of new possibilities of sense by holding within itself possible being. Gadamer writes:

> Every word causes the whole of language to which it belongs to resonate and the whole world-view that underlies it to appear. Thus every word, as the event of a moment, carries with it the unsaid, to which it is related by responding and summoning. The occasionality of human speech is not a casual imperfection of its expressive power; it is, rather, the logical expression of the living virtuality of speech [*die Virtualität des Redens*] that brings a totality

of meaning [*Sinn*] into play, without being able to express it totality. All human speaking is finite in such a way that there is laid up within it an infinity of meaning to be explicated and laid out. (TM 458/GW1 462)[25]

Language *qua* living is finite and as such it presses forth into possibilities.

But how so? In order to see precisely how Gadamer takes up an ontology of the possible let us extend the implications of the notion of the center (*Mitte*) of language. The unsaid held within the center of language whereby there is a creative multiplication of the word is not a potential waiting to be realized because the center of language is for Gadamer speculative. Ironically, this notion of the speculative immediately places Gadamer again in proximity to Hegel. But here the issue, as is often the case when Gadamer draws upon Hegel, is the retrieval of a notion that aids an ontology bent on overcoming a philosophy of subjectivity. For Hegel, the speculative in his metaphysical dialectics is the movement of the object that thought experiences in a way analogous to the mirror receiving its being from the object's appearing. The dialectical activity in speculative thought, in other words is an activity of the thing itself. Hegel sees this same speculative dimension in the Platonic dialogues where the interlocutors follow the path the thing itself (justice, for example) took them. For Gadamer to claim that language has a speculative structure means that what is (the thing) and its meaning belong together in language just as an object and its mirror image belong together. The mirror image belongs together with the original object in a way that the two are indistinguishable. The mirror image throws back an image (*Bild*) and not a copy (*Abbild*). This unity of two that is one is called a speculative unity.[26] Applying the speculative to language means that what is expressed in language does not entail that a second being is acquired. Rather, everything that is language has a speculative unity, that between its being and its presentation of itself, "but this is a distinction that is not really a distinction at all" (TM 475/GW1 479). All traditionary material displays this paradox of being one and the same yet different. Such difference always exists within identity, otherwise identity would not be identity. Thought contains deferral and distance, otherwise, thought would not be thought.[27]

To the extent that a second being is not acquired in language, language does not re-present the matter (*Sache*) as if it were determined in advance, but rather, language is that wherein the intelligibility of what is is formed, formed not as a mirror of an essence but in relation to a totality of possible meaning. "To say what one means . . . means to hold what is said together with an infinity of what is not said in the unity of the one meaning and to ensure that it be understood in this way" (TM 469/GW1 473). In speaking speculatively, which is often found in an intensified way in the poetic word, we express a relation to the whole of being, which is not simply a speaking that lacks completion, a speaking that is merely a potential that is yet to be realized.

Gadamer can make this claim precisely because the speculative character of the hermeneutic situation is fundamentally different from Hegel's dialectical self-unfolding of Geist, notwithstanding the fact that there is even a teleological component in hermeneutic experience. It is true that Gadamer sees a real correspondence between dialectic presentation in Hegel and the structure of hermeneutic interpretation that by virtue of a relative fulfillment conceives the unity of the *Sache* only in successiveness. However, Gadamer insists that this correspondence ultimately fails because of the radical finitude at the basis of hermeneutic experience. That difference in dialectical presentation for which finitude is responsible is essentially twofold: (1) the dialectical realization of sense in hermeneutic experience begins as a response and thus there is no problem of a beginning; (2) the dialectical realization of sense in hermeneutic experience is a completion that issues in a new creation of understanding in such a way that the conception of end is transformed.

Regarding the notion of response, Gadamer writes: "The apparently thetic beginning of interpretation is, in a fact, a response; and, the sense of an interpretation is determined, like every response, by the question asked. *Thus the dialectic of question and answer always precedes the dialectic of interpretation*" (TM 472/GW1 476). In reading a text, interpretation is first called for when the accord between reader and text is disrupted, but this means that the text poses a question to us. Notice then what occurs by the question. It arises as a mark of finitude, of the negativity of not knowing. But more importantly, the mark of the question itself is that it opens up the being of the questioned and doing so is the holding open of possibilities. Questioning is not a positing, but a probing of possibilities that come out of and are taken up by the *Sache*. For Gadamer the point is not so much that questions then get answered, that possibilities are actualized—this of course occurs in interpretation in the very disappearance of interpretation—but that in questioning I am able to gain access to the otherness of the other (as traditionary text).[28] The art questioning is being able to go on asking questions which is at once the art of conducting a real conversation. Reading a text, which is the interpretation of tradition, is ultimately a matter of allowing the text to speak to us like a partner in a conversation; it is hearing and responding to what the other has to say in the element of speech. Perhaps it is here that the ontology of the possible is most evident, for in no way is conversation a repetition in which something prefigured comes forth and out into the open in the manner of self-actualization. Tradition does not stand behind the partners in conversation prefiguring its possibilities—the configuration of a metaphysics of actuality—but is the standing within the possible as such as the source of the always already of the *Sache*, which in the speaking comes to speak in a new voice.

Indeed the text does speak. There is a communicative event, a dialectical realization of sense, that by its very constitution will say the same within the tradition that we witness when the interpretation disappears in the interpretive act. What emerges as "self-same," though, is not the re-actualized original, but a *common* sphere of meaning, a sharing in a common meaning.[29] "There is no being-in-itself that is increasingly revealed when Homer's Iliad or Alexander's Indian Campaign speaks to us in the new appropriation of tradition; but, as in genuine dialogue, something emerges that is contained in neither of the partners alone" (TM 462/GW1 466). We should not forget that genuine conversation, when successful, *transforms* the opinions of the speakers. This transformation is not Hegelian movement but Kierkegaardian repetition. This is the sense in which the "new voice" is to be understood. Every genuine conversation is performative in such a way that what is disclosed is always a *movement forward*, a repetition of possibilities in every event of understanding. In his analysis of the logic of question and answer in *Truth and Method* Gadamer points out that his position differs from Collingwood's in that the "reconstructed" question of the text can never stand with its original horizon.[30]

How then are we to understand this τέλος of hermeneutic experience? Unlike Hegel's objective teleology, and for that matter unlike Kierkegaard's subjective teleology, Gadamer's teleology is the teleology of language itself with respect to a state of openness (*Offenheit*), just as experience entails the openness to further experience. The accomplishment of understanding, sharing in common, can only be measured against the content of tradition itself, and, Gadamer insists, every assimilation of tradition is historically *other* than the original event. But, if other, then hermeneutic understanding cannot be accounted for as a retrieval of what is self-same. The metaphor of mining the goods of the tradition that Caputo insists characterizes the project of philosophical hermeneutics is inappropriate, for what is there (for hermeneutic understanding) is there only as a possibility that remains possible. The difference that occurs in the way tradition speaks is not to be understood as an imperfect grasp (*getrübte Erfassung*) of it in the manner of something yet to be actualized. The differences of speaking pertain to the repetition of possibilities. Such repetition is manifest in the play of language itself as a play of presence and absence, which makes possible a new creation of understanding.

Living language, conversation, is thus language on the move (κίνησις), a movement of discourse in which word and thing first become what they are. Sense emerges within the dialogue, within the κίνησις of living language, in such a way that it inevitably transforms itself. The ensuing dialectic is an inexhaustible play of words, a self-propelled language game, steered neither by the original nor by the will of the one who wishes to understand. What occurs in language is "the play of language itself, which addresses us, proposes and withdraws, and fulfills itself in the answer" (TM 490/GW1 494).

When Caputo suggests that whenever the tradition comes to speak again we have simply the infinity of an unfolding Geist, he fails to see that tradition has nothing to do with a collective subject, but, again, is simply the collective name for each individual text.[31] Tradition is the text of Iriguray, Lacan, Malcolm X as well as Plato and Aristotle. The wholeness of tradition is more regulative than constitutive of experience, for every speaking is a new voice. And thus in every speaking something comes into being that had not existed before, that is to say, new possibilities of sense emerge from within the tradition itself. Like the κίνησις of living being, the movement of tradition repeats its own δύναμις, and more importantly, this unfolding of possibility does not come from a sphere of an already delineated essence. If such were the case possibility would not be higher than actuality. If such were the case the totality of sense would be nothing other than a prescribed set of possibilities, and thus the merely indeterminate as such. The contemporaneousness of every interpretation, the repetition of its possibility, is imbedded in the multifarious mixture of past and future which opens up to a whole new field of possibilities. The inexhaustible depth found in every interpretation must be understood in this context: the infinite is a function of the finite and not vice versa.

CHAPTER FIVE

Philosophical Hermeneutics and Truth

§ 16. The Question of Truth in Philosophical Hermeneutics

At the outset of chapter 4 we indicated that the question of truth in philosophical hermeneutics is linked to the question of finitude under the more encompassing question of Gadamer's essentialism. It appears that from one perspective Gadamer speaks too much of truth (the truth of an essentialism), while from another perspective Gadamer speaks too little of truth (a historicized, relativized truth). Given that Gadamer's essentialism is to be read in terms of an ontology of living being, we should now expect to find the question of truth addressed in these terms as well.

Undoubtedly, the question of truth in philosophical hermeneutics is more enigmatic than the question of finitude, for in point of fact Gadamer does not make the question of truth explicitly thematic in *Truth and Method*.[1] Moreover, when the question of truth is raised in various essays scattered throughout his writings, Gadamer often treats it in relation to other issues (the connection between art and truth, for example).[2] Where Gadamer is most explicit about truth in *Truth and Method*, namely, in the analysis of art, the point is often lost because the analysis of hermeneutic experience has not yet been given. It is just this point, though, that gives us a clear direction for taking up the question of truth in philosophical hermeneutics.

In the part 1 of *Truth and Method*, which is concerned with the question of truth in art, Gadamer first lays out the concept of art in a historical perspective and shows by that how the concept of art gradually came to be understood in terms of aesthetic differentiation by aesthetic consciousness. From the perspective of aesthetic consciousness art has its being in the subjectivity of the subject, where the experience of art is the experience of aesthetic enjoyment unencumbered by any association with the world in which the art work is rooted. This way of regarding art is for Gadamer a distortion of the real experience of the work of art. Gadamer maintains that art is a way of understanding ourselves, that is, understanding our historical existence, not unlike Hegel's view of art as a form of spirit in which the real is presented in its not yet fully mediated absolute shape. "Is there," Gadamer asks, "to be no knowledge in art? Does not the experience of art contain a claim to truth which is certainly different from that of science, but just as certainly is not inferior to it? And is not the task of aesthetics precisely to ground the fact that the experience of art is a mode of knowledge of a unique kind" (TM 97/GW1 103).

Gadamer then takes as his starting-point for this effort at overcoming the subjectification of aesthetics in the attitude of aesthetic consciousness a concept that has played a major role in aesthetics: the concept of play (*Spiel*). In Gadamer's hands, though, the concept of play is freed of its subjective meaning (found in Kant and Schiller) in order to capture the event character of understanding in the experience of art. Taking the concept of play in its ordinary usage, Gadamer finds play to essentially involve a decentering of the player in play for the sake of play's self-presentation. The decentering of the player is such that the player loses him or herself in the play; the player in the game of sport, for example, gives him or herself over to the game, participates in the playing of the game. This losing is not to be understood literally, but connotes the way in which "self-understanding always occurs through understanding something other than the self" (TM 97/GW1 102). In the loss of self one is still present, but being present now has the character of being outside oneself:

> [B]eing outside oneself is the positive possibility of being wholly with something else. This kind of being present [*Dabeisein*] is a self-forgetfulness, and to be a spectator [at the festival] consists in giving oneself in self-forgetfulness to what one is watching. Here self-forgetfulness is anything but a primitive condition, for it arises from devoting one's full attention to the matter at hand, and this is the spectator's own positive accomplishment. (TM 126/GW1 131)

If the structure of play does not exhibit then the structure that so dominates modern philosophy, namely, the re-presentation *to* subjectivity, it is also not a re-presentation *of* subjectivity. That is to say, play is essentially self-presentation (*Selbstdarstellung*), a self-defining movement, a χίνησις, in which the players enter, subjecting themselves to its play, whether it be the play of the card game, the play of sport, or whatever. Of course, it is the player's participation in play that brings play into presentation, yet it is not the player's subjectivity that is presented, but the game, the play itself. Here play is, properly speaking, a circle of play, a back-and-forth self-renewing movement, like the χίνησις of living being.

> The freedom of movement [of play] is such that it must have the form of self-movement. Expressing the thought of the Greeks in general, Aristotle had already described self-movement as the fundamental characteristic of living beings [*Lebendig*]. Whatever is alive [*lebendig*] has its source of movement within itself and has the form of self-movement. Now play appears as a self-movement that does not pursue any particular end or purpose so much as movement *as* movement, exhibiting so to speak a phenomenon of excess, the self-presentation of living [*Lebendigseins*]. (RB 23/GW8 113–14)

How is this concept of play embodied in aesthetic experience? To answer this question it is important to keep in mind what Gadamer is after in the experience of art, namely, that it includes understanding and thereby represents the hermeneutic phenomenon. We have seen that the hermeneutic phenomenon follows the general pattern of experience. Now, this pattern is configured to some extent in the experience of art as the "play" of art. Undergoing an experience with art means being able to recognize its claim to say something to me, which is accomplished not by being a distanced onlooker, but in a kind of participatory involvement in the manner of play. As a "spectator" there is a sense in which I perform the meaning of the work just as the player performs the play/game. Just as play has its being in being-played, so too the work of art has its being, not as an object framed by aesthetic categories,[3] but in the event of re-presentation, as is most evident in the case of theatrical performance. The work of art is not in the script, nor in the hidden intentions of the playwright, nor in the play's conscious reception in the mind of the theater-goer. Here the work of art is literally in its being-played, and the spectator, if we follow the Greek understanding of this, is no mere spectator but is a participant in the performance. The spectator is in a sense "educated," that is, the spectator becomes who one is in the interpretative participation with the work of art. The point is that art *is* in the encounter with it, in the place where it is there (*da*).[4] When it is successfully "there" it speaks in the sense that something *more* has been said, more comes to be known. This understanding of what is said is a participation in an event of truth.

Since encounters are different, the question of truth in art could be interpreted as the attempt to justify the claim that art gives us a historicized, relativized truth. Yet it is the same work that presents itself to intepretation. Thus the question of truth in art could be interpreted as the attempt to justify the claim that art gives us the multiple showings of the same truth, but simply shown in different ways. The connection between play and art is in fact meant to take neither position here. To see how this is the case is to understand what Gadamer means when he says that in the experience of art, play achieves an ideality in its transformation into figurative structure (*Gebilde*). The "play" of art, not having its being in the consciousness of the player, is simply the "pure appearance [*reinen Erscheinung*]" (of what is being played).[5] In this autonomy the "play" of art is a transformation, that is, something is suddenly and as a whole something else.[6] When a child plays at dressing up, the transformation is not the disguise but what is presented! But more important, for Gadamer, in this autonomy the "play" of art is a transformation *into structure*, that is, the play as $\varkappa \iota \nu \eta \sigma \iota \varsigma$ is $\dot{\epsilon} \nu \dot{\epsilon} \varrho \gamma \epsilon \iota \alpha$ as the actuality of movement, but in its ideality it has the character of an $\dot{\epsilon}' \varrho \gamma o \nu$ as completed work and not only of $\dot{\epsilon} \nu \dot{\epsilon} \varrho \gamma \epsilon \iota \alpha$ (TM 110/GW1 116).[7] The actuality of art has become "figured," a structured shape for which one must be hesitant to use the word "thing."[8] What takes place in being structured is a leaving behind of the origin, and yet, by virtue of being structured, the work of art is capable of repetition. The reading of the *Iliad* of Homer for example does not depend on recreating the world of the Greeks in order for one to enter into the experience of the work. The work of art as structure is precisely that meaningful whole, beyond its origination, that is not judged in terms of what lies outside it. In this sense the transformation into structure "means that what now exists, what presents [*darstellt*] itself in the play of art, is that which remains true [*bleibende Wahre*]" (TM 111/GW1 117).[9] In art the transformation into figurative structure is a transformation into the true.

> Certainly the play takes place in another, closed world. But inas-
> much as it is a structure, it is, so to speak, its own measure and

measures itself by nothing outside it. Thus the action of a drama
. . . exists as something that rests absolutely within itself. It no
longer permits of any comparison with reality as the secret measure
of all verisimilitude [*abbildlichen Ähnlichkeit*]. It is raised above
all such comparisons—and hence also above the question whether
it is all real—because a superior truth speaks from it. (TM 112/GW1
117)

The world that is "mirrored" in the play of art is a world pure and simple,
not a copy of some intended other reality. In the presentation of play reality
is captured in an image: "what we experience in a work of art and what
invites our attention is how true it is, that is, to what extent one knows
and recognizes something and oneself" (TM 114/GW1 119).

Here then the question of truth is most explicit. For philosophical
hermeneutics truth pertains to a disclosure of the real in the image, to a
disclosure through a kind of $\mu\iota\mu\eta\sigma\iota\varsigma$ in which there is recognition, but not
a recognition as a recollection of an origin. The *question* of truth in philosophical hermeneutics is one of understanding precisely what this means
and how it can be maintained for hermeneutic experience as a whole.

Unfortunately, most commentators, recognizing this general insight
that truth in philosophical hermeneutics pertains to disclosure, have simply
assumed that the experience of truth in philosophical hermeneutics can
be accounted for in terms of Heidegger's analysis of truth as $\dot{\alpha}\lambda\dot{\eta}\theta\epsilon\iota\alpha$.
Richard Bernstein, for example, acknowledging the affinity with Heidegger
and yet not wanting to limit the hermeneutic experience of truth to this
affinity, accounts for the hermeneutic experience of truth in the following
way: Gadamer appeals to truth in order to distinguish philosophical hermeneutics from a historicist form of relativism, and the nature of such truth
comprises a blending of motifs that have resonances in Hegel and Heidegger.
Like Hegel, Gadamer understands truth to be revealed in the process of
experience, in the dialogical encounter with the very tradition that has shaped
us. Like Heidegger, Gadamer seeks to recover the notion of $\dot{\alpha}\lambda\dot{\eta}\theta\epsilon\iota\alpha$ as
disclosedness and unconcealment. But, Bernstein insists, unlike Hegel,
Gadamer does not regard truth as the whole revealed in science; and, in
relation to Heidegger, Gadamer is hesitant to follow his meditations in the
way that Heidegger himself would.[10] In this blending of motifs, Bernstein
thinks that what Gadamer is appealing to is a concept of truth that comes
down to what can be validated argumentatively by the community of inter-
preters who open themselves to what is "handed down" says to us.[11]

But in opting for this Rortyan-pragmatic line, which amounts to justifying claims to truth by giving the strongest arguments showing why something is true, Bernstein never pursues considerations specific to the hermeneutic event of disclosure. Bernstein's description, in other words, is hardly sufficient to account for what goes on in the *transformative* unfolding of dialogue, and even more so, it does not sufficiently account for the experience of truth in relation to Being that we find in the experience with the work of art. Bernstein fails to make explicit the thematic of *recollective recognition* as the particular eventing character of hermeneutic truth.

As a corrective to Bernstein's analysis, the intent of this chapter is to show that for Gadamer the experience of truth is indeed the recollective recognition of truth, not unlike the recollection of truth one finds in Plato. Most decisively, for Plato the recollection of truth is directly tied to the experience of the beautiful, and it is precisely this connection that needs to be maintained in an account of truth in Gadamer's hermeneutics as well. It is by no means coincidental that Gadamer concludes *Truth and Method* by retrieving his analysis of the work of art, adding at this point a discussion of Plato's concept of the beautiful. To defend this position, we must, first, situate more precisely the question of truth—as Gadamer himself would have us do—from within the analysis of the beautiful. In doing so we are then able to see how the experience of truth in philosophical hermeneutics is taken up in what can be called a "play of image." Second, we must then show how a recollective recognition of truth is operative in this play of image as the site of truth.

§ 17. The Being of the Beautiful

Gadamer begins the last section of *Truth and Method* by summarizing his just-completed analysis of language in relation to hermeneutic experience as a whole. Everything that is language, Gadamer insists, has a speculative unity whereby that which comes into language is not something pre-given before language. This means that the being of language is self-presentation. This same self-presentation, Gadamer reminds us, also characterized the being of art. In order to explicate the self-presentational character of the being of language (and art)—which means here the dimension of self-showing in hermeneutic experience whereby the claim to truth has its force—Gadamer introduces the conception of the beautiful from Greek antiquity as analogous to the specific event character of hermeneutic understanding.

What appeals to Gadamer in the classical Greek conception of the beautiful is precisely its relation to the structure of being. When Plato links the idea of the beautiful with the idea of the good, he does so because they are always to be thought in relation to the teleological order of being. Both the beautiful and the good go beyond everything that is conditional and multiple. When, in the *Symposium*, Plato describes the beautiful itself as that which lies at the end of the journey through many beautiful beings, we should immediately compare this claim with Plato's remark in the *Republic* that the good is that which lies beyond what is good in certain respects. But the connection between the beautiful and the good for Plato is actually closer than this. In the *Philebus* Plato tells us that in the attempt to grasp the good itself, the good takes flight in the beautiful. The good is conceived here according to the ideal of mixture and thus inseparable from other aspects: "the power of the good has taken refuge in the nature of the beautiful; for measure and proportion are everywhere identified with beauty and virtue."[12] Plato then adds truth to this "mixture" so that beauty, proportion and truth are named as the three aspects of the good which appears as the beautiful. In this context, the good (which is at the same time the beautiful), contrary to the description found in the *Republic*, does not merely exist beyond being, but exists as well in those things that we recognize as a beautiful mixture.[13]

And yet, for Gadamer, this close connection between the beautiful and the good points at the same time to one respect in which the beautiful is different from the good. Insofar as the good takes flight in the beautiful, the beautiful appears to have a specific advantage over the good. The beautiful has the advantage of presenting itself; it is part of its nature to be that which appears (*Erscheinendes*). As such the beautiful, unlike models of human virtue which have no light of their own—and thus "often succumb to impure imitations and appearances of virtue" (TM 481/GW1 485)—has its own radiance. Accordingly, to say that the good is displayed in the beautiful simply means that the good is visibly manifest.

This feature of the beautiful—to be visibly manifest—is also found in the *Phaedrus*. In the myth of human destiny presented there, Plato describes the procession to the vault of the heavens where true being is revealed. In this procession the human soul is drawn back by the unruly steed, and thus is a soul whose vision is clouded and has, at best, a fleeting memory of true being. There is one experience, however, that allows the "wings to grow" and thus rejoin the ascent, namely, the love of the beautiful. Beauty, we are told, is the one εἶδος that preserves something of the former lustrousness of an idea, and that shines forth in the visible stimulating love in us: "For the beautiful alone this has been ordained, to be most radiantly manifest [ἐκφανέστατον] (to sense) and most beloved."[14] For Plato, the example of the beautiful illustrates the controversial relation of participation in the εἶδος without attending to any of the logical difficulties inherent in the problem. The function of the beautiful is to mediate between the intelligible and appearance. It can do so precisely because radiance, shining-forth, constitutes the being of the beautiful in such a way that being present belongs decisively to the being of the beautiful. The beautiful itself, as an εἶδος, rises above the flux of appearances; and yet, it is itself that shines forth in the appearance. As that which is most radiantly manifest (ἐκφανέστατον), the beautiful is the appearance itself.[15] The distinctive feature of the beautiful, then, in contrast even to the good, is that of itself it presents itself; it makes itself immediately evident (*einleuchtend*). But this means, at the same time, that the beautiful does not simply mediate between the intelligible and appearance. It collapses the distinction between the difference; it collapses the distinction between the illuminated and the illuminating: "The idea of the beautiful is truly present, whole and undivided, in what is beautiful" (TM 481/GW1 485). It is the condition of the εἶδος itself to shine, to present itself, and thus it is not something that exists through something else.

How then is this illuminating character of the beautiful analogous to the event structure of hermeneutic experience, to an encounter with something that asserts its own truth? Gadamer's claim is that the beautiful, in connection with the comprehensibility of the intelligible, is *einleuchtend*. Literally, a "shining in," its meaning is conveyed in the expression "an enlightening experience." The enlightening refers to the fact that something has come to light in the sense that something becomes clear. Such clarity does not result from methodological procedure. Thus it stands in contrast to Cartesian certainty that marks the outcome of methodological procedure. The clarity of *einleuchtend* comes upon us, perhaps even surprises us. Gadamer thinks that one finds this notion of clarity in rhetoric. The art of rhetoric, which ties itself to the immediacy of its effect, advocates a claim to truth that defends the probable, the (*verisimile*), and that which is convincing to ordinary reason (TM 485/GW1 488). The true has the mark of "appearing to be true" (*wahrscheinlich*), asserting itself of its own merit, rather than certainty: an argument may have something true about it even though we may argue against it. The way in which what is true is compatible with the whole of what we consider correct is left open. Similarly, the beautiful engages us, charms us, without being immediately integrated into the whole of our orientations.

In this dimension of shining we already begin to see the connection, which was always evident for Plato, between beauty and truth. The enlightening as clear has something true about it; the shining-in is a shining-forth (ἀλήθεια). What is most intriguing for us here, however, to go back to what we said earlier, is the manner of the shining-forth. For the beautiful, it makes no difference whether it itself or its image (*Abbild*) appears. For Gadamer, this unique situation has a distinctive consequence: the being of the beautiful, this self-presentational shining-forth, must always be understood ontologically as image (*Bild*) (TM 487/GW1 491).

The whole issue of the shining-forth of the self-presentational character of being (and ultimately the question of truth) turns on Gadamer's understanding of image (*Bild*). Most certainly, in this context image is no longer the distorted copy that appears as semblance, an image with something behind or beneath it that determines the image as something less than real. But precisely how image is to be understood requires that we retrieve the analysis that we stopped short of giving in discussing the being of the work of art as transformation into structure.

In discussing the ontological valence of the picture (*Bild*), Gadamer is quick to point out that the problematic character of a picture is derived, as it was for Plato, from the problem of the original picture (*Urbild*). The concept of a picture, linked to the concept of (re)presentation (*Darstellung*), is a form of imitation (μίμησις). What Gadamer wants to show is that the presentation of the picture, as in a framed painting, is related to the original in a different way than the relation of the copy to the original.

Gadamer has already been able to show that for the performing arts the mimetic presentation is not a mere copy. In drama "the world that appears in the play of presentation does not stand like a copy next to the real world, but is that world in the heightened truth of its being" (TM 137/GW1 142). If Shakespeare's *Hamlet* re-creates a person's struggle over doubts for which one can find precedent in life outside the play, it is not the life outside the play that is portrayed but Hamlet's struggle, and it is this struggle that I see. A transformation occurs in dramatic play: what is meant is intrinsic to the presentation and only in a secondary, critical stance do we ask about the identity of the player or the quality of the production (those comparative questions that force a distinction between copy and original).

What is ontologically true of the performing arts is true of the work of art in general: every production is a self-presentation having its τέλος within itself. Such a claim is hardly striking if one recognizes, as Gadamer does, that this presentational character of art is what is expressed by the original concept of μίμησις. Originally, the concept of μίμησις has little to do with the imitation of something that is already familiar to us. Rather, it pertains to the way in which something is presented such that it is actually present in sensuous abundance.[16] The mimetic character of the presentation, the "copying" character of the presentation, is simply the appearance (*Erscheinung*) of what is presented. And even more so, "without being imitated in the work, the world does not exist as it exists in the work" (TM 137/GW1 142). Consequently, it is possible to say in some sense that the work of art does not refer to something, because the presence of what is presented stands in its own right as a completed whole in the presentation.

The question though is whether the same analysis can also be applied to the picture (*Bild*). It would appear that with respect to a picture, copy (*Abbild*) and original (*Urbild*) are quite distinct, since the original picture, unlike dramatic play that has its real being in being performed and thus produced, resists production as self-presentation. But here too the image/original structure collapses. Notice what is entailed in the nature of a copy. Its function is to announce the original by resembling it. The measure of its success is that one recognizes the original in the copy. That is, although a copy exists in its own right, its nature is to cancel out its independent existence by pointing beyond itself. An ideal copy, then, would be the mirror image "for its being can effectively disappear; it exists only for someone who looks into the mirror, and is nothing beyond its pure appearance" (TM 138/GW1 143). But in truth it is no picture or copy at all, for it has no existence for itself. And yet, that we speak here of a mirror *image* and not a copy is not insignificant. "For in the mirror image the entity itself appears in the image so that we have the thing itself in the mirror image," whereas a copy "must always be regarded in relation to the thing it means" (TM 138/GW1 143).

A picture is not itself a copy since it is not intended to be canceled out. Similar to the mode of being of performance, the picture itself is what is meant; thus one is not directed away from it to some anterior or posterior presentation. This feature of presentation is the positive distinction of being a picture as opposed to being a mere reflected image.

And yet, as presentation, the picture is not the same as what is presented. According to Gadamer, "even today's mechanical techniques can be used in an artistic way, when they bring out something that is not to be found simply by looking [*Anblick*]" (TM 140/GW1 144–45). Of course such a picture remains limited by the original, but the relation to the original here is quite different from a copy-original relation. In the case of the picture, the relation is no longer one-sided. Since the picture has its own reality, one can say that the original presents itself in the presentation. In the case of the copy, the original is always inferred and has its semblance in the copy. The presenting in the picture is no incidental occurrence, but belongs to the picture's actual being. Every picture is an ontological event that in its presentation produces an increase in being. In a sense the picture is the original's emanation.

This conception of presentation in which the picture stands in a unique relation to the original is not novel. Gadamer thinks we find this same mode of being in the concept of *Repräsentation* (*representation*) in canon law. *Repraesentare* means to make present, and for canon law this meant legal representation. But, "the important thing about the legal concept of representation is that the *persona repraesentata* is put forward and presented (*Vor- und Dargestellte*), and yet the *Repräsentant*, who is exercising the former's rights, is *dependent* upon him" (TM 141/GW1 146). This concept of *repraesentation* suggests something even more about the relation of image and original. Now we can say that the picture has an independence that effects the original, "for strictly speaking it is only through the picture that the original actually becomes original [*Ur-bilde*]" (TM 142/GW1 146–47). The religious picture is a good illustration of what is meant here. The appearance of the divine acquires its picturalness (*Bildhaftigkeit*) only through the word and the picture. The religious picture is not a copy of a copied being "but is in ontological communion with what is copied" (TM 143/GW1 147). The pictural image is thus not an imitative illustration, but an image that allows what it presents to be for the first time what it is.

If we take this analysis of the pictural image as indicative of what Gadamer means by the self-presentational character of being, as an event by which the world comes into being, then self-presentation can be described as a play of image. And what is true of the visual image would also be true of the word, for the word is not simply a sign, but more like an image (*Bild*). Consistent with Gadamer's claim that as living language the being of language is in conversation, this means that the structure of being, the intelligible, is not simply copied in language. Rather, in language the intelligible forms itself.[17] In the word, as in the beautiful in its shining-forth, there is a showing forth.

Thus, in words, too, there is an image play. Insofar as every body of words is but a phase in the execution of a communicative event, the image play is nothing less than a site of performance. This site is such that, consistent with the character of living language, there is no first word, just as there is no last word. Most decisively then, in the same way that we are caught up in our speaking, we can say that the image play, the site of performance, is something in which we find ourselves entangled. At the end of *Truth and Method* Gadamer writes:

> When we understand a text, what is meaningful engages [*einnimmt*] us, just as the beautiful engages us. It has asserted itself and engaged us before we can come to ourselves and be in a position to test the claim to meaning that it makes. What we encounter in the experience of the beautiful and in understanding the meaning of tradition really has something of the truth of play about it. In understanding we are drawn into an event of truth and arrive, as it were, too late, if we want to know what we are supposed to believe. (TM 490/GW1 494)

In such entanglement, we are not simply bound to an image play, we are also bound to the mimetic field in which the image play is located.

But precisely how is this mimetic field to be understood, this sphere of replay and repetition that has entered into the collapse of the image/original distinction? On the one hand, Gadamer would want to recognize the paradox of mimesis that Derrida finds lying within Plato's metaphysics: that the origin of truth (which is beyond imitation) cannot be understood without the mimetic activity of repetition (in the form of recollection).[18] Philosophical hermeneutics itself escapes the paradox by refusing to posit an origin of truth beyond imitation. Consequently, Gadamer recognizes that the act of figuration (*Gebilde*) can no longer rest on the priority of the imitated over imitation. This is precisely what the "truth of play" is all about: an image play, whether conversation or drama, is essentially a performance that has no being, no substantiality, outside the performing.

At the same time, however, Derrida's own deconstruction of μίμησις takes it in a direction that Gadamer cannot follow. For Derrida the mimetic field produces no upsurge of determinative sense in the determination of real being. Following Mallarmé, Derrida likens mimetic action to a perpetual allusion that constantly displaces its referent. Mimetic activity must defer any reference to what lies outside the activity, and is thus understood as a movement of *différance* that serves to undo all presence and centering. This means that it is not just the truth of *adequatio*, which structures the image/original distinction, that Derrida would undercut in the mimetic field.

Derrida would also undo the truth of ἀλήθεια insofar as the mimetic field does not produce a presentation of the thing itself, a showing-forth of being.

But to accept this latter consequence of the mimetic activity would be to undo the point to which we have just been led in Gadamer's analysis of the image. There is a question of truth in hermeneutic experience, but it is certainly not that of *adequatio* whereby there is an agreement between the re-presentation and the thing, for the character of the image play is no longer tied to the image/original distinction. Philosophical hermeneutics, in other words, is not engaged in a metaphysical quest of seeing truth itself instead of an image but in its own paradoxical way, precisely the inverse: of getting entangled in the image that entangles us in truth. And it must be added that this is no simple reversal that would now subscribe to a priority of the imagination within the still constituted framework of truth as origin. Gadamer is not positing a transcendental imagination that would apprehend the original in intuition or suggesting that art is the productive transformation of nature, as in Kant's aesthetics. Gadamer is too Greek to be this Romantic. But philosophical hermeneutics is concerned with truth.

Thus on the other hand, for Gadamer, the mimetic field, although endless by virtue of its practical performance, is not a house of mirrors without referent, where endless play deflects and diffuses the brightness of the illuminated. Rather, to be caught within the mimetic field *is* to be caught in a play of truth. The question, which is the question with which we began, is that of the character of truth in the image-play, and ultimately this is the question of the difference not only between Gadamer and Derrida, but also between Gadamer and Heidegger with respect to the question of truth.

§ 18. The Imaging of Truth

Without ἀρχαί or τέλος extending beyond the mimetic field, the image-play as a play of truth suggests that what transpires in language, art, and all the other dimensions of hermeneutic experience is a constant entanglement of *thick* images in which the intelligible is itself entangled. Such entanglement is prescribed not only by the character of the image, but also by the character of hermeneutic experience that always begins with "a supporting mutual understanding" (*ein tragendes Einverständnis*).

> There is always a world already interpreted, already organized
> into its basic relations, into which experience steps as something

new, upsetting what has led our expectations and undergoing reorganization itself in the upheaval. Misunderstanding and strangeness are not the first factors, so that avoiding misunderstanding can be regarded as the specific task of hermeneutics. Just the reverse is the case. Only the support of the familiar and common understanding makes possible the venture into the alien, and lifting up of something out of the alien, and thus the broadening and enrichment of our own experience of the world. (PH 15/GW2 230)

We are, by virtue of our beginnings, already in the truth, and we bear witness to our entanglement with truth when we find ourselves caught up in the effort of finding the common ground whereby what is said by the word or presented by the performance speaks in a new voice. In this effort at understanding, it is not a matter of disentangling the image play, of retreating from the entanglement and image, but of a performative enactment (*Vollzug*) in which an image shines forth. Such a performing, since it occurs within the already understood, has, as we have seen in the analysis of experience in chapter 3, the character of recollection, of gathering-together-anew the already interpreted. But the moment of recognition in this recollection, which is at once the recognition of the true, is not simply the fact that something makes sense—the state of being lifted out of the alien—for in such a claim, the matter of truth amounts to nothing, and it does not fully take into consideration the critical analysis that is part of the movement between the strange and familiar. Even more so, we must be careful not to reinscribe a more sophisticated notion of *adequatio* into the movement between the strange and familiar. A correspondence will always require an alignment to a reference point, a correlation from which the measure of the thing is taken. But this account of truth is insufficient to account for the dynamic of the image that is always bound to the play of figuration within hermeneutic experience.

We could go farther, but certainly not without some reservation, in determining the character of the imaging of truth if we employ a metaphor appropriate to thick images, namely, depth.[19] A thick image is one with great depth; but in its depth it can be dense in the sense of abundant or muddy and obtuse. Following this metaphor, we can describe the moment of truth in hermeneutic experience in two ways. First, in the moment of truth, the recollective recognition, there is something *fitting*. This notion of fitting we have implicitly encountered before. It describes with some accuracy the character of disclosure in practical life. Practical reasoning, we should recall, was set against ἐπιστήμη and was characterized by that as a knowing that is "indeterminate" in the sense that the rule-governed activity remains determined by the situation. For this and other reasons, Aristotle says that in the determination of moral virtue it is easy to miss the mark, but hard to hit it.[20] Hitting the mark is finding the proper measure; it is, in other words, finding the measure *fitting* the situation. In the fit is the interpretation, and it is this notion that is carried over into hermeneutic experience. In the logic of question and answer, which structures the play of language, we can speak of a fitting response. In dialogical conversation we throw out statements along the way in an effort to find the fitting response: we put statements forward, but we also discard or abandon statements along the way since some statements are found to lead us nowhere. Fitting, then, pertains to a certain disentanglement, a separating out in which something comes together—a moment of coherence not of wholeness, where the interpretation is now one with the λόγος, but a moment that forms a whole in coming together as it does. In this thickness of words, this infinity of meaning held in everything said, there arises the right word, the word heard by the inner ear, fits or rings true. The fitting thus pertains to the action of a text, or a dialogical partner, upon the hearer.

In this context, it is even possible to speak about a notion of falsifiability in hermeneutic experience. An interpretation becomes false whenever the *Sache* breaks through in conversation to show itself as other than it first presented itself. The *Sache*, though, is not to be understood as that which is self-same within the multiplicity of interpretation. Philosophical hermeneutics is not subscribing to a metaphysics of a plurality of essence, that is, the self-same showing itself in many ways as one could read in cursory fashion, for example, Gadamer's notion of tradition. The *Sache* is the singular datum: this text, this work, this spoken word. The recognition within the mimetic field of the image play then is the recognition of what is presented in its presentation. This does not mean that recognition is merely a matter of seeing something that we have seen before; rather, recognition is something qualitatively different. In recognition we cognize something as something that we have already seen in our entangled condition. According to Gadamer, the enigma of knowing lies entirely in this "as" that, in the process of recognition, lets us see things "in terms of what is permanent and essential in them, unencumbered by the contingent circumstances in which they were seen before and are seen again" (RB 99/GW8 32).[21]

At the same time—and here we point to the second way of describing the moment of truth—the thick image suggests that truth is played out within the continuum of empty and full.[22] The mimetic field, we should recall, is such that in the image play something comes forth in sensuous abundance. Inasmuch as the work of art does not simply refer to something, because what it refers to is actually there, its productive character can be described as an "increase in being." The determination of truth in the work of art appears to be pointed at this overflow; it has to do with the possibility of saying more as the landscape in a picture becomes more by being picturesque. Similarly, in the virtuality of living speech, we are "full up," so to speak, and yet always able to say more. When we say what we mean, we are at once holding together what is said "with an infinity of what is not said in one unified meaning" (TM 469/GW1 473). We can see more precisely what is meant here by again noting how there is a notion of falsifiability at work in our interpretative efforts. Error coincides with the empty, when the interpretation comes to nothing.[23] In the case of the work of art, the empty is imitation in its usual meaning; imitative art is no longer alive. The art is cheap (*contra* dear), plastic in the worst way—marked by artificiality and pretension. In "Philosophy and Poetry" Gadamer uses this notion of empty to describe a feature common to both poetical and philosophical types of speech. He says of both that they cannot be "false." What he means of course is that the measure-taking for the truth of these discourses cannot be obtained by an appeal to an external standard that would verify or falsify the discourses. And yet, the discourses are not arbitrary. "They represent a unique kind of risk for they can fail to live up to themselves," which happens because their words prove to be empty. As Gadamer explains it:

> In the case of poetry, this occurs when, instead of sounding right, it merely sounds like other poetry or like the rhetoric of everyday life. In the case of philosophy, this occurs when philosophical language gets caught up in purely formal argumentation or degenerates into empty sophistry. In both cases these inferior forms of language—the poem that is not a poem because it does not have its "own" tone, and the empty formulae of a thinking that does to touch on the matter of thought—the word breaks. (RB 139/GW8 239)

Of course, what constitutes being full—the moment of truth—is not determined by a quantitative mark, but occurs whenever the *Sache* speaks again in a new voice.

In both descriptions, the moment of truth—and the conception of error—is linked to whether or not something actually takes place, to the performance that occurs when one is drawn into the experience with the work or when one responds to the voice of the other in dialogical encounter. In this context, we should not forget the connection that Gadamer has already made to the tradition of rhetoric.[24] From this perspective, one could argue that in hermeneutic experience we come back to a richer notion of truth as *veritas* (to the notion of truth as real) and *verificare* (to the notion of affirming and attesting).[25] In the presentation of art, for example, Gadamer suggests that the presentation intends to be so true that we do not advert to the fact that it is not real. The work of art is true whenever it shows itself to be "real," a "veritable" image. In undergoing an experience with art, then, we "verify" it, which is not a matter of confirming but of testifying to the real, of bearing witness to what is by being drawn into the image-play, of making the matter itself real through the practical performance of play.

This notion of truth is suggested by Gadamer in *The Relevance of the Beautiful* in response to the question of the meaning of truth in poetic language. Poetic saying, he tells us, "says so completely what it is that we do not need to add anything beyond what is said in order to accept it in its reality as language" (RB 110/GW8 75). Such reality is at once a "recitation of the truth." The word of the poet is autonomous in the sense that it is self-fulfilling, bearing witness to itself, and thus does not admit, as we have just indicated, of anything that could verify it in the ordinary sense (a kind of confirmation by external authority). The poem is not judged against the world outside it, but, on the contrary, a world is constructed from within the poem itself.

What is true of poetic language could also be said of all speaking inasmuch as poetic language simply "stands out as the highest fulfillment of the revealing which is the achievement of all speech" (RB 112/GW8 76). Gadamer notes that in terms of the living language of the early Greeks, truth has a double sense. In connection with speech, ἀλήθεια is openness where being open means to say what one means. In *telling* the truth, we say what we mean. This is supplemented by a further sense of truth in which "*something* 'says' what it 'means': whatever shows itself to what it is, is true" (RB 108/GW8 73). Thus when we say "real gold" we mean it is gold; it is true gold as the Greeks say ἀληθές.[26]

But in describing truth in this way, ἀληθές is equivalent to its Latin translation; the true is *veritas*, not in its medieval determination as a kind of *adequatio*, but as simply the actual nature of the thing. Here the point of difference between Gadamer and Heidegger becomes most apparent. For Gadamer, it is certainly not a matter of thinking the withdrawal that demarcates the region of the open, nor is it enough to say that for hermeneutic experience, truth is openness as this occurs when words stand forth and show things as they are. It is rather a matter of the *thematic of speaking itself that holds the question of truth within it in an unthematized manner.*[27] The early Greeks understood this quite well: without any concern for the structuring of the true, for what pertains to ἀλήθεια per se, Nestor asks in the *Iliad* upon hearing the thunder of the running horses, whether he is wrong "or speaking the true [ἢ ἔτυμον ἐρέω]."[28] Nestor asks if he speaks a true thing, if the matter is true or real (ἐτεός). The Gadamerian hermeneut repeats this gesture: one stands in the truth, verifies it, only when one finds the right word, only when one says what one means. One stands in the truth, bears witness to it, only when the thing, the art work, says what it means (ἔτυμον ἐρέω). In such standing, we bear witness to our own being as well; the image play entangles us in its entanglement.[29] Thus, the imaging of truth for Gadamer is not about how things come to show themselves as they do. It is not about the conditions for the rupturing in the folds of being (as Heidegger takes up this project). It is rather about the art of saying. It is about what Cicero understood to be a task of the orator: *consule veritatem*, consider the etymology. But *veritatem* here is a translation of ἔτυμον.[30] The task of the orator is to consider the real being. For philosophical hermeneutics that is all anyone can do.

The recollective recognition is, accordingly, the event of continual reacquisition. This is precisely what Plato affirms in his doctrine of recollection. According to Gadamer, "in his theory of *anamnesis* Plato combined the mythical idea of remembrance [*Wiedererinnerung*] with his dialectic, which sought the truth of being in the *logoi*, that is, in the ideality of language. In fact this kind of idealism of being is already suggested in the phenomenon of recognition" (TM 114/GW1 119). Platonic recollection is the gathering-together—"for a human being must understand a general conception formed by collecting into a unity by means of reason the many perceptions of the senses"[31]—that renews the vision of true being. For Plato this process of reacquisition is the way mortals participate in immortality. Philosophical hermeneutics will not stray far from this insight, from this essential human task of keeping in memory. The recollection of truth with respect to poetic saying—that highest fulfillment of the revealing which is the achievement of all speech—is for Gadamer "living in poetry": the "rediscovery of the abundance which *memoria* is able to grant to human life" (EPH 91/GW9 257). In *memoria* is the preserving (*Bewahren*) of all that we are, but preserving does not mean to cling to what already is.[32] If preservation is the authentic manner in which the true can be for humans, this means nothing less than the taking care for, paying heed to that which is in being said.

CHAPTER SIX

The Voice of the Text

In the Introduction and throughout this book we have emphasized how the various thematics taken up by philosophical hermeneutics ultimately come to be framed by the dynamics of conversation. At the root of this model lies, not the dialectic of German Idealism, but the Socratic dialogue as "the true carrying out of $\overset{?}{\alpha}\nu\acute{\alpha}\mu\nu\eta\sigma\iota\varsigma$." In this conditional framing of the field of hermeneutic understanding, Gadamer takes language to be living language, the language of speaking of one to another. This means for Gadamer that it is always the language of the voice and, as dialogical, the voice of the other that constitutes the field of hermeneutic understanding. In Socratic dialogue the word is not an isolated word, nor is it a formulated proposition, but that which points beyond all possible assertions as "the totality of a way of accounting by means of speaking and answering" (DD 112–12/GW2 371).

It is with this model of conversation and its underlying assumptions about the nature of language that Gadamer enters the postmodern debate on the nature of language and texts, and the character of interpretation of texts. His engagement in this debate is in fact quite specific. It is an engagement that began as a result of a colloquium on text and interpretation held in Paris in 1981, an engagement that brought together Gadamer and Derrida for the first time. Since then Gadamer has given several other papers in which he attempts to place his own work in its proper perspective relative to that of deconstruction.[1] The focus of this chapter is on this placing of philosophical hermeneutics in relation to deconstruction. Such placement though is by no means a simple matter; what is offered here are two readings of the relation between hermeneutics and deconstruction. The first reading comments directly on the exchange between Gadamer and Derrida from the 1981 meeting, and looks to what is common to both. The second reading takes note of the distinctive feature of Gadamer's hermeneutics—that it is a hermeneutics of the voice—and attempts to give an account of it that shows the essential difference between hermeneutics and deconstruction without allowing hermeneutics to be reduced to what falls under the deconstructive critique of hermeneutics.

A. HERMENEUTICS AND DECONSTRUCTION—FIRST APPROACH

§ 19. *Situating Hermeneutics and Deconstruction*

Hermeneutics *and* deconstruction. Why do we speak of a conjunction? Ostensibly, the conjunction serves to bring together two postmodern approaches to reading the text. And so one can speak of "text and interpretation" as a point of departure for coming to terms with the real possibility of conjunction. There is a public event, the principals are present, the conjunction is cast. But what is it that is brought together when we say "hermeneutics and deconstruction." Is it not the case that the conjunction is rooted in a common quest for liberation? Both hermeneutics and deconstruction take seriously the playfulness of language and with it the possibility of liberation from the solidification of the words (and its deleterious consequences for the question of meaning) of texts.

The problem of the conjunction is that, from the perspective of deconstruction, hermeneutics is not at all engaged in an effort of genuine liberation because it is naive about the boundaries of meaning configured in text and interpretation. For deconstruction, the text is no longer simple, a constituted body of words present to the reader depending on a proper methodological access. The text is no longer so simple nor so insular to itself, bounded by its markings of title, beginning, end and authorship. What has been recognized is that the text, as a repository of meaning, as centered, cannot, like the statues of Daedalus, be tied down.[2] The text is always open to a fundamental multiplicity of meaning because of the functioning of language in which *différance* invades the sign. Neither word nor concept, *différance* is the paradoxical structure that plays on its double meaning of difference and deferral.[3] That the process of signification is a formal play of differences means that "whether in the order of spoken or written discourse, no element can function as a sign without referring to another element which itself is not simply present."[4] In this interweaving of signs every element of language is constituted by the trace within it of the other elements in the system. In this context it can be said that nothing among the elements of language is ever simply present or absent; there are only differences. But what is true of the sign must also be true of the system of signs; accordingly, there is also an undecidable relation between the event and structure of language. Derrida writes:

> One can extend to the system of signs in general what Saussure says of language: "Language [*langue*] is necessary for speech [parole] to be intelligible and to produce all its effects, but speech is necessary for language to be established. . . ." There is a circle here, for if one rigorously distinguishes language and speech, code and message, schema and usage, etc., and if one wishes to do justice to the two postulates thus enunciated, one does not know where to begin, nor how something can begin in general, be it language or speech. Therefore, one has to admit before any dissociation of language and speech . . . a systematic production of differences, the production of a system of differences—a *différance*—within whose effects one eventually, by abstraction and according to determined motivations, will be able to demarcate a linguistics of language and a linguistics of speech.[5]

Language is thus constituted as an effect the cause of which does not lie outside the movement of *différance*; there is no subject who is the master of *différance*, for every (speaking) subject depends upon the system of differences and the movement of *différance*. By inclusion, the language of philosophy is also constituted as an effect. Accordingly, the metaphysics of presence refers to that working within a discourse that ignores the conceptual opposition in play (e.g., sensible/intelligible, writing/speaking) by privileging one element as being prior to the movement of *différance*.

Corresponding to this notion of language and text, the "interpretation" of a text is essentially critique.[6] It is an analysis—what Derrida calls "a general strategy of deconstruction"—that displaces the centering found in the text by following certain terms that govern the textual production itself. The displacement is not to be construed as a merely negative critique, but entails a double gesture: on the one hand, a deconstruction of the hierarchial opposition that itself must remain interminable; on the other hand, a critical operation that continues to work "on the terrain of and from within the deconstructed system." Such interpretation amounts to a new concept of writing, one that "simultaneously provokes the overturning of the hierarchy of speech/writing, and the entire system attached to it, and releases the dissonance of a writing within speech, thereby disorganizing the entire inherited order and invading the entire field."[7] Writing, *écriture*, is what disperses and defers meaning and shatters all totalizing unity.

The question that arises in the exchange—the question that is addressed by Gadamer in his essay "Text and Interpretation" but never explicitly stated by Derrida—is whether the intertwining of text and interpretation in philosophical hermeneutics is simply one more instance of a metaphysics of presence, of a logocentric metaphysics that believes that the statues of Daedalus can in fact be tied down. This question must be addressed to any hermeneutics that sees meaning as something to be discovered. Clearly, despite the fact that Gadamer shifts the centering of meaning away from authorship—for Gadamer the normative notion of author's intention represents only an empty space, since what is fixed in writing always frees itself for a new relationship—and despite the fact that for Gadamer the question of meaning is about repetition without ultimate terminus within a historical horizon, Gadamer does insist on deciding the question of meaning. If one paints philosophical hermeneutics in broad strokes, one could even say that it is a hermeneutics that appears to be not just one example of a logocentric metaphysics but a very conservative Heideggerian logocentric metaphysics.[8] After all, it is a hermeneutics framed by a notion of tradition such that interpretation can be construed as that which does not break open possibilities of meaning but remains something that takes place within the envelopment of what is already handed down.

One cannot help seeing in this question something of a defense on Gadamer's part. But the defense should not be construed as being like the defense of the church against Galilean science, that is, as a holding fast to archaic views against a superior position. For if such were the case there would be no point to an exchange. There is something of a "defense" because Gadamer sees the concept of the text as that which "unites and perhaps divides" him from Derrida. His "defense" is one of setting the matter straight, of turning ultimately to the question of linguisticality and deciding if it is a "bridge or a barrier." Behind this, it could be said that Gadamer's defense is one of correcting misinterpretations of his position (and perhaps even of Heidegger's position with which Gadamer is aligned).[9] According to Gadamer, we are not faced simply with a choice between practicing an infinite deferral of the signified and a deep probing of a text that seeks *the* meaning of the text, a description of hermeneutics that is more apropos to nineteenth-century hermeneutics and certainly to Hirsch's hermeneutic theory. Gadamer has said on more than one occasion that Derrida's criticism of hermeneutics is a criticism of the hermeneutics of Paul Ricoeur. To take hermeneutics engaged in the reconstruction of meaning, which is one way of describing Ricoeur's methodological procedure of explanatory understanding, does not accurately describe the philosophical hermeneutics of Gadamer. The question of philosophical hermeneutics' metaphysics of presence, which is the question of the conjunction, will be discussed here within an analysis of the theme of text and interpretation.

§ 20. Text and Interpretation as Communicative Event

There is no question that Gadamer's philosophical hermeneutics sees interpretation as a search for meaning. But if we stop with this, Gadamer's position is not significantly different from other traditional theories of interpretation. What distinguishes Gadamer's account of interpretation is that the fixation of meaning is problematic. We have only to look at the dialectical character of Gadamer's philosophical hermeneutics to see the issue here.

In "Destruktion and Deconstruction," written subsequent to "Text und Interpretation," Gadamer links his work with Derrida's inasmuch as they share in common the continuation of Heidegger's effort at an overcoming—that is, a *Destruktion*—of the language of metaphysics. This *Destruktion* of the conceptuality of metaphysics, though, is broadly conceived by Gadamer so that in fact Heidegger was not the first to take up this task. In his own way Hegel, too, by means of the dialectical movement of thought, attempted to dissolve the Greek ontology of substance and its conceptuality (DD 108/GW2 366). The difference in this regard between Hegel and Heidegger lies in the fact that the dialectical character of thought only sharpens propositions to the point of opposition and does not force the meaning of words, as does Heidegger's more radical *Destruktion*, and ultimately fails to escape from the domination of its own thinking. Nevertheless, in this broadened account of *Destruktion* Gadamer sees himself as standing united with Derrida as having taken, beyond Heidegger's own efforts, one of two other paths toward overcoming "the ontological self-domestication belonging to dialectic and move into the open" (DD 109/GW2 367). His own step back from dialectic is a step back from dialectic to dialogue, to conversation.[10] It is a step back from thinking as the λόγος of the world situated in subjectivity—Hegel's λόγος—to the Platonic dialectic stripped of its metaphysical encasement, where the Socratic dialogue is the true carrying out of ἀνάμνησις: "What is accomplished in conversation is a summoning back in thought [*denkende Erinnerung*] that is possible only for the soul fallen into finitude of bodily existence" (DD 111/GW2 370).

This step back into conversation that marks Gadamer's own attempt at superseding any metaphysical realm of meaning governing words and their meaning entails the recognition that *Wesen* is not the property of presence in present objects, but, in its temporalizing sense, means *An-Wesen*, to come-to-presence, relative to a *Verwesen*, a decay. Accordingly, in his turn to conversation in which words are there only in the totality of our speaking and answering, Gadamer thinks he has found the "logic" that enables him to move "beyond linguistically fixed assertions, and so also beyond all encompassing synthesis, in the sense of the monological self-understanding of dialectic" (DD 111/GW2 370). In conversation the end keeps on delaying its arrival, for there is always a "potentiality for being other [*Andersseins*] that lies beyond every coming to agreement about what is common" (TI 26/GW2 336).

The fact that a potentiality for otherness remains suggests that for Gadamer the text remains plural and not for reasons of an ambiguity of its content. Rather, the text remains plural by virtue of the structure of inter-pretation itself. According to Gadamer, the history of the concept of text shows us that it does not occur outside the interpretive situation; it refers to "all that which resists integration in experience" (TI 31/GW2 340). Even the metaphorical "book" of nature is something that becomes readable by way of its interpretation. From the perspective of interpretation (in contrast to the perspective of grammar and linguistics), the text is the authentic given which is to be understood, and remains the firm point of relation over the possibilities of interpretation which are directed toward the text.

But it is not enough to say that the concept of text as a hermeneutical concept is that which is open to interpretation. This broad characterization of text is ultimately too inclusive. Gadamer wants to narrow the concept of text in order to bring the "eminent mode of textualizing [*Textierung*]" into view (TI 37/GW2 347). He does this by distinguishing three forms of opposition or resistance to textuality: antitexts, pseudotexts, and pretexts. Antitexts are texts that cannot stand on their own because they only make sense in the context of interactive speaking. Texts that are ironic are antitexts, for the use of irony presupposes prior common cultural understandings. To say the opposite of what one means and still be understood in writing depends on a communicative pre-understanding. Pseudo-texts are texts that do not intend to transmit meaning, but serve as rhetorical bridges over the flow of speaking. Gadamer insists that every translator has encountered such pseudotexts in the performance of translation; the translator will recognize what is filler material and deal with it in an appropriate way. Pretexts, by far the most significant oppositional form, are texts that do not mean what they say. The understanding that occurs with pretexts must always push through a wall of pretense precisely because what comes to expression is masked. Both dreams and ideological statements are examples of such texts. In both one finds a masking of interests that distort the interpretative communicative event while at the same time both presuppose the possibility of non-distortive understanding. Because Gadamer sees these not as texts (in the eminent sense) but only as pseudo-texts, he objects to treating forms of "distorted communication" as the normal case of language use, as Habermas does. A "hermeneutics of suspicion," as Ricoeur calls the hermeneutics of Marx, Nietzsche, and Freud, where hermeneutics is a decoding or deciphering, cannot be taken as the paradigmatic case for textual interpretation when text is text in an eminent sense.

What is other than decoding shows itself in the "eminent mode of textualizing," for which the literary work is the paradigmatic case. Such a text is not simply open to interpretation, but in *need* of interpretation in a special sense. The interpreter steps in when the text is not able to do what it is supposed to do, namely, to be heard and understood on its own. And when the communicative event takes place, the text does not disappear in our understanding of it, but continually stands before us speaking anew. Hermeneutics, in other words, gets caught up in the process of repetition, in the self-presenting of the word:

> A literary text is not just the rendering of spoken language into a fixed form. Indeed, a literary text does not refer back to an already spoken word at all. . . . [T]he literary text is text in the most special sense, text in the highest degree, precisely because it does not point back to an originary act of linguistic utterance but rather in its own right prescribes all repetitions and acts of speaking. No speaking can ever completely fulfill the prescription given in the poetic text. The poetic text exercises a normative function that does not refer back either to an original utterance nor to the intention of the speaker, but is something which seems to originate in itself, so that in the fortune and felicity of its success, a poem surprises and overwhelms even the poet. (TI 42/GW2 351–52)

Thus for Gadamer the eminent text is something in itself that can always say something more to the reader in its interpretation precisely because language itself comes to appearance in reading the text.[11]

Language, text, and reading, then, are intimately connected in Gadamer's understanding of text. And the particular dynamic of reading can best be described as a movement where text and interpretation coalesce into one movement of departure and return. This departure must be understood in the context of writing's ideality. In an obvious way a text attains an ideality in the way it stands apart from the necessary repetition, which links the past with the present, of oral tradition. Writing, unlike speech, is freed from the contingencies of origin. The issue here is not one of understanding writing on the basis of its supplement, for writing, despite the loss of oral immediacy in which intonation and accent lends itself more readily to human communication and understanding, has, in Gadamer's words, an "astonishing authenticity." Just as a literary text is not just the rendering of spoken language into a fixed form, writing is more than a mere fixation of what is said. Ideality, Gadamer asserts, addressing himself to Derrida, "befits not only the written structure but also original speaking and hearing insofar as their content can be separated from the concrete speech act and can be reproduced."[12] The written structure is essentially a separation from the original language-event. The written form means that a repetition (not reproduction) of the language-event of disclosure is available as a possibility. What is needed here, is to see that written texts present us with the real hermeneutic task of a transformation back into living language. "Even the pure signs of an inscription can be seen properly and articulated correctly only if the text can be transformed back into language" (TM 390–91/GW1 394). The ideality of writing, which enables it to be contemporaneous with every present, is an abstraction from the event (of language itself).

Interpretation, as that which brings written, fixed speaking into living speech, is, consequently, an event of overcoming the self-alienation, the departure, of writing. That event is a return to what is meant. But this return is not a reconstruction, for the thing meant exists nowhere else than in the appearing word. Speaking is, for Gadamer, dialogical, an endeavor that continually modifies itself, and as such it leaves behind the intended meaning of the speaker; consequently, the return is the hermeneutic event of speaking again in a new voice. Like other theorists of language, Gadamer too distinguishes between language (*langue*) and speech (*parole*), but for different reasons. For Gadamer it is important that the spoken word not be confused with the system of signs that constitute language. The spoken hermeneutical word is also not to be confused with the word as it is viewed in linguistics, that is, as a sign. And the text "is not to be viewed as an end product the production of which is the object of analysis whose intent is to explain the mechanism that allows language as such to function at all" (TI 31/GW2 341). The functioning of language, which is the concern of the linguist, is merely a precondition for comprehending what is said. The text must be readable. And then, from out of its readability, it is the subject matter of the text and not the text itself that is the point of concern. For Gadamer, writing needs to be transformed into speech, that is, the communicative event where language is not a system of signs but "real exchange and work." This means that "the text is a mere intermediate product [*Zwischenprodukt*], a phase in the communicative event [*Verständigungsgeschehen*]" (TI 31/GW2 341).

The communicative event would seem to be problematic for a theory of text interpretation like Gadamer's since the written text, by virtue of its ideality, is something cut off from the give and take of living conversation. What would a conversation with a text amount to? Above all, it would be a conversation that places a certain demand upon the reader as locus of the real exchange and work. For Gadamer, a performative dimension is at work in every interpretation.[13]

It is in the context of this performative dimension of textual interpretation that Gadamer emphasizes how both partners in a conversation must have a "good will" to try to understand one another. This phrase, not to be confused with the good will in Kant, captures the overall sense of the conditions for conversation. But in the exchange between the text and a nameless reader the "good will" would seem to be all the more problematical. Is it not simply a matter of recognizing that the writer of a text wants to impart meaning and thereby always writes *to* someone, who, at best, is someone with whom the writer shares presuppositions? Knowing full well that we cannot resurrect the author, the answer to this question would seem to be both a yes and a no. Yes, because what does our writing and speaking take place in if not a community of speakers and writers who wish to be understood. And although this implies that in an exchange we are able to bring about a real understanding—that rupture and breaking off can be brought to unity, that one can "say the same"—we have not made a naive return to a metaphysics of presence, for the event character of understanding means precisely that there is no mere repetition of the text nor a mere recreation of a text, but a new creation of understanding. The sense of the good will in Gadamer is Socratic: "one does not go about identifying the weakness of what another person says in order to prove that one is always right, but one seeks instead as far as possible to strengthen the other's viewpoint so that what the other person has to say becomes illuminating [*Einleuchtendes*]."[14] It is this good will that Gadamer considers essential for every true understanding.

But the moment we attempt to probe this dimension of a partner in conversation more deeply, the "no" to our question arises. The intention of a reader of a text is to grasp what is spoken of in the text. In Gadamer's hermeneutic theory this presents a special problem in as much as the reader is always guided in advance by anticipations of meaning. In this context, the good will is basically the projection of intelligibility of the text on the part of the reader that is necessary for the text to speak at all. We have already seen how this projection of intelligibility was characterized in *Truth and Method* as the "fore-conception of completeness" (*Vorgriff der Vollkommenheit*). In order to understand at all, a reader presupposes that the subject matter of a text has a perfected unity of meaning. The subject matter, in other words, is regarded initially as neither incoherent within itself ("immanent unity of meaning") nor inconsistent with what is true concerning the subject matter ("transcendent expectations of meaning which proceed from the relation to the truth of what is being said") (TM 294/GW1 299). Naturally a text could be otherwise. But without this initial projection, one enters a circle of having only the confirmation of one's anticipations, which is nothing less than a will to mastery. But Gadamer insists that as a will to mastery interpretation will always fail. For the perfected unity of meaning in the text itself enables the text to stand as self-presenting and authoritative whole. The lack of success in interpretation—those instances when the anticipations of meaning fail—is known to the reader when the text simply will not speak, that is, the reader finds the text "boring, empty or ridiculous, sentimental, imitative or simply not working."[15] That a text is boring or empty or whatever is, of course, determined not by a correspondence theory of meaning, but by the back and forth of dialogical exchange. Accordingly, the anticipation of completion must be regarded as regulative rather than constitutive of text and reading. One cannot dictate the meaning of a text; it must be followed according to its meaningful sense, which the communicative event attempts to actualize.

For Gadamer, then, in the coalescing of text and interpretation, the text is performed by the reader and through this it leaves a trail of effects (*Wirkungen*). The text is performed not as a play of signifiers, but in the interpretative free space of the text's meaningful sense.

§ 21. Two Faces of Socrates

In view of Gadamer's remarks on text and interpretation, there is no doubt that he sees the work of understanding texts as a working that establishes itself within a play of presence and absence. Hermeneutic understanding is the work of repetition, of a conversation in which there is no last word just as there is no first word. One has to wonder what is really so naive about Gadamer's position that would force one to disconfirm the conjunction "hermeneutics and deconstruction." The answer, of course, is that Gadamer does in fact decide for decidability (of meaning): communicative understanding is possible in the coming-to-appearance of meaning in language. Granted that Gadamer is not after meaning in itself, that hermeneutics is not a reconstruction, it can be described as "logocentric" insofar as Gadamer posits coherence, agreement. The productive act of hermeneutic understanding is directed toward hearing the λόγος in order to say the same (ὁμολόγειν).[16]

The issue then is the degree to which the conjunction still stands with respect to a common quest for liberation. As a way of maintaining the conjunction between hermeneutics and deconstruction, insofar as both are engaged in a common vigilant quest for liberation, while at the same time extending the analysis of the exchange into Gadamer and Derrida's actual responses to each other, I want to suggest that an appropriate expression of this common liberation is found in the image of Socrates. Socrates enters the community neither to teach, nor instruct, nor prescribe, but to undertake an inquiry that is prior to all positing of knowledge. This prior preparatory task is not skepticism but simply an attempt to shake discourse loose. The quest for liberation, consequently, takes the form of vigilance: the prior preparatory task is a vigilance against the pretension of knowing, against the sedimentation of knowing where it is no longer responsive to the question. Socrates appears on the scene not to answer but to question, to be vigilant against unquestioned authority that would confuse what appears to be with what really is. Recognizing the space that separates the human from the divine, Socrates takes up this questioning of others in the humility of his own ignorance. For Socrates to be consistent with his own practice, he can never escape the beginning to arrive at a philosophical doctrine; his task is always unfinished.

In contemporary garb, the Socratic figure is the antifoundationalist thinker. It is the one who does not search for origins as foundations that would have us decide once and for all, at least in principle, what constitutes meaning and truth. It is the one for whom there are no ultimate assurances and thus engages in a probing that always remains at risk. Derrida is one such Socratic figure. His deconstructive critique is a vigilance against the system of signs that leads to a pure presence, to a claim to a stabilized meaning. For Derrida there is no elixir for decidability, but only the sting of interruption. But equally so, the image of Socrates is attributable to Gadamer's hermeneut as well. This is perhaps more obvious in the case of Gadamer than with Derrida, for Gadamer explicitly ties his procedure to the Socratic dialogue whereby the logic of question and answer is made into a hermeneutic principle. Gadamer's hermeneut comes to the market-place armed with the vigilance of the question "knowing" that the proc-lamation of the correct interpretation rests on foundations that cannot be supported. Here too we find a vigilance.

There are, consequently, two faces to Socrates; the vigilance has a double sense. On the one hand, there is the vigilance of intervention, the radical probing that does not nor can not rest. This is Derrida's vigilance. He shows the face of Socrates that enters the community as gadfly, as an annoyance and a bother. He wants to disrupt and he is disruptive of the privileged λόγοι. We can see something of this vigilance of intervention in the questions that Derrida poses to Gadamer's paper. The questions center on Gadamer's claim that genuine conversation requires a good will to try to understand one another. Derrida asks whether the very positing of good will commits Gadamer to a metaphysics of the will as this is understood in the history of metaphysics; that is to say, that Gadamer overlooks the domination that such a notion brings to the text.[17] He also asks about the extent to which a psychoanalytic hermeneutics in which there is an inter-ruption of rapport must enter these considerations of understanding the other. What is behind these questions is for Derrida the necessity of the rupture, the break that constantly wedges itself between the said. In the end, Derrida confesses his uncertainty about dialogue ever being able to "say the same."

Consequently, by focusing on the good will, Derrida thinks he has focused on the structure that governs the totality of the phenomenon of understanding. The vigilance of intervention wants to shake free the totality by pointing to what the totality excludes. In this case what is excluded would seem to pertain to the hidden intentions that would conflict with the supposed transparency of the good will. But this does not mean for Derrida that we must replace one kind of hermeneutics for an archeology of the subject. The vigilance as vigilance is only to practice the shaking against the closure of sedimented truth. In his own contribution to the exchange—*Guter Wille zur Macht (II): Die Unterschriften interpretieren (Nietzsche/Heidegger)*—Derrida does not present an alternative theory of text but continues to probe the issue of domination in hermeneutics. Derrida sees in Heidegger's reading of Nietzsche that the figure of Nietzsche has been made to stand still, like the statues of Daedalus. In understanding Nietzsche as the last metaphysician, Heidegger has turned Nietzsche into his partner, who now shares with him the same question about being.

But the vigilance of intervention is a serious business. The kind of negative conclusion that Derrida would constantly enact is not done for the sake of anarchy. We should bear in mind that for Socrates, the disruptive play is mindful of the human community to such an extent that it could be said that his intervention is in service to the community. Can we not say that the Derridian disruptive play is likewise mindful of the human community? That the play of intervention in effect prepares the way for a new form of community? Such a community would have to be thought in terms of what the disruptive play makes possible, namely, non-exclusion. Only this form of community we would say is truly liberated. Repression enters the system in the form of exclusion, and exclusion is precisely what occurs when one seeks unity rather than difference. For Derrida, the community sought must be a community of difference.

At this point however we must broach the other sense of vigilance; we must broach the vigilance in the conversation that we are, for any reference to community is a reference to unity. Perhaps that is the very question: Can intervention remain outside the community? Is this not precisely what Gadamer asks and is expressed by the vigilance in the conversation that we are? Here is the face of Socrates, not of the gadfly, but of the midwife who seeks to bring wisdom to birth. It is the face of Socrates that wants to distinguish sophistry from dialectic in the piety of questioning. Certainly, in light of what we have seen, such vigilance does not fall into the trap of closure and foundation. In fact, one has to see that Gadamer is not Heidegger here. Gadamer as reader does not center the text by the question of the meaning of Being.[18] And yet, Heidegger himself was certainly aware that "every word is itself always an answer and gives rise always to putting a new question."

Undoubtedly Gadamer shows a face of Socrates. Understanding is always a form of dialogue, a coming to agreement within a structure of openness. And again, conversation is not a talking about something that is already there, but has the structure of an event, a present enactment, which remains unfinished. Any text is a structure that can be taken as a new event; written things must begin to speak again. Every reading that attempts to understand is only a first step and never comes to an end; we need the continuing effort to find the common ground. This is what the vigilance of the conversation that we are enacts. Gadamer does install λόγος, but not a centered one. Gadamer's λόγος is rootless, not tied to a transcendental subject or a methodological procedure. It is a λόγος that is in principle always unfinished. Accordingly, against the naiveté of a reading that says it is simply written there, against the reading of the text that constrains its truth to the mastery of the reader, the hermeneut remains vigilant within the communicative event. In his response to Derrida's criticism, Gadamer insists that even Derrida wishes to be understood, otherwise he would neither speak nor write. The moment of coherence in the conversation that we are, then, is not the moment at which the statue of Daedalus has been secured, but the fulfillment of genuine dialogue as being written in the soul of the one who hears.[19] The coherence is not a sedimentation of meaning but the disappearance of interpretation.

Finally, we need to see that here too there is a preparation for a form of community. In the conversation that we are, the posited community is in question, not with respect to its borders, but more so with respect to its ends. For Gadamer the ideal of democracy is that there are common opinions, that the other is right. Thus, within the experience of limitation in which full presence constantly eludes the one who wants to understand, there is included all those things that bind us together. In his reply to Derrida's remarks, Gadamer speaks elliptically of the ability to sustain social life through the element of dialogue and how this directs us to human solidarity. Elsewhere, Gadamer has characterized this as participation that posits the goal of human solidarity.

B. HERMENEUTICS AND DECONSTRUCTION—SECOND APPROACH

§ 22. *Hermeneutics at the Edge of the Breath*

The distinguishing feature of Gadamer's hermeneutics in contrast to, let us say, the hermeneutics of Paul Ricoeur, is that it is a hermeneutics of the voice.[20] In the attempt to underscore this feature of Gadamer's hermeneutics we have quoted on more than one occasion his definition of hermeneutics that reflects this feature: hermeneutics is precisely letting that which is far and alienated speak again "not only in a new voice but in a clearer voice."[21] Accordingly, it is not enough to say that for philosophical hermeneutics the experience of meaning is linguistic; one must immediately add to this the more specific claim that this experience of meaning takes shape in the language of *speech*, in living language, and as such hermeneutics is of the voice. In setting philosophical hermeneutics off in this way we can see, at the same time, how Gadamer separates himself from those thinkers closest to him who come to bear on the project of philosophical hermeneutics. Gadamer reorients Hegel's dialectic toward the art of living dialogue and Heidegger's project of overcoming metaphysics is continued in the dynamics of a language, not of metaphysics, but "which we speak with others and to others."[22]

If one were to ask for a justification for locating the experience of meaning in the voice one could only assume that it follows from the context of that Socratic-Platonic mode of thinking that comes to bear on the project of philosophical hermeneutics precisely as that corrective to the formalism of Hegelian dialectic and to the Heideggerian preoccupation with the overcoming of metaphysics.[23] This context, which takes human finitude so seriously, insists that one proceeds toward understanding only through dialogical inquiry where one encounters the living word that is of memory (Μνημοσύνη).[24] Here in this space, not just of the voice, but of the voice of an other, logical demonstration yields to the power of communication in language where one must find the right words to convince the other. Here in this space of the voice understanding occurs as a communicative event (*Verständigungsgeschehen*), an event of agreement in understanding.

In this second approach to placing hermeneutics in relation to deconstruction I want to consider what is "of the voice," and, what is more problematical, what is at stake in deferring to the voice. Under this latter consideration the question that arises, already in the Socratic gesture of the turn to the living word, is one of the status of writing. For Gadamer, writing (*Schriftlichkeit*) changes nothing; the text too stands under the voice. The question about the voice thus cannot avoid the question of privileging and of opposition, of the relation between speaking and writing.[25] It would appear, though, that in deferring to the voice the question of the relation between speaking and writing has already been decided in that hermeneutics is committed to a phonocentrism as the condition for the possibility of commensurate understanding. This immediate response to the question is, of course, framed by the project of deconstruction, and to some extent the question has been taken up by Gadamer in his essays found in *Dialogue and Deconstruction*. Here I do not wish to repeat what has already been said there, but rather to take up the question of speaking and writing as it pertains thematically to what is "of the voice." In this regard, I want to explore the question of the voice not just in terms of the Derridian critique of phonocentrism, but also within the project of philosophical hermeneutics itself where we are to find the measure for the voice.

Most provisionally, we find both dimensions of the question of the voice taken up by Plato in the *Phaedrus* where he marks out the difference between writing and speaking in a discussion about the nature of a good (καλόν) speech—a speech that would not only be in accord with things spoken of, but also written in the soul of the one who hears:

> Soc.: It is the same thing with written words; they seem to talk to you as though they were intelligent, but if you ask them anything about what they say, from a desire [βουλόμμενοs] to be instructed, they go on telling you just the same thing forever. And once a thing is put in writing, the composition, whatever it may be, drifts [κυλινδεῖται] all over the place, getting into the hands not only of those who understand it, but equally of those who have no business with it. . . . But now tell me, is there another sort of discourse that is the brother to written speech, but of unquestioned legitimacy? Can we see how it originates, and how much better and more effective it is than the other?
> Phaed.: What sort of discourse have you in mind, and what is its origin?
> Soc.: The sort that goes together with knowledge, and is written in the soul of the learner, that can defend itself, and knows to whom it should speak and to whom it should say nothing.
> Phaed.: You mean no dead discourse, but the living and breathing word [λόγον ζῶντα καὶ ἔμψυχον], the original of which the written discourse may fairly be called a kind of image [εἴδωλον].[26]

Let us consider for a moment what is most decisive in this *locus classicus* for the distinction between speaking and writing. Plato tells us, first of all, that one asks of words what they say from a wish or desire (βουλόμενοs) to be instructed. Secondly, he tells us that when these words are written they tend to drift (κυλινδεῖται) all over the place. And, thirdly, he tells us that the discourse that is the "brother" of written discourse, which appears to be the more proper, is of the living and breathing word (τὸν λόγον ζῶντα καὶ ἔμψυχον). Highlighting the text in this way is no guarantee that we have read it properly, for we know that this text has already been subject to radically opposing interpretations. On the one hand, it has been read to say that, despite the seemingly clear indication that spoken discourse has an unquestioned legitimacy, Plato ultimately wants to champion ἐπιστήμη over δόξα, which can only come about by the emerging literate revolution.[27] On the other hand, there is a more trenchant reading of it by Derrida who sees Plato promoting the supremacy of spoken discourse over all written discourse insofar as he make claims for the first order of spoken discourse. Without attending to any one interpretation at the moment, let me reassemble the three highlighted features of the passage into three theses, in no corresponding order, that allows us to attend to this question of the voice in philosophical hermeneutics: (1) speaking, which is of the voice, is of the breath; (2) the voice, being of the breath, is situated in the space of desire; (3) communication, occurring through the voice, drifts in the voice.

§ 23. The Voice in the Breath

Let us consider, first, the thesis that speaking is of the breath. The living word, according to Plato, is ἐμψθχον, literally "en-souled," or "of spirit." Ψυχή, following its use in Homer where the word is not yet directly related to the more exclusive "mind" or "intelligence," means primarily the principle that makes one to be alive. But what is of life is of the breath: Ψυχή is related to ψύχειν, to breathe, and accordingly could be translated as "breath-soul." According to Snell, Homer does not tell us what he considers to be the function of the ψυχή during life. In dying, though, it is clear that the ψυχή, as the breath of life, is breathed forth, leaving through the mouth or even through a wound.[28] And, what is of breath is capable of flight: in every attempt of Odysseus to grasp the ψυχή of his mother in Hades, the ψυχή flew out of his hands "like a dream." With death, she tells her son, the mighty energy of burning fire overcomes the flesh and bones "and the ψυχή like a dream flies away and flutters."[29]

This etymological determination of ψυχή as breath-soul enables us to grasp the character of the living word as it occurs in the Greek oral tradition. According to Onians, "it was natural to say that the speeches of a man who πέπνυται [has breath] are themselves πεπνυμένα. They come forth with the breath that is intelligence in them."[30] The living word is of spirit, and spirit is in flight. A spoken word, is said by Homer to be "winged," and an unspoken word "without wings."[31] To speak the word is to breathe it, sending it forth to be heard when the one with ears breathes in.[32] But the word is itself breath, that is to say, being of life, it is of spirit, mind, intelligence.

What then does it mean to say that the voice is of the breath? And how are we to situate philosophical hermeneutics, in particular, in this context? First of all, the voice of which we speak is not identical with φωνή, mere sound, for it is possible, following the language of Augustine, for the sound of a word to be an empty voice (*inanem vocem*). The voice that is mere sound must be withdrawn before the voice in which something is given to be understood. A poem is not heard when the mere sound of the words are received by the ear, just as a text is not read when our eyes read the letters that make up the words. What is at stake in the voice, in other words, is the taking place of language as such. The *flatus vocis*, literally, the breathing voice, occurs in the eleventh century as a term for the voice as an intention to signify and as a pure indication that language is taking place.[33] And in language is the most universal field of meaning, namely being. In this context one could say that the meaning of being is to be found in the experience of the voice.

What is of the voice, then, to use Gadamer's own language, is the inner word (*verbum interius*). In its classical formulation in Aquinas, the inner word is distinguished from the outer word, which are sounds produced by the respiratory tract that have meaning. That the spoken word has meaning allows the word to be distinguished from other sounds produced by the respiratory tract, like coughing. Only the inner word, which is related to the outer word as its efficient cause, is related to understanding; until the inner word emerges we do not understand. What appeals to Gadamer in this notion of the inner word is that this word, which is not expressing the mind but the thing intended, "still has the character of an event," and "remains related to its possible utterance [*Äußerung*]" (TM 422/GW1 426). This is the word that says something beyond its grammatical parts. This is the word *of spirit* that occurs in writing when the word is read. This is the word of breath that is heard by the inner ear.[34]

Now, what appears to be peculiar to the voice of the inner word in dialogical inquiry is that it is always between sound and meaning: in responding to Derrida's charge of logocentrism, Gadamer writes that "conversation defines itself precisely by the fact that the essence of understanding and agreement are not found in the 'vouloir-dire' or intended meaning, through which the word supposedly finds its being, but rather in what aims at being said beyond all words sought after or found."[35] What is of the voice then for Gadamer pertains to the word finding its place. In the rhetorical tradition the distinction is made between *ratio iudicandi* and *ratio inveniendi*, between the art of assuring the truth of a proposition and the more originary art of setting off the very advent of discourse in order for language to reach its place. The place for language was in fact the argument as the illuminating event of language. In the face of such a difficult task though, the ancient topics declined into a technique of "memory places," in which language was conceived as something that has already taken place and the *ratio iudicandi* was now conceived as making available this already given.[36] But what happens if the word is not already given, as is the case for philosophical hermeneutics, where the word is enacted in dialogical inquiry? It would appear that in dialogical inquiry, in the "handing over of one's own thinking to another," the voice displaces itself in the intention to signify. This negative dimension of the voice, which is not to be confused with dialectical negation, means precisely that there is no self-identity in the voice, as if the meanings of words possessed a "firmness that could be grasped." But if there is no self-identity in the breath of the voice there is still being, still the meaning of being.

Secondly, that the voice is of breath means precisely that the element of continuity is inescapable in all our speaking. The word that lives and breathes requires a space of continuity. In the oral tradition, this space is the ἀγορά, the place of assembly for debates and business, but also the place of the gift of speaking. In this space of intimacy and familiarity speaking is granted. And in the granting, by virtue of the continuity, a word has no edge, that is, a border or dividing line where a word can separate itself from other words. For Homer, word (ἔπος) means not just a word, that which could possibly have an edge, but includes the meanings "speech," "tale," "song," or "epic poetry as a whole."[37] This means, of course, that in the voice one never finds simply one word. In the ἀγορά the edge of a word fades into its renewal in another word. When Gadamer says that the word "always already refers to a greater and more multiple unity," a notion one finds in the concept of *verbum interius*, one can readily relate this to the Greek ἔπος.[38] For philosophical hermeneutics, there is, by virtue of the voice, never one word. A breathless written word, on the other hand, is encountered as ruptured discourse and accordingly exists in a space of separation. The written word not only separates words from one another, but separates words from reader. Without the reader words do indeed have edges.

But the issue here, especially as it is understood by Gadamer, is not that of a simple opposition between oral and written discourse. Gadamer insists that the same fundamental conditions that hold for oral exchange holds for written conversation. In both writing and speaking we are faced with the same problem of understanding what is said. What is at issue in both the printed text and in the repetition of what is expressed in conversation is the return to what was originally announced (*Urkunde*). For written texts this presents the real hermeneutic task, for the original announcement stands under the ideality of the word. The hermeneutic task is accordingly transforming the ideality of the word back into language as speaking—that is, into the communicative event that is not the repetition of something past, but the sharing of a present meaning. For writing, the communicative event is accomplished by the reader in reaching beyond the literal inscription of the word in the continuity of words arising in dialogue. This assumes, of course, that reading is in fact analogous to dialogue, that the text stands as an address to an other who fills out and concretizes what is said.

Within the dialogical inquiry, then, the problem is not how to understand writing on the basis of speaking, but, beyond the ideality of the word, of attending to the seduction in the voice that persists in both writing and speaking. In *Truth and Method* Gadamer reminds us that: "Just as in speech there is an art of appearances and a corresponding art of true thought— sophistic and dialectic—so in writing there are two arts, one serving sophistic, the other dialectic" (TM 393/GW1 396–97). The voice is continually threatened by what adheres to the voice, namely, a corruption by which it falls away from what is spoken about in the voice. The "binding element" in conversation is, by its very nature, surrounded by idle talk (*Gerede*), and thus by the mere appearance of speaking. In the art of writing, in particular, then, the writer has an obligation of establishing, in the sense of mooring in the drift, the original announcement such that its sense is understandable.

But to say that the printed text is to be read in terms of what was originally announced implies that the text already stands under the voice. If for Gadamer there is not a simple opposition between writing and speaking, is it because Gadamer wants to understand writing on the basis of speech, because he has privileged the voice? In this context, let us look once more at the relation between writing and speaking. In *On Interpretation*, Aristotle explains the process of signification whereby "that which is in the voice [$\phi\omega\nu\dot{\eta}$] contains the symbols of mental experience, and written words [$\gamma\rho\dot{\alpha}\mu\mu\alpha\tau\alpha$] are the symbols of that which is in the voice."[39] According to the ancient commentators, the position of the $\gamma\rho\dot{\alpha}\mu\mu\alpha\tau\alpha$ in the passage between these terms was to secure the interpretation of the voice; in a sense it became the ground that sustains the entire circle of signification. As ground, though, the $\gamma\rho\dot{\alpha}\mu\mu\alpha$ has the peculiar status of being not simply a sign but that which is in the voice. As a sign the γράμμα presupposes both the voice and its removal.[40] In this context one can legitimately speak of a voice of a text because there is always already the voice in writing. When Gadamer claims that it is "necessary to separate the concept of the word from its grammatical sense,"[41] he is objecting to the removal of the voice from writing. For Gadamer the communicative situation demands that grammatology not exclude the voice.

Thirdly, and finally, in the claim that the voice is of the breath, there is entailed a further claim—and here we return to the issue of the corruption of the voice—that at the edge of breath is memory. We should not forget that in the *Phaedrus* the issue in terms of which the distinction between speaking and writing is raised is the issue of memory. In the myth told by Socrates, Thamus holds against the invention of writing, against the substitution of the breathless sign for the living voice, because it cannot answer for itself. Consequently, writing, as a recipe for reminding (ὑπομνήσεως) rather than memory (μνήμης), will implant forgetfulness in the souls who have learned it. According to Derrida, this myth is meant to instruct us in the danger that Socrates sees in inverting the priority of speaking over writing. In inverting the priority one will have turned from the origin for truth and knowledge, and thus the danger is the threat to truth (and morality) that arises in memory as the field of presence.[42] Gadamer, on the other hand, reads the text in a more felicitous manner, which is to say that it is *not* a question for Plato of deciding for speaking over writing, where writing is understood as the fixation of speech. Rather, it is a question of an appeal to a correct use of writing relative to how the soul is to learn.[43] In the writing that would serve dialectics there is an art of writing that comes to the aid of thought, and it is to this that the art of understanding is allied (TM 393/GW1 397).

There is a particular problem, then, endemic to the voice. What occurs in the breath—that is, in the writing that is to be read and in words that are there only in spoken discourse—is a seduction to the *emptying* of the word. The problem here is more than the possibility of conversation falling away from itself in the manner of *Gerede*. It is also, by virtue of the element of power intrinsic to discourse, the possibility of truth turning into the lie, of the reading of history turning into propaganda, of the revealed word turning into the secret. To say that at the edge of breath is memory, means, accordingly, that in the breath one faces the constant demand of continual renewal, the gathering-together-anew, of that which is said. Hermeneutic recollection is precisely this rediscovery of the abundance and the attentiveness to what is in the voice. The question before us, then, pertains to what shatters the seduction.[44] For this we must turn to a consideration of the second thesis.

In the breathless sign there is no desire. There is, of course, in the chain of signifiers, an interruption, a spacing, but this want and lack, this breech of continuity, is not desire, for desire belongs, if not exclusively to life, then certainly to being.[45] But what is in the voice is altogether different than what is in the sign.

Let us recall the distinction in the rhetorical tradition between *ratio iudicandi* and *ratio inveniendi* that was made earlier. The *ratio inveniendi* assumed that the event of language was already completed, and accordingly, the *inventio* of the arguments was related to memory as a reminding. But when we engage in the experience of language precisely as an event, we notice that the notion of memory is otherwise than being reminded. This change in the notion of *inventio* is already present in Augustine. In *The Trinity* Augustine tells us that the etymological origin of *inventio* was *venere in*; it means to come into that which is sought. But this movement is a function of desire (*amore*), where the word is born if it is united with knowledge.[46] This amorous desire, in which the word arises, is more originary than *inventio* as reminding. Here, then, the event of language pertains to memory rather than reminding; and, most significantly, what is of memory is of desire. At the edge of the breath, then, is not just memory; there is also desire.

But what exactly does this connection between desire and the event of language mean for philosophical hermeneutics and what are the implications for our problematic concerning hermeneutics and deconstruction? Let us first see more precisely what is contained in the notion of desire. In the well-known section from the *Phenomenology of Spirit*,[47] Hegel describes self-consciousness as being in the first place desire, and the end of desire is for self-consciousness to rediscover itself in the heart of life. In this context, desire is both intentional as a desire for the other, and reflexive as a modality in which the subject is discovered. Considered in itself, of course, desire, has no real end, for desire generates desire. One could say of desire that it is essentially ontological rupture, the breaking and holding open of being before itself. And yet, desire, as the power of the negative, seeks to transfer this difference into identity. If desire is the pursuit of identity, desire is also what poses for us the question of identity. In effect, desire is an interrogative mode of being.

Wherein might we find the element of desire in philosophical hermeneutics? If dialogue is the condition for communicative understanding, one would have to say that desire is the condition for dialogue. Where does a dialogue begin if not in the space of desire, in the space of the interrogative that allows one to cross over into the word of the other. In *Truth and Method* Gadamer tells us that the first condition of dialogue is "ensuring that the other person is with us" (TM 367/GW1 373), which requires that one is willing to be addressed by the other. This condition is most evident in therapy that proceeds on the basis of a genuine dialogue model;[48] the exchange cannot move to the question and the modality of discovery without the desire for the question. The interrogative itself appears in the spacing of interrogation that is desire. When Gadamer says in "Text and Interpretation" that in dialogical inquiry "both partners must have the good will to understand one another" (TI 33/GW2 343), this is saying the same thing, namely, the effort of dialogue is nothing that dialogue itself can accomplish, but is dependent upon being able to turn toward the other and to be open in order to be addressed by the other. If words are winged, so too is desire.

But one would also have to say that desire is in the voice in a more direct way not only in that there is the desire *for* the word, in which all speaking is a reaching into language for what it is about to say. In this sense, the relation between desire and language testifies to the space of separation that exists in the voice. What is in the voice is never simply present to the voice. There are no edges in the breath, but there is separation.

Desire is also in the voice in the sense that every speaking is a speaking to the other as a desire for the other. There is always in the communicative situation the voice of the other as the desired voice. In this context it is difficult to understand how the event of understanding can be construed as appropriation, as making something one's own, turning the event of understanding into a unity of understanding. In Gadamer's eyes, Derrida, who sees hermeneutics as appropriation, never seemed to grasp the element of otherness that is in play in philosophical hermeneutics. If understanding would be appropriation, which involves the covering up of otherness, then one surely has entered the sphere of logocentrism. But, for Gadamer, it is precisely the voice of the other that breaks open what is one's own, and remains there—a desired voice that cannot be suspended—as the partner in every conversation. The element of sameness in understanding is not an "abiding one," but simply what takes place in conversation as it goes along. Here the intertwining of desire and breath is most evident: in the language of Merleau-Ponty, the other in the address "draws from me thoughts which I had no idea I possessed."[49] The voice of the other, as desired, draws one beyond oneself, to think with the other, "and to come back to oneself as if to an other" (DD 110/GW2 369). And insofar as the voice is of the text as well, one would want to say that in written discourse, the words—if you will forgive the metaphorical hyperbole—must make love to the reader.

Finally, in this regard, in the claim that all speaking is a speaking to the other, we are able to derive an essential insight concerning the realm of the breath. The ἀγορά, which is supported by desire,[50] is, first of all, a community of trust rather than suspicion. The fragility of the voice in terms of which propaganda, lies and secrets are possible, are possibilities because there is trust. If speech is destroyed before it is spoken, there is no speech. What turns the voice out of its element (a seduction that is itself of desire) is, paradoxically, turned back into itself through desire—a desire for the voice of the other that tenuously holds all speaking before its possible truth. Desire is what keeps the space of intimacy intact and yet, the voice is always spaced by the element of desire.

§ 24. The Drift in the Voice

As a way of approaching the third thesis, let us return to the passage from the *Phaedrus* that has served to guide our analysis. In the desire of the soul to learn, the soul finds written words to be a dead discourse, infinitely repeating the same thing. In their written form, words are caught up in mere repetition, and drift about. What counters the written word is the spoken word, as it is more effective in defending itself, and thus provides itself with the anchor that can bring a halt to the drift.

In his deconstructive reading of the Phaedrus, Derrida insists that this metaphysical opposition between speaking and writing in which writing is viewed as a deficiency of speaking, actually breaks open in the text of Plato. If writing is a danger (φάρμακον) to good speech, it is also the case that Plato writes about good speaking. The reason the opposition breaks is because writing changes *everything*. The writing Derrida has in mind, though, is not the writing in the soul, where the voice is still present as a kind of psychic γραφή, where writing is "only a writing of transmission, of education, of demonstration."[51] It is rather a writing where what is signified in the writing is displaced. Derrida demonstrates this in the text of Plato by showing how the word φάρμακον is itself caught up in the chain of signifiers. Writing changes everything once it is apparent that there is a movement of *différance* in language that institutes the system of language itself. For Derrida, then, a certain kind of writing, which is not opposed to speaking, precedes the voice and disseminates it.[52] This Socratic gesture of holding the determination of meaning open before the reader through a strategy that seeks to disseminate the economy of the text is what ultimately separates Derrida from Gadamer. In Derrida's eyes, there is for Gadamer's hermeneutics no literal writing, that is, no writing that is "external to the spirit, to breath, to speech, and to the λόγος,"[53] which would disrupt the λόγος, halt the breath. Gadamer wants to maintain the difference, in other words, between the letter and the spirit of the text, where the concern is always for what is of spirit.

Without attempting to decide the "quarrel" between hermeneutics and deconstruction—for what, in the end, would it mean to decide the matter—let us consider more precisely, by way of conclusion, what it means to say, then, as Gadamer insists that writing changes *nothing*. We have already indicated in a general way that for philosophical hermeneutics both writing and speaking are considered as text that stand under the ideality of the word. Certainly, the ideality of the word is not to be confused with the ideality or absolute identity of meaning—a transcendental signified—that constitutes the logocentrism of western metaphysics.[54] The ideality of the word is simply the word not spoken; accordingly, for philosophical hermeneutics there is no quest for objectivity as absolute ideality, but only the effort to bring the word to reverberate in the voice so that it can be heard. The question that remains for hermeneutics, then, concerns the actual proximity of the signified, whether in writing or speaking, in the voice.[55]

That there is a *question* of proximity for hermeneutics is a result, not of the dissemination, but of the drift, in the voice. It was said in the *Phaedrus*, that words, once written, drift (κυλινδειται) all over the place. As it occurs in the Greek, κυλινδειται is often spoken of in relation to speaking; it conveys the sense of being tossed about from mouth to mouth, as a ship is tossed about at sea. The word is also used in the context of rolling around or wallowing as one might wallow in the mud.[56] For hermeneutics, the drift in the voice cannot be avoided because writing changes nothing. Communication, which is accomplished in the sharing of present meaning, will always drift in the voice because the voice is no longer under the control of a controller of words. In this sense, it would seem foolish to want to control the drift, for, if it is the case that our words say more than they say at any one time—that speaking is excessive—it would be fruitful to follow the drift. And yet the drift in the voice is not entirely aimless precisely because the voice is living. What reverberates in the living voice, in other words, is no mere echo.

A speech that merely repeats what someone else had said is a mere echo. It is a voice for which there is no other—a "voice cast out across a space, only to be returned, almost as if from others."[57] In classical myth, Echo fell in love with Narcissus, who did not return her love. As a result, Echo pined away in grief and in the end what remained of her was only her voice. According to the myth, one could still hear her, for her voice was living. But this voice is actually a voice that is the death of the living voice, for it speaks bygone words in an approximation of a repetition of the same.

But not every echo is a mere echo, for, in fact, an echo can pluralize speech and decenter the source of speaking.[58] Such an echo, no longer tied to the classical image-original distinction, does not claim to be a semblance of an original sound.[59] This is what one finds in the living voice, that is, a plurality of the voice that is granted by the voice of the other. And it is from this voice that the drift of meaning becomes an advent of meaning, an advent of meaning that arises at the edge of breath. To be at the edge of breath, this means either to be at the boundary, the borderline, where one encounters what is on the other side of breath, namely silence. But breath is everywhere. Alternately, then, at the edge of breath means to be at the brink, on the verge, at the interval space at which a different state of affairs arises. The proximity in the voice resides here at the edge of breath where speaking turns into a new speaking—hermeneutics at the edge of the breath.

CHAPTER SEVEN

The Voice of the Poet

Poetry is perhaps this: a turning of breath
—Celan, *Meridian*

§ 25. *The Question of Poetic Discourse*

It is evident to even the most casual reader of *Truth and Method* that the topic of art is central to the project of philosophical hermeneutics. *Truth and Method* begins with an analysis of art in which an experience of truth is defended in it, an experience of truth that corresponds to the whole of hermeneutic experience. This experience of truth is what Gadamer returns to at the end of *Truth and Method* as a way of bringing the entire analysis to a close. The ontological background of the hermeneutic experience of the world is rooted in the metaphysics of the beautiful, in the radiance of the beautiful.

Just how central this topic is is underscored by Gadamer in a recent essay, "Word and Picture,"[1] where he tells us that his interest in the *Geisteswissenschaften* in *Truth and Method* was an interest motivated not simply by the fact that the scientific character of hermeneutics is problematic in them, but by the fact that they deal with art in all its dimensions (GW8 373). The arts, Gadamer claims, "co-govern the metaphysical heritage of our Western tradition" (GW8 373). As Gadamer reads philosophy in relation to its own history, a history in which Plato is decisive, the questions of philosophy never stray far from the topic of art.[2] But in making the topic of art central to the project of philosophical hermeneutics Gadamer presents us with something more than a philosophy *of* art, that is, an aesthetics to go along with a "theory" of understanding and a "theory" of language.

185

The centrality of art is not to be understood as simply a dominant theme within a philosophical project. Rather, the centrality has to do with the way in which philosophy and art conflate, or perhaps it would be better to say "cross," inasmuch as the experience of art is so fundamentally like that of the experience of philosophy. Both experiences are hermeneutical, both engage in the experience of understanding, both are caught up in interpretation in which the world becomes larger not smaller. The game of art is like the game of language.[3]

Within the scope of hermeneutics generally, this crossing of philosophy and art has also been given considerable attention by Heidegger particularly in his later writings. For the most part, this crossing pertains to the relation between philosophy and poetry: both the thinker and the poet (who for Heidegger is equated principally with Hölderlin, because of his greatness)[4] bring Being into words.[5] Of course, this crossing has nothing to do with relating to art in terms of an aesthetic attitude; rather, it is a direct result of the transformed task of philosophy and to a conception of language commensurate with this task. This task has already been identified in chapter 1. To briefly recall what was said there: at the outset of his career Heidegger defined philosophy in opposition to Neo-Kantianism and the abstracting theoretical orientation towards philosophy's general object of concern, namely, factical life. Philosophy does not start from consciousness that thinks life, but starts within life itself as a hermeneutics of facticity. By the end of the 1920s Heidegger developed this thematic into the question of the Being of factical life (life = Dasein). In this development and in the further expansion of this questioning through the so-called turn in the 1930s, the task of philosophy remained constant: the articulation of the Being of life which requires a radical destructuring (*Destruktion*) of the conceptual framework in which philosophy operates. In its more familiar post-1920s expression, the task of philosophy calls for an overcoming of metaphysics with its culmination of the total forgetfulness of Being. But insofar as Being and language are fundamentally related, the overcoming of metaphysics is inseparable from the overcoming of the language of metaphysics. Heidegger sought a language commensurate with the matter to be thought, and the language of technical thinking, of propositional calculation, was nothing more than one more instantiation of the language of metaphysics. He found the language he was seeking in the language that stands nearest to the language of "thinking," that is to say, the language of the poet.

When Gadamer claims in response to the criticism of Derrida that the intention of his own work was to follow Heidegger in the overcoming of metaphysics and that the trajectories in thought opened by the later Heidegger confirmed his own path of thought,[6] we should expect the character of the crossing of philosophy and art in philosophical hermeneutics to be similar to Heidegger's. Most certainly, Gadamer too turns to the poetic word as a special case of the event of language, as "language in a preeminent sense" (RB 106/GW8 71). But for Gadamer, in contrast to Heidegger, the turn to poetic discourse is not done for the sake of a new language of philosophy, for the destruction of the language of metaphysics. There is in Gadamer's eyes no language of metaphysics. In his essay "The Language of Metaphysics," Gadamer asks: "But can a language . . . ever properly be called the language of metaphysical thinking, just because metaphysics was thought, or what would be more, anticipated in it? Is not language always language of the homeland [*Heimat*] and the process [*Vollzug*] of becoming-at-home in the world? And does this fact not mean that language knows no restrictions and never breaks down, because it holds infinite possibilities of utterance in readiness?" (HW 78/GW3 236). If there is no language of metaphysics for Gadamer, there is nonetheless a language of homeland, or better, a language that is the performance of being-at-home in the world, that marks the point of crossing between philosophy and poetry. But Gadamer's language of homeland does not have the particular sense that Heidegger gives to this same notion from his reading of Hölderlin, namely, that the language of homeland is the language of the political soil, of that from which the question of the historical destiny of a people is to be interpreted. For Gadamer, undoubtedly the poet is to speak to our times, and to this extent such speaking is decisive for our existence. But such speaking is understood more modestly; the language of homeland, is simply what we speak to one another in becoming who we are. In this more modest but broader sense of the language of homeland Gadamer retains the general character of what Heidegger calls poetic dwelling: a building as a creative event (*Vollzug*) in which mortals draw near the advent of their being. Poetic dwelling names the point of crossing between philosophy and poetry for both Heidegger and Gadamer. What remains to be seen is how for Gadamer in particular poetic dwelling captures the experience of philosophy and in its own way constitutes the task of philosophy as initially conceived by a hermeneutics of facticity—that of awakening existence to itself.

But again, for Gadamer poetic discourse is only a special case of the event of language. Before proceeding to an account of poetic dwelling, we need to establish that point of crossing, that is, to give an account of the character of poetic discourse such that it stands in close relation to philosophical discourse as the discourse of a philosophical hermeneutics.

§ 26. *The Gift of the Word*

This question of the crossing, of the identity and difference of philosophy and poetry, is explicitly taken up by Gadamer in the essay "Philosophy and Poetry." Gadamer asks here how language, as the only medium of poetry and thinking, of image and concept, is able to encompass what is common to both of them. The answer lies in the peculiar status of the word. Unlike everyday speaking where our words pass over into what is said, the language of both philosophy and poetry can stand for itself, "bearing its own authority in the detached text that articulates it" (RB 132/GW8 233). Just as the language of poetry does not refer to something else, but is what it represents, so too, in philosophy, the language of concepts suspends itself and leaves everyday reality behind it. This claim, in which we already find the difference between philosophy and poetry, is supported through a consideration of the "extreme cases" of the lyric poem and the dialectical concept. The lyric poem is for Gadamer an extreme case because it suggests in the clearest possible way "the inseparability of the linguistic work of art and its original manifestation as a language, as the untranslatability of such poetry shows" (RB 134/GW8 235). In the pure poetry of Mallarmé, for example, "where the musicality of the poetic word is intensified to the highest degree," "the form of the poem is constructed by the constantly shifting balance between sound and sense" that "hauls back" the fleeting word that points beyond itself (RB 134/GW8 235). In this standing of the word—and here "word" designates the whole in which it stands—the word names; that is, it calls the phenomenon into presence. The word as image has an illuminating power even though the precise meaning of the word is often ambiguous.

The dialectical concept, on the other hand, moves beyond everyday speech in a different way. The problem, Gadamer insists, "is not that everyday prose threatens to infiltrate the language of the concept, but that the language of the proposition takes us in the wrong direction" (RB 137/GW8 237). Hegel has shown that the proposition in the form of judgment is not suited to express speculative truths. The point is not that philosophy should try to avoid the form of proposition, but rather, to recognize that philosophy moves exclusively in the medium of the concept, where "the matter of thought is immanently and dynamically articulated." As Gadamer rightly notes, it was Hegel who understood that the Aristotelian logic of definition reaches its limit in the realm of philosophical principles. In speculation, which is the properly genuine character of thought, thought is able to recover from all externalization. The language of philosophy is a language that sublates itself.

Although it is Hegel who represents philosophy in this essay, Gadamer draws from several sources for his understanding of the language of philosophy; he draws from Heidegger of course but perhaps even more from Plato. From Plato, Gadamer takes language to be living language, the language of conversation, and as such it is interwoven with the very task of philosophy—the recollective recognition of what is that occurs in speech. What this dynamic conversation implies about the object of philosophy is that it is not something ready at hand; accordingly, philosophy fails when it understands itself as a construction of a system of propositions, the formalization of which would be to deepen its insights. Gadamer takes seriously Plato's insight in the Seventh Letter that the means of philosophizing (logical demonstrations) are not the same as philosophizing itself. This is not to suggest that Gadamer is against logic, that in the end he wants to aestheticize or poeticize the experience of philosophy. Nothing could be farther from the truth. Philosophy remains for him the experience of the logos. His critique of philosophy and the language of philosophy as the language of the proposition—a critique that is also found in the later Wittgenstein—must be seen in terms of what philosophy is after. "[T]he thematization in logic restrains the horidon of questioning to allow verification and in doing so blocks the opening up of the world which takes place in our experience of the world."[7] In this context, poetry is not an inferior speaking in relation to the language of concepts, as if conceptual rigor could disclose the world better than a play of images. The issue of poetry is simply the determination of the special place of poetry in connection with the binding character of language (which involves a conceptual element).

What do poetry and philosophy, then, share in common? Certainly, they both share in the effort of communicating, whereby what is imparted becomes greater. This effort of communicating remains an effort precisely because speaking is caught up in finitude, in the essential fracture found in all speaking. In both philosophy and poetry there is always "self-bestowal and self-withdrawal," an uncovering and a withdrawal within the mystery of language. Accordingly, both poetry and philosophy share the common feature of being a type of speech that cannot be "false," for neither is judged according to the usual norm of correspondence and adequation. And yet such speech is not arbitrary. The truth of the word lies in its accomplishment such that we witness the failure of speech in poetry when poetry sounds like the rhetoric of everyday life, and we witness the failure of speech in philosophy when philosophy degenerates into empty sophistry. In both instances, Gadamer insists, "the word breaks" and does not fulfill itself.

The analysis of this proximity of poetry and thinking does not do enough to highlight their difference. How is poetry in fact a special case of the event of language? In "Text and Interpretation" Gadamer makes much of the fact that it is the literary *text* that has a special autonomy:

> But then there is literature! That is to say, texts that do not disappear in our act of understanding them but stand there confronting our understanding with normative claims and which continually stand before every new way the text can speak. What is it that distinguishes these texts from others? . . . My thesis is this: These texts are only authentically there when they come back to themselves. Then they are texts in the original and authentic sense. (TI 41/GW2 351)

The autonomy of a literary, poetic, text—one must assume here a text in some form of opposition to a philosophical text—rests on its ability to be taken as a whole that "lifts itself out of the stream of speech that is flowing past."[8] This means, as we have see in the description of text in chapter 6, that the poetic text does not refer back to an already spoken word, as if reading the poetic text would be an exercise in getting back to an original expression. Gadamer's point is precisely that in the poem we are "wholly directed toward the word as it stands" (RB 107/GW8 72). Accordingly, the special autonomy of the poetic word pertains to the way in which language comes to appearance in a unique way. In "On the Contribution of Poetry to the Search for Truth," Gadamer describes this autonomy in relation to two other autonomous texts, the religious text and the legal text. The religious text that "stands written," is something like a pledge (*Zusage*), a "binding word that presumes mutual obligation" (RB 109/GW8 74). The legal text is also a binding word, but in this case it is so as a proclamation (*Ansage*). A legal text "only becomes valid by means of a declaration. A law must be promulgated" (RB 109–10/GW8 74). In contrast to these two forms of eminent text, the poetic text is binding as a statement (*Aussage*).[9] "It is a saying that says so completely what it is that we do not need to add anything beyond what is said in order to accept it in its reality as language" (RB 110/GW8 75). This does not mean that the content of a poem completely expresses itself in every reading, but only that it "bears witness to itself and does not admit of anything that might verify it." It is in this context that the truth of poetry is to be understood; consistent with the dynamic of self-bestowal and self-withdrawal, the truth-claim of the poetic text is not judged as true to something, that is, in terms of a reference outside the text. The poem's validity rests in itself and has its saying power in the way language comes to appearance in it.

In "Text and Interpretation" Gadamer states the character of this autonomy in much the same way:

> [I]t is in the literary text that the word first attains its full self-presence. Not only does the word make what is said present; it also makes itself present in its radiant actuality as sound. Just as style constitutes a very effective factor in a good text and yet such a text does not put itself forward as a piece of stylistic decoration, so too is the actuality of words and of discourse as sound always indissolubly bound up with the transmission of meaning. Nevertheless, there is a profound difference between the functioning of words in ordinary discourse and in literature. On the one hand, in discourse as such we are continually running ahead in thought searching for the meaning, so that we let the appearance of the words fall away as we listen and read for the meaning being conveyed; on the other hand, with a literary text the self-manifestation of each and every word has a meaning in its sonority, and the melody of the sound is also used by the discourse to augment what is said through the words. (TI 43/GW2 352–53)

If the literary text possesses its own status in "the repetition of the words in the original power of their sound," and to this extent is distinctively literary as opposed to philosophical, how are we to understand the crossing of philosophy and poetry? The crossing as such appears as a function, not of the status of the text—for in the end, the crossing can have its sense only if the difference between philosophy and poetry is preserved—but of the interpretation of texts. In "Text and Interpretation" this issue of interpretation is presented in terms of the problem of how the *mediating* discourse of the interpreter could be taken over into the act of interpreting the poetic text. That there is a problem at all results from the fact that the poetic text, in contrast to all other texts, "is not interrupted by the dialogical and the intermediary speaking of the interpreter; rather it is simply accompanied by the interpreter's constant co-speaking" (TI 46/GW2 356). Stated in this way, the problem of interpretation, as the problem of the crossing, appears identical to the way in which the relation between philosophy and poetry is characterized by Plato in the *Ion*.

Excursus: Poetry as a Lending of the Voice

In the *Ion* the ancient quarrel between philosophy and poetry occurs, appropriately enough, in the context of the determination of the nature of interpretation (ἑρμηνεία). At the outset of the dialogue Ion has just returned from a contest of rhapsodes where he won first prize. Ion is accordingly deemed to be good at lending his voice, for the rhapsode does not create poetry but recites for the poet, in the absence of the poet, the poet's verse.[10] This skill of the rhapsode is a skill that, for Plato, is in the first instance an interpretation: the lending of the voice is an interpretation of the poet's thought to those who listen. Now, it is precisely the character of this interpretation that interests Socrates. He envies the rhapsode for he is conversant with Homer and understands "his thought [διάνοια] and not merely his verse [ἔπη]."[11] He understands what the poet, who is himself an interpreter of the gods, means to say (λέγει). The specific focus of the discussion centers on the nature of this understanding that must comprehend the poet, this understanding that is the condition for the success of the rhapsode when the rhapsode lends his voice. In inquiring after this under-standing, however, it should not go unnoticed that Plato has already made the separation between philosophy and poetry. It is philosophy that insists on the separation of the λόγος from the verse, whereas in poetry, to borrow a phrase from Gadamer, it is possible to recognize "the whole in the verse."

In the dialogue, Ion does in fact claim to be skilled with respect to what Homer says, and considers the acquisition of this knowledge to be direct; it is not a matter of interpretation as mediated knowing, but of simply learning completely what Homer says. Socrates seizes the opportunity to ask Ion about the nature of his expert knowledge. When it is determined that this knowledge is a knowledge in form and not in content, that this knowledge is neither an art nor an science, neither τέχνη nor ἐπιστήμη, Socrates proceeds to provide an account of the rhapsodes' specific art for Ion. The rhapsode, who in lending his voice must restore the poet in his verse, is an interpreter not from knowledge, but from a divine power. This power is like the force of magnetism that attracts iron rings. The magnetism passes through the rings enabling each subsequent ring to act like the first member. Since the rings are actually unchained, the peculiar problem confronting this imagery is to explain the μίμησις, the mimetic event of reduplication, that is, the magnetism proper. In Socrates' account, the magnet is the Muse who "first makes men inspired, and then through these inspired ones [ἐνθέους] others share in the enthusiasm, and a chain is formed" (533e). The poet's song is a song of inspiration, deprived of reason: the poet says what is, tells the "truth," as "a light, winged and holy thing" (534b) who cannot compose (ποιεῖν) until he has become inspired and beside himself.

According to Socrates, then, the poet is no different than the rhapsode, he too is someone who lends his voice; the poet lends his voice to the inspiration, to what transpires in being beyond oneself, in not being oneself. But if such is the case then one can say that in some sense the poet's voice is the voice of another. How this can be understood is of course of utmost importance. Certainly this lending of the voice as the voice of another is not to be confused with ventriloquism, where the voice simply comes from another place. The poet, in other words, must not be confused with Eurycles, one of the wizards who were called ventriloquists, because they made their voices issue from their own bellies (*venter -loqui*).[12] The poet's voice is not a displaced voice, but a voice that speaks in not being oneself. This not being oneself is the poet's enthusiasm, but it is also the borrowing of the voice as such. The voice of the poet (and equally so for the rhapsode) is a voice lent to the other for the other to speak. The lending of the voice is a matter of participation in the speaking that is from an other. In the sentence immediately preceding the one where the poet is described as the one who is inspired, Socrates says, "for the poets tell us . . . that the melodies they bring us are gathered from rills that run with honey, out of glens and gardens of the Muses, and they bring them as bees do honey" (534b). The poet is not engaged in creating (in this case the honey) but in providing us with what they have gathered. The composing (ποιεῖν) of the poet is accordingly a *giving* as a hearing and declaring in song. The poet is indeed an interpreter because, like Hermes, he brings the announcement, he carries the announcement and in so doing communicates, albeit in song.[13] In this announcing in song the voice of the poet is paradoxically at once a forgetting—that is, the voice of enchantment is a forgetfulness, certainly a forgetting of oneself (of oneself as well as the one spoken to)— and a remembering—that is, the lending of the voice is the invocation of Mnemosyne, it is the act of remembering, in this case a remembering who we are.[14]

It is easy to see how in this description the poet stands opposed to the philosopher in the figure of Socrates, even if we grant that Socrates too is a message-bearer, that is, the task of philosophy is formulated in response to the demand to convey a message from Apollo. The poet, unlike the philosopher, does not interpret in order to comprehend the λόγος, but only to declare in song what is of the divine. The poet "sings [ἀείδειν] with the Heliconian Muses."[15] In point of fact, then, Socrates' envy is ironic for poetical speaking is disturbing to the philosopher; the poet's voice is taken to be authoritative yet it cannot support itself. The philosopher can secure his place in the πόλις, whether this be the πόλις of the Greeks or our global village, by liberating poetry of its inherent element—inspiration.

And yet, this description of the poet does not stand opposed to all philosophy. Philosophy sees in poetry precisely what it wants to stake a claim to, namely, the ability to say what is. For Socrates the question is who speaks most truly. Moreover, even the manner of the philosopher's speaking is in some ways not unlike the poet's speaking; philosophical speaking is always a *participation* in a speaking that is from an other.[16]

Let us consider then how it stands with philosophy today. If we consider philosophy in terms of what Heidegger calls the task of thinking, a task that remains inseparable from hermeneutics, we find more proximity with poetry than distance. In "The Dialogue on Language," Heidegger actually refers to Socrates' remark in the Ion that the poets are messengers of the gods in the context of the discussion with the Japanese interlocutor on the character of thinking—and this means hermeneutics—after *Being and Time*. This thinking is hermeneutical as an "exposition [*Darlegen*] that brings tidings [*Kunde*] insofar as this exposition is able to attend to a message [*Botschaft*]."[17] This exposition is an interpretation of what is already said through the poets. Philosophical thinking is thus not a matter of proposing and asserting, just as philosophy itself cannot be a science of thought. On the contrary, thinking is the bearing of the message, of the announcing that brings out the Being of beings. Thinking announces as naming, a nominating of Being. Here we could also say—for Heidegger gives us many ways to say what is the same—that thinking is a hearing as a co-responding to sending of Being. The thinker too participates, that is, must lend his voice and thereby take up "the preserving of a message [*Verwahrens einer Botschaft*]."[18] With Heidegger, however, as his critics charge—and here Gadamer must be counted among them—the association between the thinker and the poet may be too intimate. Despite Heidegger's own words that the same "is the belonging together of what differs through a gathering by way of difference,"[19] the thinker's mode of speech often breaks out into a poetizing mode of speech, and this blurs the very difference between the two. In this context, it would seem that the difference between uttering Being and naming the holy amounts to nothing more than the added feature of song, as the medium for the poet's voice.[20] But, perhaps, in the end, this *is* the essential difference.[21]

In the crossing of philosophy and poetry, philosophical hermeneutics certainly recognizes the element of song as a mark of poetic discourse. In poetic discourse "every word has a meaning in its sonority, and the melody of the sound is also used by the discourse to augment what is said through the words" (TI 43/GW2 352–53). Elsewhere, Gadamer refers to the effort to read the poet Stefan George as one "in which the tone and echo of the intellectual reality and effect of the poet" is to be heard (EPH 83/GW9 249).[22] As song, the voice of the poet is indeed an enchanting voice, a *canto* that is *incanto*, a consecration with spells, a voice beside itself, outside itself. And if in this enchantment there is delight, this is not because the poetic word is charming. The charming only pleases and does not announce.[23] In the enchanting voice there is a radiance, an illuminating announcing. The poetic word, Gadamer tells us, "makes itself present in its radiant actuality as sound" (TI 43/GW2 352). Radiance, as the essential determination of the beautiful, belongs to the poetic word.

But then, we can ask, following the *Ion*, from where comes the radiant word that is not made? The *Ion* tells us that the radiant word is given, granted to the poet, who can only preserve the word. As given, the radiant word is a *gift*, in this case a gift given by the Muses. The notion of the gift, of the giving and granting of the word, I would argue, is the essential configuration in the interpretation of the poetic word, of the word that is a *Aussage*—a statement, assertion, testimony that bears witness to itself. In this context of a giving and granting the word of the poet can be understood as a word of grace. In English, the word "grace" means a gift granted from God, and is thus consonant with the description of the nature of poetic discourse given in the *Ion*. For us today, this description simply means that the word of grace is a word that is given in a certain manner. It is given in the manner of a gift that cannot be exchanged. Equally important for us, however, are the other meanings associated with this word. "Grace" has not only an aesthetic connotation, as when we speak of a graceful dancer—and thus it is quite appropriate to speak of the poetic word as graceful—but also an ethical connotation, as when we speak of a gracious person, someone of kindness and good will.

Appropriately enough, it is Heidegger who draws our attention to this character of the granting of the word. At the end of the essay ". . . Poetically Man Dwells . . ." Heidegger asks, in response to his claim that poetry is authentic or inauthentic according to the degree of appropriation of our being to that which needs our presence, "when and for how long does authentic poetry exist?"[24] He finds the answer in a verse from Hölderlin:

> So lange die Freundlichkeit noch
> Am Herzen, die Reine, dauert, misset
> Nicht unglüklich der Mensch sich
> Mit der Gottheit.

> As long as Kindness,
> The Pure, still stays with his heart, man
> Not unhappily measures himself
> Against the Godhead.[25]

Heidegger contends that, if taken literally, "*Freundlichkeit*" is a translation for the Greek word χάϱις, and then proceeds to tell us what χάϱις is by quoting a verse from Sophocles' *Ajax*: "For kindness [*Huld*] it is, that ever calls forth kindness."[26] Leaving aside Heidegger's question of authentic poetry, the word χάϱις holds within it all the meanings we found in the English word *grace*. It refers not only to one's outward grace or beauty, but also grace in the sense of a favor felt (thus the sense of kindness and good will). Its various meanings include as well the gratification or delight from a thing, and favors granted in an erotic sense. Moreover, in the verse from Sophocles, we also learn how χάϱις is given: "For kindness it is that ever calls forth kindness." This means that χάϱις is given in that space between the exchange of debt in a self-encircling exchange. Χάϱις precedes the act of χάϱις, otherwise it would not be χάϱις. A word of grace can only be given in grace. This is, of course, the nature of any gift. In a recent book, *Given Time*, Derrida points out what Marcel Mauss failed to see in his classic text on the gift—that for there to be a gift there must be no reciprocity or debt.[27] The giving cannot be indebted (ought to) in any way for there to be a gift.[28]

Accordingly, we can say that the word of grace can be heard only from grace, from that singular position whereby the word in fact can be given. We need not resort to myth nor mysticism in order to understand this notion. The poet, let us say, is one who creates kind words, gracious words, in kindness, in friendship. A kind word is a radiant word, even if the content of the word is not itself radiant.[29] If, however, the poet creates in kindness, in friendship, then we assume not just that poetic creation cannot exist without the friend, but that there are indeed friends, or at least the hope of a friend. Who, then, is the friend? Is it not simply every interpreter as "co-speaker," the one who hears the voice of the other by speaking with this other, the one who is always confronted in the effort to hear words that in co-speaking are at the same time not own's own. Is not the friend the one who in a confrontation with a poetic text is able to accept some things that are against that one, even though no one is asking this of the that one? Is this not the Gadamerian hermeneut? And thereby is this co-speaking not also the experience of philosophy, of hermeneutic experience in which we encounter something that asserts its own truth?

Friendship of course is a wonderful thing, as are gifts. Whether everything is so wonderful for philosophical hermeneutics is the question that needs to be asked. Is it the case that here in the experience of the poetic word, in the language of homeland, we have our halcyon days, that we take communion in every reading of words of grace? Is it not the case that philosophical hermeneutics is naive about gifts, that Derrida is right, the gift cannot be given? To answer this question properly we must consider what Gadamer learns from Celan—this poet of darkness who speaks haltingly, silently, this poet of darkness who dislocates meaning, this poet of darkness who, when he first speaks, must even twist his own name: Paul Antschel/Ancel/Celan.

Celan is a poet who above all is concerned with the other, with the possibility of speaking to an other. But such speaking is not easy. In his prose writings, Celan describes poetry as that which might encounter the other in language: "A poem, being an instance [*Erscheinungsform*] of language, hence essentially dialogue, may be a letter in a bottle thrown out to sea with the—surely not always strong—hope that it may somehow wash up somewhere, perhaps on a shoreline of the heart. In this way, too, poems are *en route*: they are headed toward. Toward what? Toward something open, inhabitable, an approachable you, perhaps, an approachable reality."[30]

Such an encounter is always posed against language, for the poem today "clearly shows a strong tendency towards silence." In the attempt to address the possibility of an ethical relation to other in language, the poetic word is a counterword, "the word that, conscious of its insufficiency and distortion, displaces itself from itself, finds a crack in itself, to allow the other to remain other and yet be signaled in language."[31] Such fracturing of language, within which language becomes voice as a ruptured communication, occurs in the "turning of breath" (*Atemwende*), that spacing between breath, the moment between inhaling and exhaling, where the other of the voice signals its alterity: "Poetry is perhaps this: a turning of breath." In marking itself so at the interval between words, the poem's turn to "an approachable reality" is a "desperate conversation."[32]

What Gadamer learns from Celan in commenting on his poem series "*Atemkristall*" (published in 1965 under the title *Atemwende*) is that the rupture of communication, the non-communication of the poetic word is not to be distorted by the pretense that one has in fact understood Celan's poems. At best one continually attempts to listen to the "message in the bottle," to the "breathless stillness of the word." In his own listening Gadamer detects the sense of *Atemwende*: the stillness in the verses is to be welcomed as the "stillness that can be heard at the turn of breath, this most gentle renewal of the creation of breath. This is above all the turn of the breath, the sensuous experience of the noiseless, motionless moment between inhaling and exhaling. I do not want to deny that Celan connects this moment of the turning of breath—the moment when the breath reverses [*umkehrt*]—not only with motionless reticence [*Ansichhalten*], but also with the quiet hope, which resonates in all reversal as turning around" (GW9 388).[33] Words are not necessarily transparent, hermeneutics cannot escape non-transparency and the word that may be untranslatable. The element of hope that Gadamer finds in Celan and enters Gadamer's own thinking is not a nostalgia for transparency, but simply the first gesture in hermeneutic conversation—the hope that the word spoken can reach the other. There is in fact no immediate answer to the question "Who am I and Who are You?," the title of Gadamer's commentary on Celan. And yet, one does not by this fact give up the effort of understanding. The communion is simply in the granting of the word as such.

The issue for Gadamer then, and here we broach the crossing once again, is the need to be reached by the word. At the beginning of the essay "Are the Poets Falling Silent?," Gadamer poses a question about the power and possibilities of poetry in an our age. "Is there," he asks, "still a time and place for art in an age where social unrest and the discomfort of our social life in an anonymous mass society is felt from all sides and where the demand for rediscovering or reestablishing true solidarities is advanced over and over again"? (EPH 73).[34] The need to hear the word of the poet is related to the task of rediscovery of who we are, to the task of being at home in the world. As a way of entering into this question, Gadamer rightly notes that in such an age the word of the poet must be a different kind of word than the one spoken in mere reporting. This word of the poet, which allows for the fulfillment of the demand in the question is, borrowing from the poet Rilke, a word of "discretion." Gadamer interprets the word of discretion to be the word that is spoken quietly, and such a word can be heard only if there are ears receptive to it. At the end of the essay Gadamer indicates something about the character of this listening. It is not unlike the skillfulness required of the composer and conductor in fashioning the slow passage in a symphony. How are we to interpret this comparison with musical orchestration? Certainly it is an apt comparison inasmuch as poetry is essentially of song, of music. Moreover, symphonic music establishes a configuration of wholeness and continuity, a configuration from which philosophical hermeneutics never escapes. But the point of the comparison seems to be that the quiet word requires a different tempo. Such a tempo is what we find in the experience of poetic dwelling. Accordingly, what is accomplished when we are reached by these quiet words is a creative event of the advent of our being, a poetic dwelling—the name that at the same time marks the crossing of philosophy and poetry. Let us then attend to the crossing as such under the name poetic dwelling.

§ 27. Poetic Dwelling

The term poetic dwelling is not actually used by Gadamer, but the notion is clearly present in several of the later essays that deal with art and poetry, especially "Word and Picture," written in 1992. In "On the Contribution of Poetry to the Search for Truth," Gadamer describes what appears to be a notion of poetic dwelling when he states the distinctive way poetry achieves the fulfillment of speech, that is, the summoning up what is there. Gadamer contends that the truth of poetry consists in creating a "hold upon nearness [*Halten der Nähe*]" (RB 113/GW8 78). This experience of nearness has to do not only with time—reading the poetic word allows the temporality of succession to be annulled, in effect the passing of time is halted—it has to do also with the communicative dimension in the experience of art that is described here as a "growing familiarity with the world." This familiarity is not about this or that particular thing, but pertains to the familiarity itself such that the poetic word "bears witness to our own being [*bezeugt uns unser Dasein*]." In "The Verse and the Whole," Gadamer describes the "hold upon nearness" as the experience of "living in poetry" (EPH 91/GW9 257). This experience he tells us "is more than a kind of exercise in relaxation, occurring within the helter-skelter and pressures of our performance-oriented life. Living in poetry is rather one of the ways through which we experience being moved within ourselves" (EPH 91/GW9 257). To this description Gadamer then adds the most curious statement: "In this [living in poetry] only are humans able to find their self-fulfillment." In yet another text from the 1970s, "The Relevance of the Beautiful," Gadamer speaks of dwelling most directly. In the context of a discussion of the temporality of the work of art, Gadamer indicates that dwelling, *Verweilen*, is the particular comportment of this temporal space. The more one is able to dwell the more the work's richness opens up for us. Here too we find a curious statement added to the description. To dwell or tarry with the work is perhaps "the only way that is granted to us finite creatures to relate to what we call eternity" (RB 45/GW8 136). Finally, as a clue for the understanding of poetic dwelling, in "Word and Picture" Gadamer describes the experience with poetry as a "preserving tarrying [*gewahrendes Verweilen*]," whereby one is with the work of art so completely that what is "there in the work appears, comes forth" (GW8 387).

It is quite apparent from these various passages that what we want to call poetic dwelling is captured by the experience of tarrying, *Verweilen*, which formally intends to capture the distinctive experience of poetry and by extension the experience of all art. Precisely what this experience is in these terms and how this experience is also the experience of philosophy is not so apparent. If we follow the indications from the passages, however, the essential determination of poetic dwelling comes into view.

As a general determination, we can say first of all that poetic dwelling is not to be confused with an "exercise in relaxation." It is not simply leisure, at least not in the ordinary sense of this term. In our modern planning culture, leisure has come to mean a form of idleness, a space for activity where one does not work. This space of activity is a space of time (*Weile*) that is often regarded as wasting time. In our modern planning culture, one takes up poetry when there is time to waste. However, in its original understanding, leisure was not equated with idleness. When the Greek concept was first carried over into the Latin culture, leisure (*schola, otium*) was regarded as a virtue, whereas idleness (*acedia*) pertained to a particular way in which one renounces the claim implicit in one's human dignity. According to Joseph Pieper in his classical essay on leisure, idleness is the condition of life whereby there is a refusal to be what God wants in a person's life.[35] In less religious terms, it is the condition whereby someone does not want to be what one fundamentally is; that is to say, in the condition of idleness there is no consent of the will to one's life, and as such one is not whole, not one with that dynamic activity of life. In this context the opposite of idleness is not industriousness as the life of economy and commerce; rather, it is simply the condition whereby one is able to affirm one's own being. Opposed to idleness then is leisure regarded as the capacity for steeping oneself into the whole of creation through which one's created life is affirmed. One of the ways in which this is accomplished, according to Pieper, is through silence, for in silence "the soul's power to 'answer' to the reality of the world is left undisturbed." Only in silence are we truly able to hear. But leisure is not just this attitude in which one is open to everything in silence. Because we affirm the basic meaningfulness of life through it, leisure is also an attitude of contemplative celebration.[36]

On cannot fail to notice that in this activity of leisure we are not far from the experience of philosophy, not of course as contemplation in the ordinary sense of the term (as if philosophy could take distance from life), but as a hermeneutics of facticity. In the "Aristotle-Introduction" of 1922, Heidegger tells us that "the basic sense of the movement of factical life is caring," which pertains to our getting along and coping with the world, the world that is there in life and for life.[37] Moreover, what is in the movement of care is a pause-taking (*Aufenhaltsnahme*) as the way in which the world is there.[38] What is in the movement of care, in other words, is a seizing of existence which makes factical life questionable to itself. This seizing is the experience of philosophy for Heidegger. To this description of the general movement of care, Heidegger then adds the familiar characterization of factical life: that in this movement there is a tendency to be taken along by the world as a tendency towards the falling away from one's own self. How does this bear upon leisure and the opposing concept of idleness? Idleness as a refusal of life from within life is tantamount to a falling away, a covering over of life, whereas leisure, on the other hand, is a way of taking up the world, a taking up the world by taking a pause. Accordingly, if the tarrying of poetic dwelling is not to be confused with an exercise in relaxation, it remains nonetheless a form of leisure.

But precisely what does "taking-a-pause" mean? Since life is $\varkappa \acute{\iota} \nu \eta \sigma \iota \varsigma$, taking-a-pause would be, to say the least, the movement in life through which the movement of life is encountered. Certainly all this appears very enigmatic. Our ordinary sense of pausing—that of breaking, of standing back, of holding back, from the ongoing—suggests that taking-a-pause is a step back from life as a way of seeing life. But the hermeneutics of facticity suggests otherwise, that it is a seizing of life by stepping into life. The enigma is dispelled, at least for philosophical hermeneutics when the stepping into life is considered, as intended, temporally.

In *The Relevance of the Beautiful* and elsewhere,[39] Gadamer distinguishes between the normal pragmatic experience of time and the time characteristic of the work of art. The normal pragmatic experience of time is time at our disposal, as when we say, for example, "I have time for something." The temporal structure of this time is "empty," since it is a time that needs to be filled. We experience this temporality in the extremes of both boredom, where there is too much time, and the frantic pace where there is never enough time. On the other hand, there is the experience of time that is not subject to the abstract calculation of temporal duration. It is the experience of time that we do not reckon with at all. This is the experience of time, for example, of the festival where every moment of its duration is fulfilled, where the moment of time is autonomous. "This fulfillment does not come about because someone has empty time to fill. On the contrary, the time only becomes festive with the arrival of the festival" (RB 42/GW8 132). This whiling, this space of time [*Weile*], of the festival is fulfilled when the festival is there (*da*). The space of time proper to the work of art in general—that is, when the work of art is successful—is like that of the festival; it is one that nobody measures and that one finds neither boring (*langweilig*) nor entertaining (*kurzweilig*). As such, this time does not last and does not pass away. And yet, something happens here; there is in this conversion of taking-a-pause a halt to (the succession of) time; there is a time of tarrying (*Verweilen*) in this space of time. "It is the nature of the festival that it should proffer [*vorgibt*] time, arresting it, and allowing it to tarry" (RB 42/GW8 133). In the autonomous temporality of the world of art—a temporality of simultaneity (*Gleichzeitigkeit*) of duration—there is a halt in the succession of time.

In speaking of the time of the festival, the time of art, or better, the time of life (since this experience of time is an experience that according to Gadamer resides in liveliness [*Lebendigkeit*] as such), we have brought ourselves back to the problem of transition that we saw in Kierkegaard. Time, whether empty or fulfilled, is about transition. In empty time the experience of transition is the passing of time. It is the experience of the now that stands mid-way between the old and the new. In fulfilled time, the transition is not about sequence and succession, but of being that time, where the departure of time is returned—or better, repeated—in the whiling (*Weile*) of time. Within the Greek conceptuality that underlies his analysis of art, Gadamer thinks that this structure of liveliness is what we find in

Aristotle's concept of ἐνέργεια. According to Gadamer, the concept of ἐνέργεια, which "shimmers between actuality, reality and activity [*Aktualität, Wirklichkeit und Tätigkeit*]," is conceptually tied to the character of being as being in motion, and in this dynamism stands in contrast to an ἔργον as a completed work. Following Aristotle, this dynamism is not to be confused with motion (κίνησις) as such for the moving thing is still underway and has not yet arrived at its end. The dynamism of ἐνέργεια has the distinctive property of being simultaneously becoming and having-become, as seeing and having seen and thinking something over and having thought something over are simultaneous. On Gadamer's interpretation, such activities that hold together becoming and having-become, activities of execution, are a kind of tarrying in something.

This tarrying we experience as an absorption. The time of the festival is an absorption in the becoming of time. But the time of the festival is also the time of the work of art in general. In the experience of art we are to be taken up into it, to be absorbed by the work, filled with it. We tarry with the work, take-a-pause, by going with the work. Attending to the work in this way allows for what is in the work to come out.[40] This description of tarrying can easily be misunderstood as a kind of romanticism where one has simply abandoned oneself before the work, waiting for it to speak. But the experience of the festival is not a waiting at all; on the contrary, the character of the absorption is the decisive taking up, taking hold of something. The absorption is at once participation. This participation is nothing less that what has always gone under the name of θεωρία.

Let us recall just how important participation is in the practice of hermeneutics. For Gadamer, hermeneutical inquiry transpires "in the exercise" and nowhere else. Just as language is in conversation, interpretation, as the movement of the being (ἐνέργεια) of the interpreted, is in the performative activity (*Vollzug*). This activity, the going with as a performative activity, has a double component. On the one hand, as inquiry, the activity is to be understood as the basic meaning of θεωρία. We know from Gadamer's previous work, where he identifies hermeneutics with practical philosophy, that θεωρία does not necessarily stand in opposition to πρᾶξις. The Greeks, Gadamer insists, understood all too well how, in being human, we succeed in knowing the world only in finite measures, and that within this fate we are still capable of pure contemplation of the world. But this look at the world, this θεωρία, is not a matter of construction whereby, on the basis of self-consciousness, one is able to take distance from beings and subject them to anonymous domination. For the Greeks, the distance proper that must be taken in the look is, paradoxically, one of proximity and affinity. In Gadamer's words: "The primitive meaning of θεωρία is participation in the delegation sent to a festival for the sake of honoring the gods. The viewing of the divine proceedings is no participationless establishing of some neutral state of affairs or observation of some splendid demonstration or show. Rather it is a genuine sharing in an event, a real being present" (RAS 17–18). For the Greeks, then, the theoretical is not a mere seeing, but more so, a comportment (*Haltung*), or condition, in which one holds oneself.[41]

Now, when Gadamer claims in "Word and Picture" that "art belongs in the neighborhood of θεωρία" (GW8 395), he is obviously understanding θεωρία, not as logical research, but in its original sense as a form of participation in Being. Θεωρία is here the activity of being present to what is real. The gaze (*Schauen*) of θεωρία is such that one is totally there (*ganz dabei*); the gaze of θεωρία is a tarrying. To tarry with the work of art is like being in a richly varied conversation. "The whole of a conversation is that in which one is for a while, totality with it [*ganz dabei*]" (GW8 387).

But in making this claim about art there is in fact something more being said. That art belongs in the neighborhood of θεωρία—and here we introduce the second component of the activity—is to say that art, in this sense, remains close to science, for both are opposed to all practical-technical activity. The performative activity is not to be confused with production for which there is a product (ἔργον). The work of art, which has its end in its continuous fulfillment (*Vollzug*), is not produced "like a commodity or goods (even if it is brought to market to be sold)" (GW8 395). Production is not performance, just as conceptually ἔργον is not ἐνέργεια. In this fashion, the work of art can be understood analogous to nature where nature is understood as φύσις (alive in its being in motion). What is alive in this sense is nature "as seed, as shoot [*Keim*] that comes out of the ground, and in its maturity, ripeness, fruit"[42] (GW8 395). Accordingly, the work of art is such that something comes forth (*herauskommen*); that is, when the work of art succeeds, "it" has come out. What comes forth, however, is not a reproduction of what is already there beforehand in the work prior to its depiction in art. As Gadamer has said on numerous occasions, the work of art does not present us with a reproduction. In its "elevated rank in being [*Seinsrang*]," "something comes forth [*es kommt heraus*]." But what is this "it"? Gadamer tell us in passing that the "it" is the true, where truth is no longer understood in terms of the proposition. In the same essay he tells us that what comes forth is what we agree with (in the sense of being a co-speaker), and again, not because it is a reproduction of something we have seen before (GW8 389). The work of art is a statement (*Aussage*) that can always speak again. With respect to music, for example:

> Whoever makes music does not just spell it out; as an interpreter one really fulfills it, performing it so that "it comes out." The perfect technical reproduction, and unfortunately along with it, in principle, the phonograph records and every other technical form of reproduction—for example the color reproduction of pictures—are really only reproduction without interpretation. (GW8 394)

When there is successful interpretation, the work speaks. What, then, is tarrying as the taking place (*Vollzug*) of the work of art? According to Gadamer it is not an objectifying knowing, but "the multiplicity which belongs to the performance itself" (GW8 394). It is, to use the words from the earlier analysis, "a steeping oneself into the whole of creation" in which we become more.

But then one must ask whether this has not always been the experience of philosophy as Gadamer understands it. It has been so, let us say, precisely because the experience of philosophy, like the experience of art is about the self-presentation of the being of life, and entering into this experience is what goes by the name poetic dwelling.

We can see precisely what this means if we extend the previous remarks on θεωρία into this context. Following Gadamer's analysis, we had said that θεωρία is a comportment in which one holds oneself. As such, it is not a comportment through which one takes power over an object or turns an object into something present-at-hand by means of an explanation. In this context θεωρία is more like the Latin *contemplatio* that does not exhaust itself in the service to πρᾶξις; and yet, the contemplative life is a way of taking up the world. It takes up the world by "coping" with it. This "coping" is a way of being devoted to what is. But this, according to Gadamer, is, if we follow Aristotle here, the ideal of a theoretical life. It is, to quote "In Praise of Theory," the "fulfillment of our being-'there'— not a 'self-consciousness,' but precisely that intensification of life that the Greeks called *theoria*."[43] Philosophy is about awakening existence to itself, and this task of a hermeneutics of facticity is accomplished in tarrying.

And it is in this context that the language of homeland is to be understood. We should recall here Gadamer's question at the end of the essay "On the contribution of poetry to the search for truth" about the character of the successfulness of a poem whereby the content comes to stand. This question is at once a question of how poetry is able to overcome the time-bound and occasional circumstances of its origin? This success cannot be attributed to the fact that poetic works supply us with the answers to the ultimate questions of life. This indeed may be the case for certain works. The success is attributed, rather, to the way in which the poetic word "summons up what is 'there' so that it is palpably near." From this claim Gadamer concludes that the truth of poetry consists in creating a "hold upon nearness." Now we know what this means. To be in the hold is the essential meaning of tarrying. What is *in* the hold is that commonality that supports us as speakers. What is *in* the hold in this context is language. But in "The Verse and the Whole," Gadamer tells us that language signifies memory. This claim is made in the context of articulating the possibilities of language that surpass that of a tool. To quote the complete passage once again:

> Language signifies memory. *Mnemosyne* is, however, the mother of all muses and so the patron of the art. Art . . . means, in the final analysis, a way of confronting ourselves in which we become more mindful of ourselves. In word as in picture . . . the world as a whole—the whole of our world experience—has become present. (EPH 90/GW9 256)

What is in the hold, then, to be more precise, is a kind of return to ourselves, but this means for a hermeneutics of facticity to be "there" (in life). When Gadamer claims that "living in poetry" is one of the ways of being moved within ourselves and in this we are able to find our self-fulfillment, we can only understand this as a fulfillment of our being "there." In tarrying we are indeed making ourselves at home.

Conclusion

Philosophical hermeneutics, as we have seen, is about understanding. In working through the various dimensions in which the experience of understanding is articulated and legitimated—here at the end in poetry and art, but also in historical experience and in the experience of philosophy—we have come to see that for Gadamer philosophical hermeneutics is actually more than a theory of understanding. Beginning with chapter 3 of this book, we have seen how philosophical hermeneutics carries with it a certain determination of philosophy itself, on its operation (as a form of praxis) and intention (the hermeneutical awakening of existence to itself). In this reading of Gadamer's hermeneutics, of his hermeneutic philosophy, I have tried to emphasize and whenever appropriate to come back to the importance of the roots of Gadamer's thinking in the developments of the 1920s where philosophy in effect returns to the experience of life as a way of underscoring this determination of philosophy. In Heidegger's hands this return to the experience of life is presented as a hermeneutics of facticity, and Gadamer readily acknowledges the enormous shadow that Heidegger casts over his own work. But at the same time, this experience of philosophy is one that Gadamer has always found in Plato. In the search for a "last word" here, we need to be reminded once again of these roots of Gadamer's thinking.

It is from these roots that philosophy becomes for Gadamer practical philosophy. As we have seen in Gadamer's distinctive shaping of this attribute, this means that philosophy follows the way of experience itself. But it also means that what philosophy achieves for itself is not unlike what is achieved in practical knowledge ($\phi\varrho\acute{o}\nu\eta\sigma\iota\varsigma$). Such knowledge is of course fundamentally interpretive, but equally important is the fact that such knowledge has to do with a certain building, formation (*Bildung*). What this means for Gadamer can best be seen in the interpretation of a statement that Socrates makes in the *Phaedo*. When called upon by Cebes to explain why, having never written verse before, he now composes verse, Socrates says that he was told in a dream to make music ($\mu o \upsilon \sigma \iota \varkappa \grave{o} \eta \nu$).[44] In his own interpretation of this command Socrates says that "it was urging and encouraging me to do what I was doing already . . . that is to make music, because philosophy was the greatest kind of music."[45] In his 1921/22 lecture course on Aristotle, Heidegger interprets this characterization of philosophical activity: "$\mu o \upsilon \sigma \iota \varkappa \grave{\eta}$, rhythmic 'shaping' [*Bilden*], holding itself to an inner ordering and enacting itself to it. Title for education. . . . Philosophy is a how of conducting oneself. (Plato would never define philosophy as $\tau\acute{\epsilon}\chi\nu\eta$!)"[46] On this interpretation we can say that philosophical hermeneutics thinks highly of a Socrates who practices music. Philosophical hermeneutics is accordingly an attempt to legitimate and to engage in this task of building, of music-making, for which there is no $\tau\acute{\epsilon}\chi\nu\eta$.

When Gadamer turns to a consideration of the nature of poetry and to an analysis of poetical texts, we must read these efforts in the spirit of this image of Socrates. Commenting on the fact that he is concerned with philosophy and poetry, Gadamer himself says that "these reflections have served to remind me, and might remind us all, that Plato was no Platonist and philosophy is not scholasticism" (GW2 508).[47] Hopefully it is now clear what this means. To understand philosophy in this way, we should then be careful about making too much of the "metaphysics of proximity" that Gadamer seemingly presents in the experience of philosophy, in the dynamics of bringing the word to speak again. As a hermeneutics of finitude, the task of philosophy is always posed in relation to the insight that all things escape us. What is in the hold in the "hold upon nearness" always threatens to escape our grasp. For Gadamer, poetic experience as an event of language is self-bestowal and self-withdrawal. And more importantly, in the self-bestowal in poetry I am exposed not to a comfort of home as such, but to that other in/of language, that other that in self-bestowal temporarily halts the fleeting escape of all things.

Philosophical hermeneutics does indeed follow the way of experience itself, but lest we forget, experience is the encounter with something that asserts its own truth. It is for this reason that I have placed philosophical hermeneutics within the horizon of what I have called the voice of the other. Understanding comes not from the subject who thinks, but from the other that addresses me. This other that is a speaking person in every dialogical encounter is also the other in the address of language, the other that speaks when "language becomes voice." It is this voice that awakens one to vigilance, to being questioned in the conversation that we are.

Notes

Introduction

1. "Insofar as they are my constant companions, I have been formed more by the Platonic dialogues than by the great thinkers of German Idealism" (GW2 500).

2. The original draft of *Truth and Method* is a longhand manuscript that Gadamer presented to the University of Heidelberg Library in 1980. Although Gadamer made significant changes in the manuscript, these changes concern primarily the expansion of themes and not so much the departure from initial formulations. For a more detailed account of the relation of the original manuscript to the text of 1960, see Jean Grondin, "On the Sources of *Truth and Method*," in *Sources of Hermeneutics* (Albany: SUNY Press, 1995).

3. This claim is not simply the claim that Gadamer takes up issues in the humanities within the project of philosophical hermeneutics, but that his whole orientation never goes beyond issues of the humanities. It appears that this is the claim of Grondin in several essays in *Sources of Hermeneutics*. Grondin makes this claim, in part, to distinguish Gadamer's work from that of Heidegger.

4. In the introduction to "The Problem of Historical Consciousness," written in 1975, Gadamer tells us that it was deliberate on his part to begin *Truth and Method* with the experience of art, for the reference to the reproductive arts "stands in total contradiction to the theoretical orientation under which the *Geisteswissenschaften*, particularly in Dilthey's conception, seek parity with the natural sciences" (PHC 3).

5. Weinsheimer claims that Gadamer's point of departure is the history of the humanistic alternatives to method is an indication that Gadamer sees history itself as the alternative to method. I would think that it is more accurate to say that experience, which properly understood is inseparable from the element of historicity, is the alternative to method. Historical knowledge is, however, a classic example of hermeneutic knowing since its goal is to understand an historical phenomenon in its singularity. The question of Gadamer's own procedure is another matter. This metaquestion is answered by Gadamer in the preface. He considers the method of the book to be phenomenological. See Joel Weinsheimer, *Gadamer's Hermeneutics: A Reading of "Truth and Method"* (New Haven: Yale University Press, 1985), p. 2.

6. Although the issue for Gadamer in *Truth and Method* is the self-understanding of the human sciences, the hermeneutic dimension is not limited to the human sciences. Since the publication of *Truth and Method* he has become increasingly aware of the implications of hermeneutics for the natural sciences. According to Gadamer: "Even in the natural sciences there is something like a hermeneutical problematic. Their way is not simply that of methodological progress, as Thomas Kuhn has shown in an argument corresponding in its truth to insights that Heidegger had implied in his 'The Age of the World Picture' and in his interpretation of Aristotle's Physics (Physics B1). The 'paradigm' is of decisive importance for both the employment and the interpretation of methodological research and is obviously not itself the simple result of such research" (GW2 496). For a more detailed account of Gadamer's hermeneutics in relation to natural science, see Theodore Kisiel, "Scientific Discovery: Logical, Psychological, or Hermeneutical," in *Explorations in Phenomenology*, ed. David Carr and Edward Casey (The Hague: Martinus Nijhoff, 1973), pp. 263–84.

7. The title Gadamer actually suggested to the publisher was simply *Philosophical Hermeneutics*. Gadamer recollects this situation in a recent interview with Dieter Misgeld and Graeme Nicholson. See EPH 64.

8. See Gadamer, "Martin Heidegger and Marburg Theology," in PH, pp. 198–213. This essay also appears in another translation, following the slight change in title by Gadamer, as "The Marburg Theology," in HW, pp. 29–45 (GW3 197–208).

9. Although Heidegger had a definite influence on Gadamer in shaping the philosophical significance of this notion of *phronesis*, it was not something Gadamer was coming to for the first time. In a letter to Richard Bernstein, Gadamer writes: "As important as Heidegger and his 1923

phronesis interpretation were for me, I was already prepared for it on my own, above all by my earlier reading of Kierkegaard, by the Platonic Socrates, and by the powerful effect of the poet Stephan George on my generation." Richard Bernstein, *Beyond Objectivism and Relativism: Science, Hermeneutics, and Praxis* (Philadelphia: University of Pennsylvania Press, 1983), p. 265.

10. Why still an assistant to Husserl in Freiburg in 1922, Heidegger had the opportunity to apply for the position vacated by Nicolai Hartmann at Marburg. Paul Natorp, head of the Marburg school, wanted to give serious attention to Heidegger's candidacy, but was worried that he had not produced any original work of his own. In a three-week period Heidegger wrote what was to be a publishable manuscript, "Phenomenological Interpretations with Respect to Aristotle," and sent it to Marburg. Natorp wrote to Husserl to convey the overwhelming positive impression that the manuscript had on him, and on the basis of this he received the appointment at Marburg. The manuscript was never published by Heidegger. Natorp gave his copy to Gadamer which was subsequently lost as a result of an Allied air raid when he was in Leipzig during the war. Heidegger had also applied for a position at Göttingen in 1922 and sent a copy of the manuscript there as well. This copy was only recently rediscovered among the papers of a student of Georg Misch. In the introduction written for its publication in the Dilthey-Jahrbuch in 1989, Gadamer claims that the manuscript was one of the primary source-works for his hermeneutics. See Martin Heidegger, "Phänomenologische Interpretationen zu Aristoteles (Anzeige der hermeneutischen Situation)," ed. Hans-Ulrich Lessing, *Dilthey-Jahrbuch für Philosophie und Geschichte der Geisteswissenschaften* 6 (1989): 235–69. English translation by Michael Baur, "Phenomenological Interpretation with Respect to Aristotle: Indication of the Hermeneutic Situation," *Man and World* 25 (1992): 355–93.

11. *Platos dialektische Ethik: Phänomenologische Interpretationen zum "Philebos"* (Habilitationschrift Marburg 1929) (Leipzig: Felix Meiner, 1931). English translation appears as PDE.

12. See Gadamer, *Philosophische Lehrjahre* (Frankfurt: Vittorio Klostermann, 1977). English translation by Robert Sullivan, *Philosophical Apprenticeships* (Cambridge, MA: MIT Press, 1985). See also Hanna Arendt, "Martin Heidegger at Eighty," in *Heidegger and Modern Philosophy* (New Haven: Yale University Press, 1978).

13. For this most part, this is the direction of Gadamer's work in the 1970s, especially in light of his confrontation with critical theory. See

especially his "Hermeneutics and Social Science," *Cultural Hermeneutics* 2 (1975); "Theory, Technology, Practice: The Task of the Science of Man," *Social Research* 44.3; and *Reason in the Age of Science*.

14. It is interesting to note how Gadamer critiques his own starting point some thirty years after the publication of *Truth and Method*. He now realizes, in this era of social science, of structuralism and linguistics, that his effort to link up with the Romantic heritage of the historical school is no longer sufficient. But the recognition of the limitation of the starting point does not imply that Gadamer would want to alter the direction of the project of a philosophical hermeneutics. If hermeneutic experience is really universal, it is reachable from any starting point. See his "Reflections on My Philosophical Journey," *Hans-Georg Gadamer*, The Library of Living Philosophers, edited by Louis Hahn (La Salle: Open Court, 1997).

15. Commenting on Plato's dialectic, for example, Gadamer writes: "Diotima knew [that being itself may never be apprehended in the unrestricted presence of some *unus intuitus*] when she compared to the knowing proper to humans with the life of a species that has its ongoing being only in the relentless process of the reproduction of individual instances. Hermeneutics tries to establish this point inasmuch as it characterizes the context of tradition within which we exist as an ongoing reacquisition that proceeds into infinity" (RAS 60).

16. In the "A Dialogue on Language" Heidegger comments on the need to drop the notion of the hermeneutic circle as the manner of his procedure in thinking. But this does not mean that he abandons a manner of thinking that is still fundamentally hermeneutical. The hermeneutics of the later Heidegger is a hermeneutics of the belonging together (*Zugehörigkeit*) of being and Dasein in which the advent of meaning is caught up in the metaphorics of listening (*Hören*). See *Unterwegs zur Sprache*, Gesamtausgabe vol. 12 (Frankfurt: Klostermann, 1985), pp. 79–146.

17. "Correspondence Concerning *Wahrheit und Methode*" in *Independent Journal of Philosophy* 2 (1978): 8. This correspondence is an exchange between Gadamer and Leo Strauss.

18. This is the question that Bernasconi asks in "Bridging the Abyss: Heidegger and Gadamer." See Robert Bernasconi, *Heidegger in Question: The Art of Existing* (Atlantic Highlands, NJ: Humanities Press, 1993), pp. 170–189.

19. The complete definition is "to let what is alienated by the character of the written word or by the character of being distantiated by cultural or historical distances speak again. This is hermeneutics: to let what seems

to be far and alienated speak again. But in all the effort to bring the far near . . . we should never forget that the ultimate justification or end is to bring it near so that it speaks in a new voice. Moreover, it should speak not only in a new voice but in a clearer voice." "Practical Philosophy as a Model of the Human Sciences," *Research in Phenomenology* 9 (1979): 83.

20. "Letter to Dallmayr," *Dialogue and Deconstruction*, trans. Diane Michelfelder and Richard Palmer (Albany: SUNY Press, 1989), p. 98.

21 "Letter to Dallmayr," p. 96.

22. In *Gadamer's Hermeneutics: A Reading of "Truth and Method"*, for example, Weinsheimer devotes very little attention to explicating even the most direct passages in *Truth and Method* where Gadamer refers explicitly to Heidegger. One finds this same pattern is Warnke's book as well. See Georgia Warnke, *Gadamer: Hermeneutics, Tradition and Reason* (Stanford: Stanford University Press, 1987). In *Sources of Hermeneutics*, Grondin speaks about the relation between Heidegger and Gadamer, but is more intent on pointing out their difference without attending to the indebtedness as such. The most provocative work on the subject is found in Bernasconi's essay, "Bridging the Abyss: Heidegger and Gadamer," in *Heidegger in Question*.

23. Not only does Gadamer constantly refer to Heidegger in the course of his own writings on philosophical hermeneutics, as we see most obviously in part two of *Truth and Method* and at the outset of the more recent and highly significant essay "Text and Interpretation," but he writes about Heidegger as well. See especially his recently translated volume of essays on the later Heidegger, *Heidegger's Ways*, and the essays on Heidegger ("Heidegger im Rückblick") in his *Gesammelte Werke*, vol. 10.

24. Obviously the latter is more serious. The dismissal of much of the criticism in the former rests on the conviction that it is the wrong reason for criticism. Given what some commentators say one has to wonder if they read beyond part 2 of *Truth and Method*. Here I follow the principle in philosophical hermeneutics that one must let the text speak on its own terms and then be challenged accordingly.

25. See Mark Taylor, *Tears* (Albany: SUNY Press, 1990), pp. 127–44.

26. John D. Caputo, "Beyond Aestheticism: Derrida's Responsible Anarchy," *Research in Phenomenology* 18 (1988): 67.

27. See Caputo, *Radical Hermeneutics* (Bloomington: Indiana University Press, 1987), pp. 108–19.

28. Stated in this context one can understand why tradition is nothing other than language (*logos*) itself for Gadamer.

29. See Gianni Vattimo, *The End of Modernity*, trans. Jon R. Snyder (Baltimore: Johns Hopkins University Press, 1991), pp. 130–44. Vattimo is the Italian translator of *Wahrheit und Methode*.

1. The Philosophical Background of Philosophical Hermeneutics

1. The issue of the influence of Plato and Aristotle on Gadamer's project is taken up in the subsequent chapters where the particular conceptuality in the philosophies of Plato and Aristotle enters into the thematic.

2. Hartmann was a Marburg-trained Neo-Kantian when he succeeded Paul Natorp at Marburg. Hartmann's acknowledgement of phenomenology is found in his *Grundzüge einer Metaphysik der Erkenntnis* (1921) in which phenomenology is to serve as the basis for his metaphysics of knowledge. From 1923 to 1925 Hartmann shared the department in Marburg with Heidegger, but his association with the phenomenological movement was tied more to his contact with Max Scheler. Gadamer reminisces about his association with Hartmann while at Marburg in his *Philosophical Apprenticeships*. See pp. 12–15.

3. The diversity of views in Neo-Kantianism is evident in the Davos lectures in which Ernst Cassirer and Heidegger debated some of the more controversial aspects of Heidegger's Kant interpretation. Heidegger is asked by Cassirer to account for his understanding of Neo-Kantianism since it appears, in Cassirer's eyes, that there is a Neo-Kantianism in Heidegger's reading of Kant. Heidegger responds to Cassirer by saying: "For the present, if I should name names, then I say: Cohen, Windelband, Rickert, Erdmann, Riehl. We can only understand what is common to Neo-Kantianism on the basis of its origin. The genesis [of Neo-Kantianism] lies in the predicament of philosophy concerning the question of what properly remains for it in the whole of knowledge. Since about 1850 it has been the case that both the human and the natural sciences have taken possession of the totality of what is knowable, so that the question arises: what still remains of philosophy of the totality of beings has been divided up under the sciences? It remains just knowledge of science, not of beings. And it is from this perspective that the retrogression to Kant is then determined. Consequently, Kant was seen as a theoretician of the mathematico-physical theory of knowledge. Theory of knowledge is the aspect according to which Kant came to be seen." Heidegger, *Kant and the Problem of Metaphysics*, trans. Richard Taft (Bloomington: Indiana University Press, 1990), pp. 171–72. For a more detailed account of Neo-Kantianism, see Klaus Köhnke, *The*

Rise of Neo-Kantianism, trans. R. J. Hollingdale (Cambridge: Cambridge University Press, 1991).

4. Gadamer's reading of the phenomenological movement and Husserl in particular is found principally in three essays in GW3: "Die phänomenologische Bewegung" (1963), "Die Wissenschaft von der Lebenswelt" (1972), and "Zur Aktualitt der Husserlschen Phänomenologie" (1974). The first two appeared initially in *Kleinen Schriften III* and were translated, along with several essays on Heidegger, for inclusion in part 2 of *Philosophical Hermeneutics*.

5. Heidegger, *History of the Concept of Time: Prolegomena*, trans. Theodore Kisiel (Bloomington: Indiana University Press, 1985). This text comprises the lecture course delivered by Heidegger at Marburg University in the summer semester of 1925. The German edition appeared originally in 1979 as volume 20 of the *Gesamtausgabe*.

6. Theodore Kisiel, "On the Way to Being and Time: Introduction to the Translation of Heidegger's *Prolegomena zur Geschichte des Zeitbegriffs*," *Research in Phenomenology* 15 (1985): 197.

7. *History of the Concept of Time: Prolegomena*, p. 16.

8. Gadamer echoes this sentiment in "The Philosophical Foundations of the Twentieth Century" when he claims that what one finds in Neo-Kantianism a "one-sidedness of scientific methodologism" (PH 115/GW4 10). Gadamer also writes about Neo-Kantianism in *Philosophical Apprenticeships* in the chapter on Paul Natorp, see p. 21ff.

9. *History of the Concept of Time: Prolegomena*, p. 30.

10. This section of *The History of the concept of Time* directly corresponds to section 7 in *Being and Time*.

11. Heidegger, *The Basic Problems of Phenomenology*, trans. Albert Hofstadter (Bloomington: Indiana University Press, 1982), p. 201. This text comprises the lecture course delivered at Marburg University in the summer semester of 1927. The German edition appeared originally in 1975 as volume 24 of the *Gesamtausgabe*. In conversation, Gadamer recalls how at this time Heidegger always wanted to push the *Ideas* to the margins and to renew the approach of the *Logical Investigations*.

12. There may be some hyperbole in Heidegger's remarks on Dilthey for whatever reason. The text is a lecture course and Heidegger clearly wants to emphasize certain differences between thinkers in order to put his own project in proper perspective. When he goes on to say that Dilthey's psychology is not invested with an epistemological task, we should not accept this outside the context of the theme of the lecture course. One gets the

impression here that Dilthey stands halfway between Husserl and Heidegger. Such an impression is not entirely accurate.

13. See "On the Way to Being and Time," p. 196.

14. David Carr writes: "It is not actually in the *Crisis* that the term *Lebenswelt* makes its first appearance in Husserl's vocabulary; in fact, it appears in a manuscript meant as a supplementary text to *Ideas*, volume 2, dated by the Louvain archivists at 1917. It appears there closely related to a term that is familiar to readers of Heidegger and Merleau-Ponty: *naturlicher Weltbegriff*, natural world-concept, and it is linked to the investigations of part 3 of *Ideen II* concerning the construction of the personal, spiritual, or cultural world as opposed to the scientific or natural world. A comparison would reveal that many of the themes and descriptions of *Ideen II* and the *Crisis* are similar on this point, and that Husserl's later writings on the subject were thus able to draw on reflections initiated at a much earlier date. David Carr, "Husserl's Problematic Concept of the Life-World" in *Husserl: Expositions and Appraisals*, ed. Frederick Elliston and Peter McCormick (Notre Dame: University of Notre Dame Press, 1977), p. 203. Compare this to Gadamer's remarks on the origination of the concept in "The Phenomenological Movement" (PH 156/GW3 127).

15. In "The Phenomenological Movement," Gadamer writes: "Above all, it was reflection on the Danish philosopher Kierkegaard, the religious author and critic of speculative idealism in the post-Hegelian epoch, that prompted the philosophical critique of neo-Kantian idealism" (PH 137/GW3 110).

16. See for example Heidegger's "Letter on Humanism" in which he responds to the French reception of his work that at that time was influenced by the philosophy of Sartre.

17. See for example, Gadamer's remarks in "Erinnerungen an Heideggers Anfänge," *Dilthey-Jahrbuch für Philosophie und Geschichte der Geisteswissenschaften* 4 (1986–87): 14.

18. *Philosophical Apprenticeships*, p. 5.

19. See "The Heritage of Hegel," in RAS, p. 44. In *Truth and Method* Gadamer discusses the notion of contemporaneity in connection with aesthetic experience, see TM, p. 127 (GW1 132).

20. Considering the acknowledged influence of Aristotle on Heidegger, it is interesting to note George Stack's comment on Kierkegaard that "the shadow of Aristotle falls upon almost every purely philosophical page Kierkegaard wrote." *On Kierkegaard: Philosophical Fragments* (Atlantic Highlands, NJ: Humanities Press, 1976), p. 103.

21. John D. Caputo, "Hermeneutics as the Recovery of Man," *Man and World* 15 (1982): 343. Calvin Schrag has also made this point. In *Existence and Freedom: Towards an Ontology of Human Finitude* (Evanston: Northwestern University Press, 1961), Schrag demonstrates how Heidegger's effort at a fundamental ontology is an ontologization of Kierkegaard's notion of repetition. In his more recent work, which takes account of Gadamerian hermeneutics, he continues to stress the importance of the notion of repetition for an understanding of hermeneutics. See *Communication Praxis and the Space of Subjectivity* (Bloomington: Indiana University Press, 1986).

22. The radicality of Heidegger's hermeneutic "method" is evident by the fact that Heidegger subjects his own analysis to a repetition. The repetition of the preparatory analysis of Dasein discloses the Being of Dasein as repetition. See *Radical Hermeneutics*, p. 82ff.

23. Mark Taylor, *Journeys to Selfhood, Hegel and Kierkegaard* (Berkeley: University of California Press, 1980), p. 100.

24. This edition contains a supplement with selected entries from Kierkegaard's *Papers* pertaining to *Repetition*.

25. In the *Papers* pertaining to *Repetition*, Kierkegaard writes: "That repetition not only is for contemplation but that it is a task for freedom, that it is a task for freedom, that it signifies freedom itself, consciousness raised to the second power" (R 324).

26. It is interesting to see how Kierkegaard goes on to characterize this dynamic of selfhood in freedom. The issue appears to be how one can become a self amidst it constant dispersal—a view that Heidegger places at the center of his hermeneutics of facticity: "In the individual, then, repetition appears as a task for freedom, in which the question becomes that of saving one's personality from being volatilized and, so to speak, a pawn of events. The moment it is apparent the individual can lose himself in events, fate, lose himself in such a way that freedom is taken completely in life's fractions without leaving a remainder behind, then the issue becomes manifest, not to contemplation's aristocratic indolence, but to freedom's concerned passion" (R 315).

27. This issue of making real is tied to the character of truth for Kierkegaard; it is also a way of speaking about truth in philosophical hermeneutics in a way that allows for a distinction between Gadamer and Heidegger on the question of truth. See chapter 5, "Philosophical Hermeneutics and Truth."

28. In "The Heritage of Hegel," Gadamer writes: "In relation to the Aristotlelian theory of *phronesis*, of practical rationality, I had begun to

learn how to clarify conceptually the pathos of *Existenzphilosophie* typical of the reception accorded Kierkegaard at the time. What Kierkegaard has taught us and what we then called "existential" (*existenziell*) (decades before "existentialism" was formulated in France), found its prototype in the unity of *ethos* and *logos* that Aristotle had thematized as practical philosophy, and especially as the virtue of practical rationality" (RAS 47–48). A more detailed analysis of this parallel is found in George Stack, *Kierkegaard's Existential Ethics* (University, AL: University of Alabama Press, 1977). Stack argues that Heidegger's *Being and Time* completely appropriates Kierkegaard's existential category of repetition, and is somewhat miffed by the fact that there is little explicit reference to Kierkegaard by Heidegger.

29. Aristotle, *Nicomachean Ethics*, trans. H. Rackham, Loeb Classical Library (Cambridge, MA: Harvard University Press, 1962), 110a29–34.

30. In noting this difference it would seem that Aristotle's use of repetition comes closer than Kierkegaard's to repetition as it is used by Heidegger and Gadamer. Habit suggests that repetition occurs in the circularity of the "always already."

31. *Existence and Freedom*. p. 138.

32. The allusion to the unhappy consciousness in Hegel's *Phenomenology of Spirit* is intentional. See G. W. F. Hegel, *Phenomenology of Spirit*, trans. A. V. Miller (Oxford: Clarendon Press, 1977), pp. 126–38.

33. Kierkegaard, *Concluding Unscientific Postscript*, trans. David Swenson and Walter Lowrie (Princeton: Princeton University Press, 1941), p. 182.

34. In *Radical Hermeneutics*, Caputo develops this same analysis of repetition from Kierkegaard in order to align Kierkegaard with the project of deconstruction against Gadamer. "Kierkegaardian repetition, like Derrida's, is productive. It does not limp along after, trying to reproduce what is already present, but is productive of what it is repeating." *Radical Hermeneutics* pp. 29–30. Caputo regards Gadamer's hermeneutics as a reactionary gesture, turning hermeneutics back into the fold of metaphysics. It is my contention that Gadamer's hermeneutics is also a philosophy of repetition that functions in the same way as Caputo attributes to Derrida. See chapter 4, "Philosophical Hermeneutics and Finitude."

35. This point is clearly made by Gadamer in *Truth and Method* and has been emphasized by a number of commentators; see for example Theodore Kisiel, "Repetition in Gadamer's Hermeneutics" in *Analecta Husserliana*, vol. II, ed. Tymiemiecka (Dordrecht: Reidel Publishing, 1972).

36. In effect Heidegger's "hermeneutics of facticity" designates the period from 1919 to 1923 when Heidegger was first at Freiburg. The lectures

courses from this time appear as volumes 56 through 63 of his *Gesamtausgabe*. The most significant here are volume 61: *Phänomenologische Interpretationen zu Aristoteles: Einführung in die phänomenologische Forschung* (Frankfurt: Klostermann, 1985), a lecture course from the winter semester 1921/22; and volume 63: *Ontologie: Hermeneutik der Faktizität* (Frankfurt: Klostermann, 1988), a lecture course from the summer semester 1923.

37. Gadamer goes so far to claim that, relative to the thematic in volume 61 of the Gesamtausgabe, *Phänomenologische Interpretationen zu Aristoteles: Einführung in die phänomenologische Forschung*, namely, "Leben = Dasein, in und durch Leben 'Sein' [Life = Dasein: in and through life, 'being']," we have before us the unity of Heidegger's entire path of thought. See "Der eine Weg Martin Heideggers," GW3, p. 422.

38. In the preface to the 1923 course "Ontology: Hermeneutics of Facticity," Heidegger writes: "Companions in my searching were the young Luther and the example of Aristotle. Kierkegaard gave me impulses and Husserl gave me my eyes." *Ontologie: Hermeneutik der Faktizität*, p. 5.

39. Heidegger, *Frühe Schriften* (Frankfurt: Klostermann, 1972), p. 260.

40. *Ontologie: Hermeneutik der Faktizität*, p. 7.

41. Otto Poggler along with Gadamer want to emphasize the point of contact between Heidegger and Kierkegaard, rather than Heidegger and Dilthey, for an understanding of a hermeneutics of facticity. According to Poggler, Heidegger "wanted to derive the method, that is, a binding logic, of philosophy directly from Kierkegaard. Coming out of Kierkegaard, Heidegger took a critical stance toward Dilthey. . . . Dilthey regarded life externally and in terms of states, that is, imagistically and aesthetically." Otto Poggler, "Destruction and Moment," trans. Daniel Magurshak in *Reading Heidegger from the Start: Essays in His Earliest Thought* (Albany: SUNY Press, 1994), p. 141.

42. See "Phenomenological Interpretation with Respect to Aristotle: Indication of the Hermeneutical Situation," p. 368.

43. "Phenomenological Interpretation with Respect to Aristotle: Indication of the Hermeneutical Situation," p. 361.

44. In his essay "Heidegger and Marburg Theology," Gadamer writes: [In Marburg] Heidegger was dealing with a scholastic distinction and spoke of the difference between *actus signatus* and *actus exercitus*. These scholastic concepts correspond approximately to the concepts of "reflective" and "direct" and mean, for instance, the difference between the act of questioning and the possibility of directing attention explicitly to the questioning as

questioning. The one can lead over into the other. One can designate the questioning as questioning, and hence not only question but also say that one questions, and say that such and such is questionable. To nullify this transition from the immediate and direct into the reflective intention seemed to us at that time to be a way to freedom. It promised a liberation from the unbreakable circle of reflection and a recapturing of the evocative power of conceptual thinking and philosophical language, which would secure for philosophical thinking a rank alongside poetic use of language" (PH 202/GW3 200–201).

45. See Heidegger, *Phänomenologische Interpretationen zu Aristoteles: Einführung in die phänomenologische Forschung*, pp. 18–19. With respect to this sense of "having" we witness again Heidegger's genius of interrogating "simple" words. From very early on, what Heidegger seizes upon in Aristotle is the coinage of οὐσία, which he refuses to let slip into a simple philosophical conceptuality. In breaking its conceptuality, Heidegger is able to hear in this word its original practical sense of having or holding (*Haben*). For a discussion of this and for an extensive treatment of Heidegger's work during the 1920s see Theodore Kisiel, *The Genesis of Heidegger's "Being and Time"* (Berkeley: University of California Press, 1993).

46. The text of this course has not yet appeared. There is a close paraphrase of this text in *The Genesis of Heidegger's "Being and Time"*, pp. 238–48. Heidegger also provides a reading of the *Metaphysics* in the lecture course from the winter semester 1924–25. See *Platon: Sophistes, Gesamtausgabe*, vol. 19 (Frankfurt: Klostermann, 1992), p. 65ff.

47. *The Genesis of Heidegger's "Being and Time"*, p. 239.

48. Aristotle, *Metaphysics*, trans. Hugh Tredennick, Loeb Classical Library (Cambridge, MA: Harvard University Press, 1936), 982b24.

49. *The Genesis of Heidegger's "Being and Time"*, p. 242.

50. In the "Aristotle Introduction" Heidegger writes: "The movement of care [which describes the basic sense of the movement of factical life] is not an *occurrence* of life which transpires for itself, over against the existing world. The world is there in life and for life, but not in the sense of merely Being-intended and Being-observed. How the world is there, its Dasein, gets temporalized only when factical life takes-a-pause within its concerned movement of dealings. This Dasein of the world is what it is only as have grown from a particular taking-a-pause." "Phenomenological Interpretations with Respect to Aristotle: Indication of the Hermeneutic situation," p. 363.

51. *The Genesis of Heidegger's "Being and Time"*, p. 243.

52. See *Phänomenologische Interpretationen zu Aristoteles: Einführung in die phänomenologische Forschung*, p. 80. The passage from Rickert is taken from his *Die Philosophie des Lebens* (1920), p. 194.

53. *Phänomenologische Interpretationen zu Aristoteles: Einführung in die phänomenologische Forschung*, p. 80.

54. See ibid., p. 90: "Serving objectivity is an insecure flight from facticity."

55. See Heidegger, SZ, p. 38: "Philosophy is universal phenomenological ontology, and takes its departure from the hermeneutic of Dasein, which as an analytic of *existence*, has made fast the guiding-line for all philosophical inquiry at the point where it *arises* and to which it returns."

56. Betti for example considers understanding to be a product of objective interpretation. See his *Die Hermeneutik als allgemeine Methode der Geisteswissenschaften* (Tübingen: J.C.B. Mohr: 1962).

57. In the context of Heidegger's discussion of historical existence, I have followed Macquarrie and Robinson's translation of *Geschehen* as "historizing." One could have easily substituted for this "happening," "event," or "occurrence." *Geschehen*, as we have already indicated, is a central term in Gadamer's hermeneutics and has been consistently rendered as "event."

2. History and the Voice of Tradition

1. This issue of the difference between integration and reconstruction in terms of which the question of historical understanding is to be decided, is prepared for by remarks that Gadamer makes at the end of part 1 of *Truth and Method*, see TM, pp. 164–69 (GW1 169–74).

2. Friedrich Schleiermacher, *Hermeneutics: The Handwritten Manuscripts*, ed. Heinz Kimmerle, trans. James Duke and Jack Forstman (Missoula: Scholars Press, 1977), p. 112.

3. Dilthey writes: "[In its subject matter] History is life. And history consists of life of all kinds in the most varying relationships. History is only life interpreted from the point of view of the continuity of mankind as a whole." Wilhelm Dilthey, *Gesammelte Schriften*, VII (Göttingen: Vanderhoeck & Ruprecht, 1927), p. 256. In the dedication to his *Introduction to the Human Sciences* Dilthey refers to his book as a "critique of historical reason."

4. Gadamer suggests that the intention of complementing a critique of pure reason with a critique of historical reason is set up as an analogy.

The *Critique of Pure Reason*, while destroying metaphysics as a purely rational science of the world, at the same time establishes the field in which knowledge (i.e., a science of experience) is possible. In the recognition of the incommensurability of thought and being, a critique of historical reason destroys an apriori philosophy of history and limits historical knowledge to experience. Thus, in the *spirit* of the Kantian project, Dilthey is asking how historical experience can become a science. See TM, p. 221 (GW1 225).

5. In point of fact Dilthey does not stand half-way between the historical school and the Hegelians. He himself is considered part of the historical school. The upshot of the remarks that follow is to show the way in which he is an interpreter of the historical school, formulating what Ranke and Droysen really think. In addition to Gadamer's retracing of this history in TM, see for example Michael Ermarth, *Wilhelm Dilthey: The Critique of Historical Reason* (Chicago: University of Chicago Press, 1978), p. 52ff.; and, Herbert Schnädelbach, *Philosophy in Germany 1831–1933* (Cambridge: Cambridge University Press, 1984), p. 33ff.

6. The notion that history is not a science because it deals with the particular can be found in Aristotle. See Aristotle, *Poetics*, trans. W. Hamilton Fyfe, Loeb Classical Library (Cambridge, MA: Harvard University Press, 1973), 1451a36.

7. Dilthey repeats the general sense of this claim at several places, See for example *Gesammelte Schriften*, VIII (Göttingen: Vanderhoeck & Ruprecht, 1960), p. 276.

8. In *Ideas about a Descriptive and Analytical Psychology*, written in 1894, Dilthey writes: The human studies [*Geisteswissenschaften*] differ from the [natural] sciences because the latter deal with facts which present themselves to consciousness as external and separate phenomena, while the former deal with the living connections of reality experienced in the mind. It follows that the [natural] sciences arrive at connections within nature through inferences by means of a combination of hypotheses while the human sciences are based on directly given mental connections. We explain nature but we understand mental life." Dilthey, *Selected Writings*, ed. and trans. H. P. Rickman (Cambridge: Cambridge University Press, 1976), p. 89. See *Gesammelte Schriften*, V (Göttingen: Vanderhoeck & Ruprecht, 1924), p. 144.

9. In the writings after 1900, Dilthey's hermeneutics is developed to the point where it not only shifts but presupposes a re-evaluation of his earlier hermeneutic "psychology." In 1883, Dilthey first published his

Introduction to the Human Studies in which he lays out the problem that occupied him throughout his life—laying a foundation for the human studies. With the appearance in 1894 of *Descriptive Psychology and Historical Understanding*, he develops further the concept of *Erlebnis* which he takes to be the starting point and foundation for human (i.e., psychic) life. In contrast to this, one can look to one of his last theoretical writings "The Understanding of Other Persons" (1910) in which the expressions of life are inclusive of all products of human activity and for which Dilthey adopts the term "objective spirit." This is not to suggest that Dilthey renounces his psychology for a mature hermeneutics. See Rudolf Makkreel's introduction in Wilhelm Dilthey, *Descriptive Psychology and Historical Understanding*, trans. Richard Zaner and Kenneth Heiges (The Hague: Martinus Nijhoff, 1977).

10. Dilthey writes: "In seeking here to build forth my foundation to a realistic or critical-objective theory of knowledge, I must once again and for all indicate *in toto* how much I owe to the *Logical Investigations* (1900–1901) of Husserl, which are epoch-making in their application of description to epistemology" (*Gesammelte Schriften*, VII, p. 10). An excellent discussion of Dilthey's relationship to Husserl is found in Michael Ermarth, *Wilhelm Dilthey: The Critique of Historical Reason*, pp. 197–208.

11. *Selected Writings*, p. 221.

12. The problem of historicism identifies in general the crisis of historical research in the nineteenth century. It refers to the position that, because all cultural phenomena are historically conditioned, all claims to absolute validity must be rejected. It is a problem as such because there are no normative considerations for knowing; that is, in a scientific age, relativism (of history) should be overcome. The term "historicism," though, has several senses. It is also used in a broader context to refer in general to the position that makes history into a principle, that all cultural phenomena are to be understood, not as natural, but as historical. Historicism, in other words, is associated with the view that human life is not nature per se, but the product of human action which is historical.

13. *Gesammelte Schriften*, VIII, pp. 290–291, quoted in H. A. Hodges, *Wilhelm Dilthey: An Introduction* (New York: Howard Fertig, 1969), pp. 33–34.

14. *Gesammelte Schriften*, VII, p. 6.

15. Gadamer here follows a point of criticism made by Georg Misch, a student of Dilthey. In a footnote, Gadamer tells us: "Misch distinguishes between becoming concious and making conscious. Philosophical refection

may be both at once. But Dilthey, he says, wrongly seeks an unbroken transition from the one to the other. 'The esentially *theoretical* orientation towards objectivity cannot be derived solely from the idea of the objectification of life' (p. 298). The present work gives this criticism by Misch another facet, in that it reveals in romantic hermeneutics the Cartesianism that makes Dilthey's thought here ambiguous" (TM 239/GW1 242).

16. *Selected Writings*, p. 226.

17. Gadamer is often criticized by proponents of Dilthey's philosophy that he erroneously attributes to Dilthey the view that understanding remains a methodological issue. See for example Thomas Seebohm, "Boeckh and Dilthey: The Development of Methodical Hermeneutics," *Man and World* 17 (1984): 327. To be precise, Gadamer does indeed recognize Dilthey's "radicality" in which life is to unfold from itself, an unfolding accomplished by understanding the expressions of life. The issue for Gadamer is not the issue of method per se, but the tension in Dilthey whereby, in articulating the movement of life, he also wants to articulate life in a way that moves back from its movement.

18. Although philological interpretation is considered by Heidegger a derivative mode of interpretation, it remains, in Ricoeur's words, "the touchstone." According to Ricoeur: "It is there that we can perceive the necessity of drawing back from the vicious circle in which philological interpretation turns, insofar as it understands itself in terms of a model of scientificity borrowed form the exact sciences, to the non-vicious circle formed by the anticipatory structure of the very being which we are." Paul Ricoeur, *Hermeneutics and the Human Sciences*, ed. and trans. John B. Thompson (Cambridge: Cambridge University Press, 1981), p. 70.

19. Gadamer presents his analysis of the hermeneutic circle as if there is no substantial difference between what he is saying and Heidegger's own description of it. In *Seeing and Reading*, Graeme Nicholson suggests that there is a fundamental difference in the two accounts of the hermeneutic circle. In Heidegger's account, the hermeneutic circle gives primacy to *Verstehen*, projection, over *Auslegung*, interpretation. But, according to Nicholson, when Gadamer speaks of the fore-structure of understanding "what he has in mind is not the point that every interpretation is constituted by a sense first projected by me, but rather that all my projections are intially constituted behind my back by the historical process of which my life is a part." Graeme Nicholson, *Seeing and Reading* (Atlantic Highlands, NJ: Humanities Press, 1984), p. 202.

20. The centrality of *phronesis* in Gadamer's thinking has been well documented. See the discussion of this in chapter 3, "Hermeneutic Experience."

21. This is the claim of John Caputo in *Radical Hermeneutics*. According to Caputo: "[Gadamer] describes the continuity of the tradition, but he leaves unasked the question of whether the tradition is all that unified to begin with. He never asks to what extent the play of tradition is a power play and its unity something that has been enforced by the powers that be. His 'tradition' in innocent of Nietzsche's suspicious eye, of Foucaultian genealogy. He does not face the question of the ruptures within tradition, its vulnerability to difference, its capacity to oppress." *Radical hermeneutics*, p. 112.

22. This is the claim of Terry Eagleton in *Literary Theory*. Although Eagleton does not devote himself to an extensive treatment of Gadamer's analysis, it deserves mentioning here because, in my mind, it is the most extreme misreading of Gadamer's position imaginable, and needs to be identified as such so that it cannot be taken seriously by anyone who would care to read Gadamer's text. The issue for Gadamer is not that we should "surrender to the winds of history because these scattered leaves will always in the end come home—and they will do so because beneath all history, silently spanning past, present, and future, runs a unifying essence known as 'tradition.'" Terry Eagleton, *Literary Theory: An Introduction* (Minneapolis: University of Minnesota Press, 1983), p. 72. For Gadamer tradition is not an essence, and certainly there is no necessity to its "coming home"; that is, Gadamer does not claim that the failure of communication (the speaking of tradition) cannot be tolerated. The question for Gadamer is to identify the conditions under which tradition *can* speak. In this connection Eagleton also reads the submission to tradition literally, and in this he is simply wrong.

23. The complete passage says: "It seems very misleading to me for someone to say that just because I emphasize the role of tradition in all our posing of questions and also in the indication of answers, I am asserting a super-subject and this (as Manfred Frank and Philippe Forget go on to maintain) reducing hermeneutical experience to an empty word [*parole vide*]. There is no support in *Truth and Method* for this kind of construction. When I speak there of tradition and of conversation with tradition, I am in no way putting forward a collective subject" (DD 111/GW2 370).

24. Here I am following Ricoeur's analysis in *Time and Narrative*. See Paul Ricoeur, *Time and Narrative*, vol. 3, trans. Kathleen Blamey and David Pellauer (Chicago: University of Chicago Press, 1988), p. 216ff.

25. *Time and Narrative*, vol. 3, p. 220.

26. *Time and Narrative*, vol. 3, p. 221.

27. At several places Gadamer speaks about there never being a first word. See for example "Mensch und Sprache," GW2, p. 149. This point will be developed later. See chapter 6, "The Voice of the Text."

28. The origin of the Gadamer-Habermas debate is found here. When Gadamer connects prejudice, authority, and tradition in this way Habermas claimed that Gadamer denied the power of critique found in reflection, and consequently the authority of tradition can never by truly emancipatory. The long history of that debate cannot be recounted here. Habermas's criticism appeared initially in *Zur Logik der Sozialwissenschaft* (Tübingen: J. C. B. Mohr, 1967). Gadamer's response "*Rhetorik, Hermeneutik und Ideologiekritik*" appeared initially in *Kleine Schriften*, vol. I (GW2 232–50). A second response then appeared as "*Replik*" in *Hermeneutik und Ideologiekritik* (Frankfurt: Suhrkamp, 1971) (GW2 251–75). Ricoeur provides an excellent commentary on this debate initially in "Ethics and Culture: Habermas and Gadamer in Dialogue," *Philosophy Today* 17 (1973): 153–65; and more recently, in *Time and Narrative*, vol. 3. Discussions by others can be found in several of the essays in *Critical and Dialectical Phenomenology*, ed. Donn Welton and Hugh Silverman (Albany: SUNY Press, 1987).

29. See TM, p. 374 (GW1 379).

30. I am in complete agreement with Gerry Bruns in his reading of Gadamer's position on this point. Bruns insists that for Gadamer tradition is not to be thought of as the master narrative that wants to integrate the other into the edifice of the same. According to Bruns: Self-identity "can only be preserved by sealing the subject off from the horizon of tradition, and this means the repression of what cannot be contained within its self-definition. Self-possession cannot survive the encounter with what comes down to us from the past. In this encounter the subject discovers itself as 'only something laid over a continuing tradition'; it is not just itself but also that which it finds strange and unintelligible in its own terms." Gerald Bruns, *Hermeneutics Ancient and Modern* (New Haven: Yale University Press, 1992), p. 209.

31. Gadamer's use of "preservation" (*Bewahrung*) can be understood in a way similar to Heidegger's discussion of the preservation of a work of art. For Heidegger, preserving (*Bewahren*) a work does not mean to place it in a museum, but rather to let the work be the work that it is, to let the work stand with the openness of Being. Preservation lets the work remain independent by not dragging it into the sphere of mere experience, but brings

one to the truth that comes-to-pass in the work. Heidegger, "Der Ursprung des Kunstwerkes," *Holzwege* (Frankfurt: Klostermann, 1972), pp. 55–56. English translation by Albert Hofstadter, "The Origin of the Work of Art," *Poetry, Language, Thought* (New York: Harper & Row, 1971), p. 68.

32. A complete account of Gadamer's position here requires not only an account of experience, but also an account of language, where the notion of hearing the voice of the other is most pronounced. The issue here must always remain attached to the problematic of historical understanding in Dilthey in which case, the holding open pertains to the way in which historical consciousness moves in history without forgetting (as Dilthey does) its fundamental historicity.

33. Gadamer, "Philosophy and Literature," trans. Anthony J. Steinbock, *Man and World* 18 (1985): 253 (GW8 253).

34. Ricoeur argues that the tension between alienating distanciation (*Verfremdung*) and belongingness (*Zugehörigkeit*) is the "core experience around which the whole of Gadamer's work is organized." See "The Task of Hermeneutics" in *Hermeneutics and the Human Sciences* (Cambridge: Cambridge University Press, 1981), p. 60.

35. In his "Reflections on My Philosophical Journey," where he looks back on the work of *Truth and Method*, Gadamer states that the analysis of temporal distance was a poor preparation for the later discussion of the significance of the otherness of the other and for the fundamental role played by language in conversation. If he were to rewrite this text, he would state the matter in a more general way to indicate that interpretive distance does not always have to be temporal distance. He writes: "even in simultaneity, distance can function as an important hermeneutical element; for example, in the encounter between persons who try to find a common ground in conversation, and also in the encounter with persons who speak an alien language or live in an alien culture. Every encounter of this kind allows us to become conscious of our own preconceptions in matters which seemed so self-evident to oneself that one could not even notice one's naive process of assuming that other person's conception was the same as one's own, which generated misunderstanding." The quotation is from a privately circulated copy of this essay that will appear in *Hans-Georg Gadamer*, Library of Living Philosophers. Gadamer does in fact re-write his text in a minor way on this issue. In the edition of *Truth and Method* prepared for the *Gesammelte Werke*, Gadamer added a footnote following the phrase "Often temporal distance . . ." in which he states: "I have here softened the original text ("it is only temporal distance that can solve . . ."): it is

distance, not only temporal distance, that makes the hermeneutic problem solvable. See also GW, II, 64" (TM 298/GW1 304).

36. This notion of risk and exposure to the other runs throughout Gadamer's writings. In "Hermeneutics as Practical Philosophy" for example, Gadamer says that "understanding, like action, always remains a risk and never leaves room for the simply application of a general knowledge of rules to the statements or texts to be understood" (RAS 109).

37. The term *"Wirkungsgeschichte Bewußtsein"* has been translated in a number of different ways by Gadamer's commentators: "the consciousness of standing within a still operant history" (Hoy), "historically operative consciousness" (Kisiel), "authentically historical consciousness" (Palmer), "the consciousness of the past which changes us" (Rorty). Although it is difficult to translate, its meaning can be made clear in the context of the discussion of the term.

38. I have modified the English translation of this essay, "Die Kontinuität der Geschichte und der Augenblick der Existenz," which appears as "The Continuity of History and the Existential Moment," trans. Thomas Wren, *Philosophy Today* 16 (1972): 230–40.

39. Although Hegel is a decisive figure for Gadamer, there is no mediation in hermeneutic experience as Hegel understands this term. One always has to account for the Kierkegaardian element in Gadamer's thought when one makes comparisons between Gadamer and Hegel. This issue is discussed further in chapter 4, "Philosophical Hermeneutics and Finitude."

3. Hermeneutic Experience

1. How Simmel figures in the development of a hermeneutics of facticity is yet to be seen. Gadamer reports in a footnote that as early as 1923 "Heidegger spoke to me with admiration of the later writings of Georg Simmel" where he calls the "transcendence of life the true absolute" (TM 242n138/GW1 247).

2. Heidegger speaks of experience in the same way, at least when he is not speaking about "aesthetic experience." In "The Nature of Language" Heidegger writes: "To undergo an experience [*Erfahrung*] with something—be it a thing, a person, or a god—means that this something befalls us, strikes us, comes over us, overwhelms us and transforms us. When we talk of 'undergoing' an experience, we mean specifically that the experience is not of our own making; to undergo here means that we endure it, suffer it, receive it as it strike us and submit to it. It is this

something itself that comes about, comes to pass, happens." "Das Wesen der Sprache," in *Unterwegs zur Sprache*, p. 149. English translation from original edition, *On the Way to Language*, trans. Peter Herz (New York: Harper & Row, 1971), p. 57.

3. Aristotle, *Posterior Analytics*, Loeb Classical Library, trans. Hugh Tredennick (Cambridge, MA: Harvard University Press, 1976), 100a15–b4. Translation modified. This passage is only referred to in *Truth in Method* (TM 350/GW1 356). The omission of the passage of the text from Aristotle needlessly obscures the point Gadamer is trying to make.

4. "Thus sense-perception gives rise to memory [μνήμη], as we hold; and repeated memories of the same thing give rise to experience; because the memories, though numerically many, constitute a single experience." *Posterior Analytics*, 100a4–5.

5. See *Posterior Analytics*, 100a13–14.

6. The idea of surprise is unquestionably a philosophical virtue for Gadamer, and is really the mark against which any reading of Gadamer that wants to cast philosophical hermeneutics as a conserving doctrine must be judged. It is interesting to note that the pragmatists who also see their work as a re-expression of the fundamental nature of experience, equally emphasize the idea of surprise. I am thinking here principally of the work of James, Pierce and would also want to include the work of the process philosopher Whitehead. William James, for example, writes: "According to my view experience as a whole is a process in time, whereby innumerable particular terms lapse and are superseded by others that follow upon them by transitions which, whether *disjunctive* or conjunctive in content, are themselves experiences [emphasis added]." *Essays in Radical Empiricism* (New York: Longmans, Green, 1942), p. 62. The point is that experience in all its flux as a process of becoming necessarily entails novelty.

7. Hegel, *Phänomenologie des Geistes, Werke* 3 (Frankfurt: Suhrkamp, 1986), p. 78. *The Phenomenology of Spirit*, p. 55.

8. *Phänomenologie des Geistes*, p. 73. *The Phenomenology of Spirit*, p. 49.

9. Gadamer is here affirming a point made by Heidegger. See Heidegger, *Hegel's Concept of Experience* (New York: Harper & Row, 1970). The text was originally published under the title *"Hegels Begriff der Erfahrung,"* in *Holzwege* (Frankfurt: Vittorio Klostermann, 1950). This text is analyzed briefly by Robert Bernasconi in *The Question of Language in Heidegger's History of Being* (Atlantic Highlands, NJ: Humanities Press, 1985), pp. 81–90.

10. The title of the *Phenomenology* was originally "The Science of the Experience of Consciousness." See *Hegel's Concept of Experience*, p. 141. Despite Gadamer's reservation towards Hegel's overall position, the importance of Hegel for Gadamer's project cannot be emphasized enough. See his own comments on his proximity to Hegel in *Reason in the Age of Science*. In this context of the analysis of experience, the positive affinity between Gadamer and Hegel is more apparent. That is to say, the question of Gadamer's relation to Hegel should not be considered mainly in terms of a dialectic of spirit in which Gadamer simply recoils from the telos of dialectics in absolute knowing. This is of course the case, but equally if not more important is the fact that Gadamer sees in Hegel a philosophy that is able to critique the metaphysics of subjectivity that characterizes modern philosophy. This entails a critique not only of the assumptions about the constitution of the subject relative to its relationship to the world and others, but also of the assumptions regarding the securing of the access to the world by a subject through methodological research. This critique of method by Hegel is well known, especially regarding the project of Kant. A science of the experience of consciousness demonstrates, what Gadamer has always claimed, by virtue of the hermeneutics of facticity, that knowing does not take place outside of the process of life which it (the knowing) reflects. Reason for Hegel is not an instrument of knowledge divorced from its content. In effect, Hegel's criticism of the transcendental framework of Kantian philosophy is played out all over again in the critique of Neo-Kantianism by Heidegger with his hermeneutics of facticity.

11. It is in this sense that Gadamer's project can be read as a Hegelianism that wants to say the honor of the "bad infinity" (*schlechten Unendlichkeit*). Gadamer himself says as much: "In order to determine at first the place of my own attempts at thinking, I could in fact say that I took it upon myself to save the honor of 'bad infinity'. Of course in my eyes I made a decisive modification. For the unending dialogue of the soul with itself, which is thinking, is not to be characterized as an endlessly continuing determination of a world of objects waiting to be recognized" (GW2 505). Although one cannot deny this proximity to Hegel, we err in making too much of it; see note above. One cannot adequately account for the ontology of philosophical hermeneutics on the basis of a dialectic of finitude alone. See chapter 4, "Philosophical Hermeneutics and Finitude."

12. John Caputo, who interestingly enough has come to be one of Gadamer's harshest critics, wants to make this same point, in a somewhat different context, in *Radical Hermeneutics*. A hermeneutics of facticity,

which serves as the point of departure for a "radical hermeneutics," is "convinced that life is toil and trouble" and "would keep a watchful eye for the ruptures and the breaks and the irregularities in existence." This notion becomes the watchword for *Radical Hermeneutics*: hermeneutics must stick with "the original difficulty of life" and not betray it with metaphysics. How Caputo is able to misread Gadamer's project is discussed in chapter 4, "Philosophical Hermeneutics and Finitude."

13. Gerry Bruns develops the sense of the motto of Aeschylus in connection with Gadamer's hermeneutics in *Hermeneutics: Ancient and Modern*. Bruns argues that the question of tragedy with Oedipus is not about self-knowledge; Oedipus's problem is that self-knowledge is never enough, that is, his "self-understanding cannot contain the other that his fate inscribes." Thus according to Bruns: "The story of Oedipus is about the implacable reality of this otherness, its inescapability as Fate. Fate is not just the inevitability of events; it is the otherness of identity, or reality, that which we seek to avoid but meet willy-nilly at the crossroads." Bruns claims that hermeneutic experience is principally about this event of exposure that belongs to tragedy. If experience teaches us to acknowledge the real, as Gadamer says, Bruns would add to this, as an interpretation of Gadamer's insight, that "what is recognized is reality as other, not as the same: reality as that which is more Fate than Fact." *Hermeneutics: Ancient and Modern*, p. 185ff.

14. The issue of dogmatism is also what is in play for Hegel in the very idea of "skepticism in action." Skepticism in action is of itself that preservation against dogmatism.

15. This point is made by Kathleen Wright in "Gadamer: The Speculative Structure of Language." Actually, Wright argues that Gadamer has both Heidegger and Hegel in mind. Gadamer turns explicitly to Hegel, according to Wright, because of the insufficiency in Heidegger's account of being-with in section 26 of *Being and Time*. The insufficiency is that even in Heidegger's second description of being-with, the being-with that gives's back to the other his or her freedom for the first time, there is no true reciprocity. See *Hermeneutics and Modern Philosophy*, ed. Brice Wachterhauser (New York: SUNY Press, 1986), pp. 195–204.

16. This is Derrida's formulation of Heidegger's hermeneutic circle. See Jacques Derrida, "The Ends of Man," in *Margins of Philosophy*, trans. Alan Bass (Chicago: University of Chicago Press, 1982), p. 126. What we will see is that this description by Derrida does not accurately describe the knowing in hermeneutic experience.

17. Recall from Aristotle's analysis of experience that he had noted that the unity of experience is affected by memory. See note 4 above.

18. Nietzsche writes: "All acting requires forgetting, as not only light but also darkness is required for life by all organisms. A man who wanted to feel everything historically would resemble someone forced to refrain from sleeping, or an animal expected to live only from ruminating and ever repeated ruminating. So: it is possible to live with almost no memories, even to live happily as the animal shows; but without forgetting it is quite impossible to live at all." *Unzeitgemässe Betrachtungen, Sämtliche Werke. Kritische Studienausgabe*, vol. 1 (Munich: de Gruyter, 1980), p. 250. English translation, *On the Advantage and Disadvantage of History for Life*, trans. Peter Preuss (Indianapolis: Hackett Publishing, 1980), p. 10.

19. Nietzsche, *Zur Genealogie der Moral*, Kritische Studienausgabe, vol. 5, pp. 291–92. English translation, *On the Genealogy of Morals*, trans. Walter Kaufmann & R. J. Hollingdale (New York: Random House, 1969), pp. 57–58.

20. *Kant and the Problem of Metaphysics*, p. 159.

21. *Kant and the Problem of Metaphysics*, p. 159. In *Being and Time* remembering again (*Wiedererinnerung*) is the retrieval (*Wiederholung*) of Dasein's possibilities for its authentic futurity.

22. In his 1942–43 lecture course "Parmenides," Heidegger draws the distinction between forgetfulness (*Vergeßlichkeit*) and oblivion (*Vergessenheit*): "In general we conceive forgetting in terms of the behavior of a 'subject', as a not-retaining, and we then speak of 'forgetfulness' as that by which something 'escapes' us, when, because of one thing, we forget another. Here forgetfulness is poor attention. In addition, there is the forgetting explained as a consequence of 'memory-disturbances'. Psychopathology calls this 'amnesia'. But the word 'forgetfulness' is too weak to name the forgetting that can befall man; for forgetfulness is only the inclination toward distraction. If it happens that we forget what is essential and do not pay heed to it, lose it and strike it from our minds, then we may no longer speak of 'forgetfulness' but of 'oblivion'." *Parmenides*, trans. André Schuwer and Richard Rojcewicz (Bloomington: Indiana University Press, 1992), p. 71–72.

23. The etymology of ἀ-λήθεια pertains not only to that which is not hidden but to that which is not forgotten. See Paul Friedlander, *Plato: An Introduction*, trans. Hans Meyerhoff (Princeton: Princeton University Press, 1973), p. 222. Heidegger is most explicit about this matter in the essay "Aletheia (Heraclitus, Fragment B 16)." See *Early Greek Thinking*, trans.

David Krell and Frank Capuzzi (New York: Harper & Row, 1975). The essay was published originally in *Vorträge und Aufsätze*. (Pfullingen: Günther Neske, 1954).

24. "Preface by Martin Heidegger," in William Richardson, *Heidegger: Through Phenomenology to Thought* (The Hague: Martinus Nijhoff, 1967), p. xii.

25. The English translation fails to show the interconnectedness of these words as they appear in the German. "Thought" (*Gedachtes*) is in need of "memory" (*Gedächtnis*). But it is in the *"thanc"* (*Gedanc*) that we hear the essence of these words. Heidegger writes: "Aus dem wesentlich gehörten Wort »der Gedanc« spricht nun aber zugleich das Wesen dessen, was die beiden Wörter nennen, die sich uns beim Hören des Zeitwortes »denken« leicht nahelegen: Denken und Gedächtnis, Denken und Dank." *Was Heisst Denken* (Tübingen: Niemeyer, 1971), p. 157.

26. *Was Heisst Denken*, p. 92. English translation, *What is Called Thinking*, trans. J. Glenn Gray and F. Wieck (New York: Harper & Row, 1968), p. 140.

27. *Was Heisst Denken*, p. 157. *What is Called Thinking*, pp. 144–45.

28. That for Heidegger remembrance becomes tied to the history of Being is evident for example in his essay "Recollection in Metaphysics." "Recollection of the history of Being in metaphysics is a bestowal which explicitly and uniquely gives the relation of Being and man to awareness to be pondered." "Recollection in Metaphysics," in *The End of Philosophy*, trans. Joan Stambaugh (New York: Harper & Row, 1973), p. 76. This essay was published originally as "Die Erinnerung in die Metaphysik," in *Nietzsche*, vol. 2 (Pfullingen: Günther Neske, 1961).

29. See note 19 in the "Introduction" above.

30. See William Spanos, "Heidegger, Kierkegaard, and the Hermeneutic Circle: Towards a Postmodern Theory of Interpretation as Disclosure," in *Martin Heidegger and the Question of Literature*, ed. William Spanos (Bloomington: Indiana University Press, 1979), p. 122.

31. *Phaedrus*, 249b–c.

32. See Mary Rousseau, "Recollection as Realization—Remythologizing Plato," *Review of Metaphysics* (December 1981): 337–48.

33. Here we should recall what was said in chapter 1. When Kierkegaard drew the distinction between repetition and recollection in *Repetition*, he inaugurated a decisive turn in hermeneutic theory. Repetition as a movement forward, unlike the "Greek experience of recollection," is not concerned with a past actuality but with an actuality that is not yet present. Hermeneutic

recollection in its structure is Kierkegaardian repetition. This distinction will be emphasized again in chapter 4, "Philosophical Hermeneutics and Finitude."

34. It is because "application" in its everyday sense connotes a process that is secondary to the act of knowing, e.g, applied physics, that Richard Bernstein suggests the English expression "appropriation" better conveys what Gadamer means and refers us to Ricoeur's use of this expression as integral to hermeneutic experience. See *Beyond Objectivism and Relativism*, p. 251. John Caputo suggests something similar; he would translate application as "creative appropriation." This is consistent with Caputo's later remark that describes application as consumption. See *Radical Hermeneutics*, pp. 110–15. If philosophical hermeneutics is truly about the conditions for hearing the voice of the other—granting that in this the one who hears "becomes more"—then the notion of consumption is entirely misleading.

35. David Hoy makes this same point. See David Hoy, *The Critical Circle* (Berkeley: University of California Press, 1978), pp. 89–95.

36. Paul Ricoeur, "Appropriation," in *Hermeneutics and the Human Sciences*, p. 185. Later on in the same essay Ricoeur qualifies the sense of the word, and one has to wonder why he chose this word at all. For example, he writes: "According to a third fallacious view, the appropriation of the meaning of a text would subsume interpretation to the finite capacities of understanding of a present reader. The English and French translation of *Aneignung* by 'appropriation' reinforces this suspicion. Do we not place the meaning of the text under the domination of the subject who interprets? This objection can be dismissed by observing that what is 'made our own' is not something mental, not the intention of another subject, nor some design supposedly hidden behind the text; rather, it is the projection of a world, which the text discloses in front of itself by means of its non-ostensive references." *Hermeneutics and the Human Sciences*, p. 192. The answer, of course, is that appropriation is always a good word for the interpretation that goes on within a philosophy of the subject. In the end, this is what separates the projects of Gadamer and Ricoeur.

37. Gadamer is of course referring here to Hegel. For Hegel the movement of the dialectic is a movement from the abstract and immediate to the concrete and mediated. What is real is inseparable from its concretization; since the dialectic advances not by discarding what has gone before but preserves the earlier moments within itself, what is fully real is the concrete universal. Gadamer follows this in principle but at the same time it is important

to see that for Gadamer the concretization is not a third moment in a chain of determinations. It is simply that for hermeneutic understanding the universal is inseparable from its application. What is understood is this text, this law.

38. It is in the discussion of legal hermeneutics that Gadamer takes up the criticism of Emilio Betti, the Italian theorist. Betti, in seeking to establish principles for objective interpretation, wants to make a distinction between cognitive, normative, and reproductive interpretation. To do so, in Gadamer's view, would be to make a return to Romantic hermeneutics and thus retain the distinction between the subjectivity of the interpreter and the objectivity of the meaning to be understood. Gadamer maintains that legal hermeneutics demonstrates precisely that the normative and cognitive meaning of the law are inseparable. Because the practice of interpretation in legal hermeneutics is for Gadamer similar to what actually occurs in the humanities, he takes Betti's criticism serious enough to merit a more substantial analysis. This occurs in the third section under the "Rediscovery of the Fundamental Hermeneutic Problem," which follows the analysis of $\phi\varrho\acute{o}\nu\eta\sigma\iota\varsigma$. The question of this third section is whether the process of the judge's understanding of the law is different from that of the legal historian's. Betti maintains that the legal historian is not engaged in a process of application. Gadamer counters that the legal historian interprets the text from the present, and this means that "the actual object of historical understanding is not events, but their 'significance'" (TM 328/GW1 334). Application is nothing other than this significance, of "applying" the tradition to the present. For a more detailed discussion of this issue, see Lawrence Schmidt, *The Epistemology of Hans-Georg Gadamer* (Frankfurt: Peter Lang, 1985), pp. 92–97, and Weinsheimer, *Gadamer's Hermeneutics*, pp. 192–99.

39. In *Truth and Method* Gadamer says essentially the same thing: if the text is understood properly, i.e., according to the claim it makes, it "must be understood at every moment, in every concrete situation, in a new and different way" (TM 309/GW1 314).

40. "Hermeneutics and Social Science," p. 311.

41. Gadamer argues in his recent work on Greek ethics, *The Idea of the Good in Platonic-Aristotelian Philosophy*, that Plato and Aristotle are both getting at the same thing although they do so from two different kinds of discourse. See *The Idea of the Good in Platonic-Aristotelian Philosophy*, trans. P. Christopher Smith (New Haven: Yale University Press, 1986).

42. Strictly speaking the distinction with respect to knowing that Aristotle draws in book VI of the *Nicomachean Ethics* is based on the initial

distinction between one part of the soul having logos and the other part being without it (1139a5). The part of the soul having logos is subdivided into the scientific (theoretical) and deliberative (practical). The scientific is then divided into science (ἐπιστήμη), which is concerned with what is necessary and eternal, and what is communicable by teaching; and theoretical wisdom (σοφία) which is the union of intuition and science. In similar fashion the deliberative is also divided into practical reasoning (φρόνησις), which pertains to deliberation about the good, and technical skill (τέχνη), which involves deliberation in making by the aid of a rule. To this taxonomy Aristotle adds a fifth intellectual virtue, intuitive reason (νοῦς), which is concerned with first principles.

43. *Nicomachean Ethics*, 1134b29.

44. See *Nicomachean Ethics*, 1134b34–1134a6.

45. Heidegger's reading of Aristotle draws heavily on this notion of seeing. In the "Aristotle Introduction," Heidegger translates φρόνησις as *fürsorgende Umsicht*, solicitous circumspection; and then, repeating this definition a few sentences later, as *fürsorgliches Sichumsehen (Umsicht)*, solicitous looking around oneself (circumspection). See "Phänomenologische Interpretationen zu Aristoteles (Anzeige der hermeneutischen Situation)," p. 255; English translation, p. 377. One also finds this notion in his Sophist lecture course from 1924–25. Here φρόνησις is circumspective insight into one's own situation of action. See *Sophistes*, Gesamtausgabe, vol. 19. For an excellent interpretation of Heidegger's reading of Aristotle on φρόνησις, see Bernasconi, "Heidegger's Destruction of Phronesis," *The Southern Journal of Philosophy* 28 (1989), supplement: 127–47.

46. Gadamer reads Aristotle to be saying the φρόνησις involves knowledge of both ends and means. See TM 321/GW1 326–27.

47. Gadamer concludes his essay "The Hermeneutics of Suspicion" on a similar note: "Aristotle asks, 'What is the principle of moral philosophy?' and he answers, 'Well, the principle is *that*—the thatness.' It means, not deduction but real givenness, not of brute facts but of the interpreted world." "Hermeneutics of Suspicion," in *Hermeneutics: Questions and Prospects*, ed. Gary Shapiro and Alan Circa (Amherst: University of Massachusetts Press, 1984), p. 65.

48. This characterization of science is derived principally from Heidegger. See for example "Die Frage nach der Technik" and "Wissenschaft und Besinnung" in *Vorträge und Aufsätze*. Both essays are found in English translation in *The Question Concerning Technology and Other Essays*, trans. W. Lovitt (New York: Harper & Row, 1977).

49. Gadamer describes this problem of planning in the context of an ideal of world administration in the essay "Notes on Planning for the Future," originally published in *Daedalus*, 95 (Spring 1966): 572–89. See this essay along with several related essays in part 3 of EPH.

50. In responding to the criticism of Habermas, Gadamer writes: "only a scientific consciousness under a delusion could fail to recognize that the debate concerning the true goals of human society . . . is directed to a knowing that is not science but [the knowing] that guides all human practical life." "Replik" in *Hermeneutik und Ideologiekritik*, p. 283.

51. "Hermeneutics and Social Science," p. 314.

52. "Hermeneutics and Social Science," p. 314. There are similarities here not just with Kierkegaard's assessment of contemporary life. Gadamer sounds very much like Marcel when he writes: "the society of experts is simultaneously a society of functionaries as well, for it is constitutive of the notion of the functionary that he be completely concentrated upon the administration of his functions" (RAS 74). Compare this with Marcel's comments in chapters 3 and 4 of *Man against Mass Society* (Chicago: Henry Regnery, 1952).

53. Gadamer's comment on the translation of προαίρεσις into German points to the difficulty in translating this word: "*prohairesis*, generally translated as *Vorzugwahl* [preferred choice]—naturally a horrible artificial expression for something which equally encompasses preferring as well as choosing by anticipating the consequences" (EPH 188). Προαίρεσις is not free choice among possibilities at a given time, but more of a choosing ahead of time, a choosing before other things.

54. See Aristotle, *Politics*, trans. H. Rackham, Loeb Classical Library (Cambridge, MA: Harvard University Press, 1972), 1325b21 ff.

55. Hegel gives a fascinating description of his age in the *Lectures on the Philosophy of Religion*, 3 vols., trans. E. B. Spiers and J. B. Sanderson (New York: Humanities Press, 1968), vol. 3, p. 150. In the description Hegel compares his age with the Roman Empire and at one point remarks that his own age is "nearest to the condition of infinite sorrow."

56. Greek reason, Gadamer tells us, "appears as the image of a unique future possible for us and of a possibility for life and for survival" (RAS 17).

57. Richard Rorty, "Pragmatism, Relativism, and Irrationalism," in *Consequences of Pragmatism* (Minneapolis: University of Minnesota Press, 1982), p. 161. See also Rorty's use of Gadamer's philosophical hermeneutics as an example of edifying philosophy in *Philosophy and the Mirror of Nature* (Princeton: Princeton University Press, 1979).

58. *Consequences of Pragmatism*, p. 162.

59. John Dewey, *Reconstruction in Philosophy* (Boston: Beacon Press, 1964), pp. 122–23.

60. *Beyond Objectivism and Relativism*, pp. 158–59.

61. "Hermeneutics of Suspicion." p. 64.

4. Philosophical Hermeneutics and Finitude

1. "Letter to Dallmayr," p. 94.

2. Caputo, "Gadamer's Closet Essentialism: A Derridean Critique," in *Dialogue & Deconstruction*, pp. 258–64.

3. Caputo takes this phrase from Joseph Margolis. See Joseph Margolis, *Pragmatism without Foundations: Reconciling Realism and Relativism* (Oxford: Basil Blackwell, 1986), p. 76.

4. "Gadamer's Closet Essentialism," p. 260.

5. Caputo, "Finitude and Difference," unpublished paper delivered at a conference on translation at the University of Warwick in England in July 1989.

6. "Gadamer's Closet Essentialism," p. 260.

7. See for example *Validity in Interpretation* (New Haven: Yale University Press, 1967). In essence, Hirsch wants to guarantee objectivity in the interpretation of texts through the notion of the author's intention. In view of Gadamer's account of the nature of language one could readily anticipate the Gadamerian rejoinder to Hirsch's criticism: that in the encounter with a text, an encounter that has the structure of a dialogue, the meaning goes beyond the intended meaning of the speakers. A detailed discussion of this criticism is found in David Hoy, *The Critical Circle*, pp. 11–40. This "traditionalist" view is also held by T. K. Seung in *Structuralism and Hermeneutics* (New York: Columbia University Press, 1982). Seung argues not so much that Gadamer is a relativist (in point of fact in Seung's reading he is a relativist) but that Gadamer gets caught up in contradictions and implying by that that his position is not to be taken seriously. He claims for example that insofar as tradition is for Gadamer the only ground for "contextual identity," he has no way of explaining cross-cultural understanding. Seung appears to confuse Gadamer's notion of tradition with a specific culture. See pp. 183–212.

8. Caputo's claim is that Gadamer's contention is hollow insofar as he retreats from the radicalization of *Wesen* that is underway in Heidegger.

9. Gadamer assumes that the reader is familiar with Hegel's distinction between a bad or negative infinity and a real infinite. The bad infinite is only a negation of the finite, never really absorbing it completely, and is thus an infinite that is not really free from finitude and limitation. See Hegel, *Wissenschaft der Logik I*, *Werke* 5, p. 149.

10. See ibid., *Werke* 6, p. 200ff.

11. "The importance of the logical consists in the transition of logic into becoming, where existence and actuality come forth. . . . Every moment, if for the moment one wishes to use this expression, is an immanent movement, which in a profound sense is no movement at all. One can easily convince oneself of this by considering that the concept of movement is itself a transcendence that has no place in logic." Kierkegaard, *The Concept of Anxiety*, ed. and trans. R. Thomte in collaboration with A. Anderson (Princeton: Princeton University Press, 1980), p. 13.

12. In *Journey to Selfhood: Hegel and Kierkegaard*, Taylor points out that Kierkegaard's argument attributes a more necessitarian position to Hegel than Hegel intended to affirm, thus contributing greatly to the widespread misinterpretation of Hegel as a determinist. See p. 126.

13. This point is made by George Stack in *Kierkegaard's Existential Ethics*. See p. 44ff.

14. See Aristotle's *Metaphysics*, 1049b5 ff. An excellent commentary on this text of Aristotle is given by Werner Marx in his *Introduction to Aristotle's Theory of Being as Being* (The Hague: Martinus Nijhoff, 1977). See especially chapters 2 and 3.

15. Marx, *Heidegger and the Tradition*, trans. Theodore Kisiel and Murray Greene (Evanston: Northwestern University Press, 1971), p. 111.

16. *The Basic Problems of Phenomenology*, p. 277. *Die Grundprobleme der Phänomenologie*, p. 392.

17. *The Basic Problems of Phenomenology*, p. 277. *Die Grundprobleme der Phänomenologie*, p. 392.

18. The following remarks are drawn primarily from Thomas Sheehan's work on Heidegger that explores the Aristotelian roots of Heidegger's thought. See especially "Getting to the Topic: The New Edition of *Wegmarken*," *Research in Phenomenology* 7 (1977). This is not to say that the issue of possibility in Heidegger is exhausted by the turn back to Aristotle. There is yet another figure that ultimately must be brought into consideration, namely, Nicholas of Cusa. For an excellent treatment of this connection to Cusanus see Peter J. Casarella, "Nicholas of Cusa and the

Power of the Possible," *American Catholic Philosophical Quarterly* 46 (Winter 1990): 7–34.

19. See Aristotle's *Physics*, 201b32.

20. Heidegger, "On the Being and Conception of Φύσις in Aristotle's Physics B,1," trans. Thomas Sheehan, *Man and World* 9 (1976): 266. This essay is a translation of "Vom Wesen und der Begriff der Φύσις. Aristoteles, Physik B,1" in *Wegmarken*, 2nd ed. (Frankfurt am Main: Klostermann, 1978).

21. *The Basic Problems of Phenomenology*, p. 308. *Die Grundprobleme der Phänomenologie*, p. 438.

22. The German text reads "Sein, das verstanden werden kann, ist Sprache." He refers to this phrase at a number of places. See for example, the forward to the second edition of *Truth and Method* (TM xxxv/GW2 445), and "Aesthetics and Hermeneutics" (PH 103/GW8 7).

23. In "Dialectic and Sophism in Plato's Seventh Letter," Gadamer give a more nuanced account of Plato's understanding of the relation between words and things according to Plato's remarks in the Seventh Letter. In the letter Plato asks about how insight is reached in the context of a prefatory appeal of giving oneself over to philosophical instruction with the proper attitude. Philosophy does not appear to be able to compel one to understand in the way that mathematics for example can. The answer to this question, on Gadamer's reading of the letter, is that Plato wants to show that in fact the ideal cannot be realized. What is known, Plato tells us, can be communicated in four ways: in name or word (ὄνομα), in conceptual determination (λόγος), in the illustrative image (εἴδωλον), and in the knowledge or insight itself; yet none of these are able to give us the thing itself. Even where one would most expect to find that identity between knower and known, namely, at the level of insight, Plato would insist that the thing itself remains distinct for insight cannot be separated from becoming, from the intellect's stream of life. The precise reason why these means—taken collectively or individually—are incapable of compelling someone to understand is attributed by Plato to the weakness of the λόγοι. As Gadamer explains it: "But who does not see at once that this process of attaining and communicating understanding always takes place entirely in the medium of one person's speaking with another? Plato leaves no doubt that even knowledge of the ideas, although it cannot merely be derived from language and words, is still not to be attained without them. . . . The weakness of the *logoi*, which is the weakness of all four, is precisely the weakness of our intellect itself which depends upon them. They themselves offer no

assurance that the thing itself is there in its true 'disconcealedness'" (DDP 104–5). The nature of the means of knowing is such that there is always something inessential about them. How can it ever be said that the thing is truly there? This is the question that draws Plato into a confrontation not so much with the poets but with the sophists and the answer for Plato is precisely that knowledge, especially as it pertains to the building of human community, is constantly endangered. Even Plato's doctrine of the One and the indeterminate Two can be interpreted in this same context: it establishes the limits of insight which is always midway between single and multiple meaning. Gadamer insists that "Plato is not interested in . . . elevating Socrates' *docta ignorantia* to a dialectic of reflection (Hegel) or erecting a structured universe deriving from a first, highest principle" (DDP 120). He is, nevertheless, still interested in insight, in persevering in a single direction to what is by putting opinions to the test in shared inquiry so that what is is raised up in partial aspect and placed "in the light of unconcealment [*ins Licht der Unverborgenheit*]."

24. It is in this context that the question of truth must then be situated. See chapter 5, "Philosophical Hermeneutics and Truth."

25. In "Dawn and Dusk: Gadamer and Heidegger on Truth," *Man and World*, 19 (1986): 21–53, Francis Ambrosio points out that Heidegger's notion of *Ereignis* and Gadamer's notion of *Virtualität des Sprechens* parallel each other with respect to the question of truth. I would agree that there is a parallel, but for a different reason. What enables us to speak of both is the common framework of an ontology of living being.

26. For Hegel, in a speculative proposition, unlike what one finds is other propositions, the subject concept disappears into the predicate which becomes the truth of the subject. To say "God is one," for example, does not mean that it is the property of God to be one; rather, it is God's nature to be unity. Ultimately, the speculative proposition, unlike other propositions, presents the unity of the concept in the dialectical movement of the proposition.

27. See Gadamer, "Hermeneutics and Logocentrism," in *Dialogue and Deconstruction*, pp. 114–25.

28. Compare Gadamer's remarks here with what Heidegger says in "Letter on Humanism": "When I speak of the 'quiet power of the possible' I do not mean the *possibile* of a merely represented *possibilitas*, nor *potentia* as the *essentia* of an *actus* of *existentia*; rather, I mean Being itself, which in its favoring possibilizes thought [*mögend über das Denken*] and hence also the essence of humanity, and that means in our relation to Being. To

possibilize [*vermögen*] something here means to preserve it in its essence [*Wesen*], to maintain it in its element." "Letter on Humanism," trans. Frank Capuzzi, in *Martin Heidegger: Basic Writings*, ed. David F. Krell (New York: Harper & Row, 1977), pp. 196–97. "Brief über den »Humanismus«," in *Wegmarken*, p. 314.

29. Nancy is quite right to say that every conception of interpretation is a concept of communication. See Jean-Luc Nancy, "Sharing Voices" in *Transforming the Hermeneutic Context*, ed. Gayle Ormiston and Alan Schrift (Albany: SUNY Press, 1990), p. 246.

30. See TM 369–79/GW1 375–84.

31. See Gadamer, "Destruktion and Deconstruction" in *Dialogue & Deconstruction*, pp. 102–13.

5. Philosophical Hermeneutics and Truth

1. I am not the first commentator to attempt to take up this question. See, for example, Richard Bernstein, "From Hermeneutics to Praxis," in *Philosophical Profiles: Essays in a Pragmatic Mode* (Philadelphia: University of Pennsylvania Press,1986); Jean Grondin, "Hermeneutic Truth and Its Historical Presuppositions: A Possible Bridge between Analysis and Hermeneutics," in *Anti-Foundationalism and Practical Reasoning*, ed. Evan Simpson (Edmonton: Academic Printing & Pub., 1987); Brice Wachterhauser, "Must We Be What We Say? Gadamer on Truth in the Human Sciences," in *Hermeneutics and Modern Philosophy*; Francis J. Ambrosio, "Dawn and Dusk: Gadamer and Heidegger on Truth." The most comprehensive treatment of the question of truth in Gadamer's hermeneutics is by Jean Grondin. See his *Hermeneutische Wahrheit? Zum Wahrheitsbegriff Hans-Georg Gadamers* (Königstein/Ts.: Forum Academicum, 1982).

2. See, for example, "Wahrheit in den Geisteswissenschaften" (1953) and "Was ist Wahrheit?" (1957) in GW2, pp. 37–43 and 44–56 respectively. In the first essay Gadamer appears to be concerned more with the consequences of the fact that truth in the human sciences is historically conditioned then he is with truth itself. In this context, though, he is more direct than is immediately apparent in *Truth in Method* in linking truth in the human sciences to dialogical conversation, which means at once linking truth to the element of speech. In the second essay Gadamer is even more explicit about the character of truth that occurs in speaking. Here he carries through a theme initially developed by Heidegger, namely that truth in the proposition or statement is secondary to a more dynamic relation between truth and

language. Gadamer accounts for this dynamic relation in his claim that "every proposition is motivated." Thus ultimately it is the question and not the judgment that has logical priority in speaking. These essays have recently been translated by Brice Wachterhauser and appear in *Hermeneutics and Truth*, ed. Brice Wachterhauser (Evanston: Northwestern University Press, 1994), pp. 25–46. See also the essays in GW8: "Wort und Bild—»so wahr, so seiend«" (1992), pp. 373–99; "Der »eminente« Text und seine Wahrheit" (1986), pp. 286–95; "Von der Wahrheit des Wortes" (1971), pp. 37–57; "Über den Beitrag der Dichtkunst bei der Suche nach der Wahrheit" (1971), pp. 70–79.

3. This understanding of the work of art as an object and as a thing is criticized by Heidegger in "The Origin of the work of Art." See, "Der Ursprung des Kunstwerkes," in *Holzwege*, pp. 7–68. English translation by Albert Hofstadter, "The Origin of the Work of Art," in *Poetry, Language, Thought* (New York: Harper & Row, 1971), pp. 15–88.

4. The *da* as present enactment is inseparable from temporal enactment. Gadamer understands this temporality in the Kierkegaardian sense of being contemporaneous. In its Kierkegaardian theological context, contemporaneity "does not mean 'existing at the same time.' Rather, it names the task that confronts the believer: to bring together two moments that are not concurrent, namely one's own present and the redeeming act of Christ, and yet so totally to mediate them that the latter is experienced and taken seriously as present (and not as something in a distant past)" (TM 127–28/GW1 132). The contemporaneity of a work of art is such that in presenting itself to us, it achieves "full presentness, however remote its origin may be."

5. This notion of appearance can be read in both a Heideggerian and a Hegelian context. In the Epilogue to "The Origin of the Work of Art," Heidegger writes: "When truth sets itself into the work it appears. Appearance [*Erscheinen*] is, as this being of truth in the work and as work, beauty." *Holzwege*, p. 67; *Poetry, Language, Thought*, p. 81. In the preface to the *Phenomenology*, Hegel writes: "Appearance is the arising and passing away that does not itself arise and pass away, but is 'in itself,' and constitutes the actuality and the movement of the life of truth." *Phänomenologie des Geistes*, p. 46; *The Phenomenology of Spirit*, p. 27.

6. Gadamer distinguishes transformation (*Verwandlung*) from alteration (*Veränderung*) in which what is altered also remains the same (TM 111/GW1 116).

7. These Greek concepts are developed further by Gadamer in his essay "Wort und Bild—»so wahr, so seiend«" (GW8 373-99). A further discussion of their significance for philosophical hermeneutics is found in the analysis of poetical speaking in chapter 7. See chapter 7 "The Voice of the Poet."

8. See note 3 above.

9. The notion of "remaining true" becomes a decisive expression in Gadamer's later essays for the claim to truth in language. See especially "Von der Wahrheit des Wortes" (GW8 37-57).

10. Bernstein argues, quoting from a text of Gadamer, that Gadamer is more concerned with what is feasible here and now rather than with that mediation on the cosmic night of the forgetfulness of being. See *Philosophical Profiles*, p. 106-7.

11. See *Philosophical Profiles*, p. 108.

12. Plato, *Philebus*, trans. W. R. M. Lamb, Loeb Classical Library (Cambridge, MA: Harvard University Press, 1962), 64e.

13. Gadamer does not think that the text of the *Philebus* represents a change in Plato's doctrine of ideas. Gadamer writes: "It is still true that the good must be separated out of everything that appears good and seen in distinction from it. But it is in everything and is seen in distinction from everything only because it is in everything and shines forth from it" (IG 116/GW7 193).

14. *Phaedrus*, 250d-e.

15. The word ἐκφανέστατον is related to φαίνω, bring to light; in the middle voice φανέσται means to bring itself to light in the sense of a shining that shows itself. What is radiantly manifest is what shines forth in its self-showing. Heidegger makes this connection between the beautiful and appearance in "The Origin of the Work of Art." The beautiful as shining forth, as coming to show itself, does not occur apart from truth as the unconcealment of being: "Appearance—as this being of truth in the work and as work—is beauty." *Holzwege*, p. 67; *Poetry Language Thought*, p. 81.

16. In his essay "The festive character of the theater," published in *The Relevance of the Beautiful and Other Essays*, Gadamer writes: "All true imitation is a transformation that does not simply present again something that is already there. It is a kind of transformed reality in which the transformation points back to what has been transformed in and through it. It is a transformed reality because it brings before us intensified possibilities never seen before" (RB 64/GW8 302).

17. See TM 475/GW1 479. This notion that in language a second being is not acquired was discussed above in chapter 4, "Philosophical Hermeneutics and Finitude."

18. See Jacques Derrida, "The Double Session," in *Dissemination*, trans. Barbara Johnson (Chicago: University of Chicago Press, 1981).

19. The reservation concerns the way in which the metaphor of depth could be construed as a reintroduction of origin and the notion of a recovery from oblivion. Caputo, least we forget, insists that Gadamer's hermeneutics is simply a hermeneutics of retrieval of a *deep* truth. See *Radical Hermeneutics*, p. 111.

20. See *Nicomachean Ethics*, 1106b31. Gadamer develops this point in *The Idea of the Good in Platonic-Aristotelian Philosophy*. "Practical philosophy by itself can give us no assurance that we know how to 'hit' what is right. Such knowledge remains the end of practice itself and the virtue of practical reasonableness, which is precisely not mere inventiveness" (IG 166/GW7 221).

21. Gadamer makes no further elaboration of the connection between recognition and the "as" in this context. One can only assume that were he to say more he would repeat the analysis of the as-structure that Heidegger gives in *Being and Time*, while at the same time collapsing the distinctions that Heidegger makes there. For Gadamer, the point would seem to be that recognition, which is the knowing appropriate to the universality of interpretation, functions in a similar way to the as-structure; namely, it constitutes the interpretation whereby something is explicitly understood.

22. This notion of a continuum of empty and full can be correlated to Gadamer's notion of empty and fulfilled time. See "*Über leere und erfüllte Zeit*," GW4, pp. 137–53. In *The Relevance of the Beautiful and Other Essays*, Gadamer considers these two fundamental ways of experiencing time in order to describe the kind of recurrence that belongs to the festival and the work of art in general. Empty time is time that is at our disposal ("I have time for something"). Such time has to be spent; it is empty and needs to be filled. In both "bustle and boredom" we fill our time. In contrast to this, time can be experienced as fulfilled or autonomous as in the case of the festival that fulfills every moment of its duration. "This fulfillment does not come about because someone has empty time to fill. On the contrary, the time only becomes festive with the arrival of the festival" (RB 42/GW8 132).

23. "Indeed, what characterizes the arbitrariness of inappropriate fore-meanings if not that they come to nothing in being worked out?" (TM 267/GW1 272)

24. The connection between hermeneutic truth and rhetoric is also made by Gianni Vattimo in *The End of Modernity: Nihilism and Hermeneutics in Postmodern Culture*; see pp. 130–44. Vattimo supports this claim by quoting from Gadamer's essay on the Frankfurt School criticism of hermeneutics, *Rhetorik, Hermeneutik und Ideologiekritik*. This essay appears in translation as "The Scope and Function of Hermeneutical Reflection" in *Philosophical Hermeneutics*, pp. 18–43. The passage Vattimo quotes makes essentially the same point that is made in the discussion of rhetoric in *Truth and Method* that we have already made note of above, namely, that the tradition of rhetoric advocates a claim for truth that would defend the probable. Vattimo's interpretation of this sense of truth, however, is not without its difficulties. He characterizes the common language that serves as the content for rhetorical persuasion as a "collective consciousness" and suggests that the moment of recognition is the acceptance of this collective consciousness. Such an interpretation makes hermeneutics susceptible to the charge of being an apology for what already exists. Vattimo's reading seems to disregard Gadamer's own comments made in response to this Habermasian charge.

25. In *Radical Hermeneutics* Caputo claims that "Gadamer is interested in *verum, aletheia*, what is true here and now and ready for consumption (application), not *a-letheia*, the event of concealment and unconcealment." *Radical Hermeneutics*, p. 115. Caputo has this wrong on two counts. Not only is there no truth prior to the application, but the verum is not what is to be verified (consumed).

26. It is interesting to note that Gadamer uses the same example as Heidegger does in his essay "On the Essence of Truth." For Heidegger, though, this example is used as a point of departure for the question concerning truth: "what is true about genuine gold . . . cannot be demonstrated merely by its actuality." "On the Essence of Truth," trans. John Sallis, in *Martin Heidegger: Basic Writings*, p. 119.

27. Gadamer hints at this relation between speaking and truth in "Denken und Dichten bei Heidegger und Hölderlin." See GW10, p. 79.

28. Homer, *The Iliad*, trans. A. T. Murray, Loeb Classical Library (Cambridge, MA: Harvard University Press, 1960), X, 534.

29. Ultimately for Gadamer the truth of poetry—and one would infer that this would also pertain to all speaking that "verifies" through its power

of realization—consists in creating a "hold upon nearness." At the end of his essay, "On the Contribution of Poetry to the Search for Truth," Gadamer describes what this "hold upon nearness" means: "The word of the poet does not simply continue this process of *Einhausung*, or 'making ourselves at home.' Instead it stands over against this process like a mirror held up to it. But what appears in the mirror is not the world, nor this or that thing in the world, but rather this nearness or familiarity itself in which we stand for a while. . . . This is not a romantic theory, but a straightforward description of the fact that language gives all of us our access to a world in which certain special forms of human experience arise: the religious tidings that proclaim salvation, the legal judgment that tells us what is right and what is wrong in our society, the poetic word that by being there bears witness to our own being" (RB 115/GW8 79).

30. See *Harper's Latin Dictionary* (New York: American Book Co., 1907).

31. *Phaedrus*, 239b–c.

32. The intent of Gadamer's comment here follows closely Heidegger's comments on preservation in "The Origin of the Work of Art."

6. The Voice of the Text

1. The colloquium from 1981 was initially published as *Text und Interpretation*, ed. Philippe Forget (Munich: Wilhelm Fink, 1984). The essays directly related to the exchange between Gadamer and Derrida from this text, along with Gadamer's subsequent essays on the topic: "*Destruktion* and Deconstruction" (1986), and "Frühromantik, Hermeneutik, Dekonstruktivismus" (1986), have been brought together and translated in *Dialogue and Deconstruction*. Volume 10 of his *Gesammelte Werke*, which appeared only recently, contains yet another essay on this topic. See "Hermeneutik auf der Spur" (GW10 148–74).

2. See Plato, *Meno*, 97d.

3. "*Différer* in [one] sense is to temporalize, to take recourse, consciously or unconsciously, in the temporal and temporalizing mediation of a detour that suspends the accomplishment or fulfillment of 'desire' or 'will', and equally effects this suspension in a mode that annuls or tempers its own effect. . . . The other sense of diffrer is the more common and identifiable one: to be not identical, to be other, discernable, etc." *Margins of Philosophy*, p. 8.

4. Derrida, *Positions*, trans. Alan Bass (Chicago: University of Chicago Press, 1981), p. 26.

5. *Positions*, p. 28.

6. That deconstruction is a form of criticism is the position taken by Rodolphe Gasché and others. See Gasché's "Deconstruction as Criticism," in *Inventions of Difference: On Jacques Derrida* (Cambridge, MA: Harvard University Press, 1994), pp. 22–57. In the introduction to *Dissemination*, Barbara Johnson writes: "It can thus be seen that deconstruction is a form of what has long been called *critique*. A critique of any theoretical system is not an examination of its flaws or imperfections. It is not a set of criticism designed to make the system better. It is an analysis that focuses on the grounds of that system's possibility. The critique leads backwards from what seems natural, obvious, self-evident, or universal, in order to show that these things have their history, their reasons for being the way they are, their effects on what follows from them, and that the starting point is not a (natural) given but a (cultural) context, usually blind to itself." *Dissemination*, p. xv.

7. *Positions*, p. 42.

8. See the discussion of this issue in chapter 4, "Philosophical Hermeneutics and Finitude."

9. In "Text and Interpretation" Gadamer writes: "the encounter with the French philosophical scene represents a genuine challenge for me. In particular, Derrida has argued against the later Heidegger that Heidegger himself has not really broken through the logocentrism of metaphysics. Derrida's contention is that insofar as Heidegger asks about the essence of truth or the meaning of Being, he still speaks the language of metaphysics that looks upon meaning as something out there that is to be discovered. This being so, Nietzsche is said to be more radical" (TI 24/GW2 333).

10. Of this other path taken by Derrida, Gadamer says: "On this path the awakening of a meaning hidden in the life and liveliness of conversation is not an issue. Rather, it is in an ontological concept of *écriture*—not idle chatter nor even true conversation but the background network of meaning-relations lying at the basis of all speech—that the very integrity of sense as such is to be dissolved, thereby accomplishing the authentic shattering of metaphysics" (DD 109/GW2 368).

11. The specific way in which this is understood by Gadamer was described in connection with the analysis of the speculative structure of language. See chapter 4, "Philosophical Hermeneutics and Finitude."

12. "Philosophy and Literature," p. 247. (GW8 246).

13. Gadamer takes this term from Austin. In *How to Do Things with Words*, Austin distinguishes between performative and constative utterances. Constative utterances describe a state of affairs and are true or false. Performative utterances perform the action to which they refer and are neither true nor false. For a discussion of this distinction as it relates to deconstruction, see Jonathan Culler, *On Deconstruction: Theory and Criticism after Structuralism* (Ithaca: Cornell University Press, 1982), p. 112ff.

14. Gadamer, "Reply to Jacques Derrida" in *Dialogue and Deconstruction*, p. 55. *Text und Interpretation*, p. 59.

15. "Philosophy and Literature," p. 253. (GW8 252).

16. See Heidegger, "Logos (Heraclitus, Fragment B50)" in *Early Greek Thinking*, pp. 59–78. *Vorträge und Aufsätze*, pp. 207–30.

17. In the German text the title for Derrida's remarks is *Guter Wille zur Macht (I): Drei Fragen an Hans-Georg Gadamer.*

18. The issue here is the extent to which Heidegger reads the texts of the history of philosophy in only one way, thus reducing the multiplicity of thematics in these texts.

19. See *Phaedrus*, 274b–278b.

20. In an interview with Gadamer from 1986 in which he discusses his teaching and writing, he says: "And so I developed a style of my own by speaking freely (not reading to an audience) and teaching this way. I learned to develop the melody of my own thoughts and although I do not think I am a bad writer there always is the *living voice* behind the writing" (EPH 66; emphasis added).

21. See Introduction, note 19.

22. "Letter to Dallmayr," p. 98.

23. See Introduction, note 1.

24. See chapter 5 "Hermeneutic Experience and Truth."

25. In the same interview mentioned above, Gadamer is asked whether one can claim that he has a theory of speech and writing and of their relation. Gadamer responds in the affirmative while noting that "this has not been well considered yet," and goes on to ask rhetorically: "What does it mean, for example, that in all antiquity no silent reading was done, and what does it mean that we no longer hear a real voice when reading? This has implications for writers." When asked further if he is reasserting the primacy of speech, Gadamer says only that "literature and writing must take note of the different conditions under which they occur," and then defines hermeneutics accordingly as "the skill to let things speak which come to us in a fixed petrified form, that of the text" (EPH 65).

26. *Phaedrus*, 275d–276a. This translation by R. Hackforth is in *The Collected Dialogues of Plato* (Princeton: Princeton University Press, 1961).

27. See Eric Havelock, *Preface to Plato* (New York: Grosset & Dunlap, 1967).

28. See Bruno Snell, *The Discovery of the Mind*, trans. T. G. Rosenmeyer (New York: Harper & Row, 1960), p. 9. Note also that the Latin word "anima" retains this connection between life, soul, and breath.

29. Homer, *The Odyssey of Homer*, trans. Richard Lattimore (New York: Harper & Row, 1967), XI.222.

30. Richard Onians, *The Origins of European Thought* (Cambridge: Cambridge University Press, 1989), p. 67.

31. See *The Odyssey of Homer*, XVII.57. A longer study on this topic would require that one pursue this imagery in Plato's dialogues. One immediately thinks here of the winged steeds in the myth in the *Phaedrus*.

32. Onians points out that we literally do not hear so well when yawning, that is, when not breathing in. In the Greek oral tradition the reception of the word—that is, the taking in what pertains to consciousness and intelligence—depended more on the lungs than the ears. See *The Origins of European Thought*, p. 72.

33. See Giorgio Agamben, *Language and Death*, trans. Karen Pinkus with Michael Hardt (Minneapolis: University of Minnesota Press, 1991), p. 34.

34. Gadamer does not elaborate on this notion of an inner ear, but increasingly comes to use this term to indicate the reception of what I call the performed word. One would assume that the inner ear is simply correlated with the inner word. But the inner word remains metaphysically encased, and the one place the Gadamer does refer to the inner ear in *Truth and Method* is not in conjunction with the discussion of the inner word. In the Supplement to *Truth and Method*, "To What Extent does Language Perform Thought?," Gadamer writes: "The persuasive speech which binds one man with another or even with himself in so intuitive and living a way that they seem inseparable from one another can nevertheless take on the form of written relations. These latter can be deciphered and read and raised into a new enactment of meaning, indeed so much so that our whole world is more or less . . . a literary one, that is, one administered by means of writing and transcription. Setting aside for a moment all the differences within transcription. I would say that everything in writing, to be understood, requires something like a kind of heightening for the inner ear" (TM 547). The inner ear is mentioned by Gadamer at the end of "*Destruktion* and

Deconstruction" (DD 113/GW2 371), and "Hermeneutics and Logocentrism" (p. 124). See also "Philosophy and Literature," p. 248 (GW8 247).

35. "Hermeneutics and Logocentrism," p. 118. Compare this with Gadamer's similar remark in *"Destruktion* and Deconstruction": "[What occurs in dialogue] is the very meaning of the speculative unity that is achieved in the 'virtuality' of the word: that it is not an individual word nor is it a formulated proposition, but rather points beyond all possible assertions" (DD 111–12/GW2 370).

36. See *Language and Death*, p. 67.

37. See Anne Carson, *Eros the Bittersweet* (Princeton: Princeton University Press, 1986), p. 50.

38. In *"Von der Wahrheit des Wortes"* a paper presented at and published privately by the Martin Heidegger Gesellschaft in Messkirch, Gadamer writes: "»Das Wort« meint vielmehr immer schon eine größere, vielfältigere Einheit, die in dem Begriff des verbum interius der Tradition seit langsam bekannt ist. Es lebt auch ganz selbstverständlich in userer Altagssprache weiter, wenn einer zum Beispiel sagt: »Ich möchte mit dir ein Wort reden.« Da meint man nicht, daß man ihm nur ein einziges Wort sagen will." *Denken und Dichten bei Martin Heidegger* (Der Martin Heidegger Gesellschaft in Messkirch), p. 8.

39. Aristotle, *De interpretatione, The Works of Aristotle*, trans. E. M. Edghill (Oxford: Oxford University Press, 1971), 16a5.

40. See *Language and Death*, p. 38ff.

41. "Hermeneutics and Logocentrism," p. 124.

42. For Derrida the issue here is not to argue for an alternative to self-present speech, but, in carrying out a reading of textual disruption, showing that the text fails to achieve what is argued for in the text, namely, the priority of speech over writing. See "Plato's Pharmacy," *Dissemination*, pp. 61–172.

43. In "Unterwegs zur Schrift?," Gadamer writes: "Ist es aber wirklich eine Verwerfung der Erfindung der Schrift und des Gebrauches der Schrift, die daraus folgt, oder is es eher ein Appell an den rechten Gebrauch der Schrift, etwas, was man mit einem Ausdruck unserer Tage einen hermeneutischen Appell nennen könnte?" (GW2 263). See also *The Idea of the Good in Platonic-Aristotelian Philosophy*, p. 119 (GW7 195).

44. This question can be asked in a number of ways. Rather than seduction one could pose the problem of the speaking in the voice in terms of the shattering of words as such. The problem is captured in the lines from Eliot's "Burnt Norton":

> Words strain,
> Crack and sometimes break, under the burden,
> Under the tension, slip, slide, perish,
> Decay with imprecision, will not stay in place,
> Will not stay still. Shrieking voices
> Scolding, mocking, or merely chattering,
> Always assail them.

T.S. Eliot, *Four Quartets* (New York: Harcourt, Brace & World, 1943), p. 19.

45. It would be interesting to think the ontological problem of hylemorphism in Aristotle in terms of desire. In the *Physics* Aristotle says literally that "matter desires [εφιεσθαι χαι ορεγεσθαι] form." *Physics*, 192a22. In a different context this same idea is broached by Merleau-Ponty in his *Phenomenology of Perception*: "If then we want to bring to light the birth of being for us, we must finally look to that area of our experience which clearly has significance and reality for us, and that is our affective life. Let us try to see how a thing or a being begins to exist for us through desire or love and we shall thereby come to understand better how things and being can exist in general." *Phenomenology of Perception*, trans. Colin Smith (London: Routledge & Kegan Paul, 1962), p. 154.

46. Augustine writes: "The word therefore which we now wish to discern and study is knowledge with love." *The Trinity*, trans. Stephen McKenna (Washington DC: Catholic University of America Press, 1963), p. 285.

47. See *Phenomenology of Spirit*, p. 104ff.

48. In several places Gadamer speaks of the therapeutic situation, and always understands this in terms of a hermeneutics of suspicion. That is because the therapeutic model is assumed to be hierarchical and non-dialogical as in psychoanalysis where the therapist/analyst is not a true partner in conversation. There are of course other therapeutic models. See *Truth and Method*, p. 383 (GW1 389), and *Reason in the Age of Science*, p. 108–9.

49. *Phenomenology of Perception*, p. 354.

50. Here the question of the *Republic*, which is the question of the community that wants to exclude desire, naturally arises. See John Sallis, *Being and Logos: The Way of Platonic Dialogue* (Atlantic Highlands, NJ: Humanities Press, 1986).

51. *Dissemination*, p. 154.

52. The kind of writing that Derrida has in mind is described as a "general writing of which the system of speech, consciousness, meaning, presence, truth, etc., would only be an effect, to be analyzed as such. It is this questioned effect that I have elsewhere called *logocentrism.*" *Margins of Philosophy*, p. 329.

53. Derrida, *Of Grammatology*, trans. Gayatri Spivak (Baltimore: The Johns Hopkins University Press, 1976), p. 35.

54. This is the issue in Derrida's reading of Husserl. See *Speech and Phenomenon*, trans. David Allison (Evanston: Northwestern University Press, 1973).

55. The issue of proximity in the voice is the issue of familiarity. In "On the Contribution of Poetry to the Search of Truth," Gadamer speaks of the self-fulfillment of the poetic word in terms of a hold upon nearness as a familiarity with the world. See chapter 5, note 29.

56. See *The Iliad*, XXII.414.

57. Sallis, *Echoes: After Heidegger* (Bloomington: Indiana University Press, 1990), p. 1.

58. In *Echoes* Sallis pursues the sense of the figure of Echo in turning to the work of Thoreau. There one finds, according to Sallis, an echo of nature in contrast to the Echo of classical culture. This echo is to some extent original sound. Sallis uses this as an occasion to think within the collapse of the image-original distinction. See my remark that follows.

59. See the discussion of Gadamer's treatment of the image-original distinction in chapter 5, "Philosophical Hermeneutics and Truth."

7. The Voice of the Poet

1. The full title of this essay is "Wort und Bild—»so wahr, so seiend«." See GW8 373–99.

2. Gadamer's own life-long concern with art is evident from his numerous writings on art from "Plato and the Poets" in 1934 to "Word and Picture" in 1992. These essays have been collected and appear in volumes 8 and 9 of the *Gesammelte Werke*. "Word and Picture, one of Gadamer's most recent essays takes on considerable importance, like "Text and Interpretation" written a decade earlier, when read in relation to the project of philosophical hermeneutics as a whole.

3. It is precisely on this point that Gadamer is critical of his analysis in *Truth and Method* (see "Reflections on My Philosophical Journey"). He feels he did not define with enough precision the difference between

the game of art and the game of language which becomes conflated at the end of *Truth and Method*. Gadamer's later writings on art and poetry, as this chapter shows, attempts to correct this "failing."

4. "Hölderlin is one of our greatest, i.e., one of our most promising thinkers, because he is our greatest poet. The poetical turning toward his poetry is only possible as mediative debate [*denkerische Auseinanderstezung*] with the revelation of Being which has been achieved in this poetry." Heidegger, *Hölderlins Hymnen »Germanien« und »Der Rhein«*, Gesamtausgabe, vol. 39 (Frankfurt: Klostermann, 1989), p. 6.

5. The relation between thinker and poet, between thinking and poetizing is complex. In the postscript to "What is Metaphysics," Heidegger says that "the thinker utters [*sagt*] Being. The poet names the holy," and then adds, "we may know something about the relations between philosophy and poetry, but we know nothing of the dialogue between poet and thinker, who 'dwell near on mountains farthest apart'." Heidegger, "What is Metaphysics," in *Existence and Being*, trans. Werner Brock (Chicago: Henry Regnery, 1949), pp. 391–92. The postscript appears separately in *Wegmarken* as "Nachwort zu: »Was ist Metaphysik?«," *Wegmarken*, p. 309. For a discussion of Heidegger's relation to poetry, see David White, *Heidegger and the Language of Poetry* (Lincoln: University of Nebraska Press, 1978); Peter McCormick, *Heidegger and the Language of the World* (Ottawa: University of Ottawa Press, 1976); Robert Bernasconi, *The Question of Language in Heidegger's History of Being*; and Véronique Fóti, *Heidegger and the Poets* (Atlantic Highlands, NJ: Humanities Press, 1992). Some of the more recent discussions of Heidegger in relation to poetry, to the poetry of Hölderlin in particular, emphasize the political aspect in Heidegger's turn to Hölderlin's poetry. Poetry is not simply implicated in the necessary transformation of language in order to think the question of Being, it is "the original language of an historical people," and "the essence of language must be understood through the essence of poetry." See Heidegger, *Erläuterungen zu Hölderlins Dichtung*, 4th ed. (Frankfurt: Klostermann, 1971), p. 43. For a discussion of this political context for Heidegger's reading of Hölderlin, see Bernasconi, "Poet of Poets. Poet of the Germans," in *Heidegger in Question*; and *Heidegger Toward the Turn: Essays on the Work of the 1930s*, ed. James Risser (Albany: SUNY Press, 1997).

6. "Letter to Dallmayr," p. 194.

7. "Reflections on My Philosophical Journey" *Hans-Georg Gadamer*, Library of Living Philosophers.

8. Gadamer, "The Eminent Text and Its Truth," *Bulletin of the Midwest Modern Language Association* 13 (1980): 6 (GW8 290).

9. The importance of this word for Gadamer's reflections on poetic discourse and art in general is evidenced by its use in the title of volume eight of the Gesammelte Werke: *Ästhetik und Poetik I: Kunst als Aussage*.

10. For the Greeks, the poets did not simply speak, they placed their words in song as the fitting locution for celebration and praise. Hesiod, for example, opens the *Theogony* proclaiming "Let us begin to sing [ἀείδειν] with the Heliconian Muses." Not only did the poet's voice endure in song (for the oral tradition had not yet conceived of silent forms of speech), but the voice that did endure in song was never simply the voice of the poet alone. Precisely because the poet was embedded in an oral tradition, the poet's voice was at once the voice of that tradition of which he sang. In this sense the Greek poet was forever lending his voice, for it was the voice of tradition that spoke in song; and poetry itself endured, if not in the poet himself, then certainly in the professional reciter, the rhapsode. This doubled imitated voice exhibits, in the most obvious way, the essential meaning of lending one's voice: the rhapsode must invoke Mnemosyne, and accordingly, to lend one's voice is to keep in memory.

11. Plato, *Ion*, trans. W. R. M. Lamb, Loeb Classical Library (Cambridge, MA: Harvard University Press, 1962), 530b–c. Hereafter noted in body of text.

12. Plato makes a reference to Eurycles in the *Sophist* in a discussion about the one and the many in statements; see 252c. Eurycles is also referred to in Aristophanes' *The Wasps*; see 1019.

13. It is interesting to note how Rilke, a poet dear to both Heidegger and Gadamer, speaks of poetic creation in much the same way. In a little-known essay, "Concerning the Poet," written in Duino in January 1912, Rilke gives a description of the poet through the story of his river crossing in a large sailing vessel. The focus of his attention is brought to bear on the effort of the oarsmen, whose movements never seemed to lose their ordered rhythm. He noticed that "they gave voice to a kind of counting in order to keep in time, but so exacting was their work that their voices frequently failed them." On these occasions they either suffered this lack or else recovered through an "unpredictable intervention" (*abzusehende Eingriff*), which transformed the powers within them so that they brought "untouched sources of strength into play." This unpredictable intervention is enacted by a man sitting at the front of the boat who rarely looked backward. This man, who we begin to surmise represents the position of

the poet, breaks out into song at irregular intervals and by no means does so only when the exhaustion of the oarsmen increased. This man's song was always at the right time. What was it, then, that influenced the man to sing? In Rilke's words: "What did seem to influence him was the pure movement of his feeling when it met the open distance, in which he was absorbed in a manner half melancholy, half resolute. In him the forward thrust of the vessel and the force opposed to us were continually held in counterpoise—from time to time a surplus accumulated: then he sang. The boat overcame the opposition; but what could not be overcome (was not susceptible of being overcome) he, the magician, transmuted into a series of long floating sounds, detached in space, which each appropriated to himself. While those about him were always occupied with the most immediate actuality and the overcoming of it, his voice maintained contact with the farthest distance, linking us with it until we felt its power of attraction." Rainier Maria Rilke, *Über den Dichter*," in *Werke in Sechs Bänden*, vol. 6 (Frankfurt: Insel Verlag, 1984), p. 554. English translation by G. Craig Houston, "Concerning the Poet," in *Where Silence Reigns* (New York: New Directions, 1978), p. 66. For Rilke the position of the poet is linked to the peculiar character of the poet's voice. The poet is the one who *lends his voice* in song. Moreover, the occasion for which the poet lends his voice is one of *need*, in this case a need to restore song to voices that have become silent. How the poet lends his voice is described in terms of the feature by which the poet has stood opposed to philosophy for over two thousand years. The poet is a magician (*der Zauberer*); as such he is the enchanted one (*der Bezauberte*) who enraptures and bewitches. The poet does this by speaking with his enchanting voice, a speaking in song, a *canto* that is *incanto*, a consecration with spells. He speaks with inspiration. The poet must not only invoke Mnemosyne, he must also invoke her offspring, the Muses, to endow him with the power of speaking.

14. One finds this paradoxical experience of poetry in Hesiod's *Theogony*:

> If a man has reason to grieve, and dries out his heart
> troubled with the spirit's fresh pain, yet the singer,
> the Muses' servant, sings the famous deeds of bygone men
> and the blessed gods who hold Olympus,
> at once the mourner forgets his grief and
> remembers none of his cares; but swiftly the goddesses' gifts divert
> him.
>
> (*Theogony*, 98–103)

The audience forgets its troubles and is also reminded of the accomplishments of the gods. For a discussion of this passage, see George Walsh, *The Varieties of Enchantment: Early Greek Views of the Nature and Function of Poetry* (Chapel Hill: University of North Carolina Press, 1984), p. 22ff. In terms of our analysis, this holding together of forgetting and remembering obviously broaches the crossing of philosophy and poetry. Perhaps in the end this is what it means to dwell poetically.

15. See note 10 above. The word ἀείδειν is related to αὐδή (human voice, speech), and to αὐδᾶν (to utter sounds); and from this to the verb ὔδειν (to call, name). The one who names is the ἔδης, the poet.

16. In the Platonic dialogues Socrates often says that the words he speaks are not his own. The speech of Diotima in the *Symposium* is the most obvious example here. But the participation in speaking that is from an other can also be understood ontologically as a participation in the *logos* of the world.

17. Heidegger, "Aus einem Gespräch von der Sprache," in *Unterwegs zur Sprache*, p. 115. English translation by Peter Hertz, "A Dialogue on Language," *On the Way to Language* (New York: Harper & Row, 1971), p. 29.

18. "Aus einem Gespräch von der Sprache," p. 119. "A Dialogue on Language," p. 32.

19. Heidegger, ". . . dichterisch wohnet der Mensch . . .," in *Vorträge und Aufsätze*, p. 193. English translation by Albert Hofstadter, ". . . Poetically Man Dwells . . .," in *Poetry, Language, Thought*, p. 218.

20. A more careful and sustained reading of Heidegger would, of course, be able to reveal much more about this difference. With respect to history, for example, Heidegger says that the poet institutes (*stiftet*) history, whereas the thinker founds (*gründet*) history. See Heidegger, *Hölderlins Hymne »Andenken«*, Gesamtausgabe Bd. 52 (Frankfurt: Klostermann, 1982). This distinction is mentioned by Véronique Fóti in *Heidegger and the Poets*; see p. 60.

21. The argument then could be made that because Heidegger is always occupied with individual words, he takes away from poetic discourse its essential element, that is, the song in its entirety. To his critics who insist that in his later writings Heidegger becomes too poetical, one can say that he is not poetical enough.

22. See also "Culture and Words—from the Point of View of Philosophy," *Universitas* 24 (1982): 179–88. Regarding the impossibility of making the distinction between meaning and sound in myth and poetry, Gadamer writes: "Even when the words are like Mörike's famous poem on a lamp

. . . [these words are] a world in itself, our world, the world of man, the world which grows to completion within that which is said, until it attains self-representation in sense and sound" (p. 187).

23. The issue here reflects the distinction drawn by Kant in the *Critique of Judgment*. The pure judgment of taste as a judgment about the beautiful is not to be confused with charms and emotions. "The taste is always barbaric which needs a mixture of charms and emotions in order that there may be satisfaction, and still more so if it make these the measure of its assent." Kant, *Critique of Judgment*, trans. J. H. Bernard (New York: Hafner Publishing, 1972), p. 58. Although Gadamer does not want to get caught up in Kant's subjectification of art, conceptually he does want to preserve a certain understanding of the beautiful that is in play even in Kant's aesthetics.

24. ". . . dichterisch wohnet der Mensch . . .," p. 203. ". . . Poetically Man Dwells . . .," p. 228.

25. Ibid.

26. ". . . dichterisch wohnet der Mensch . . .," p. 203. ". . . Poetically Man Dwells . . .," p. 229.

27. Derrida, *Given Time* (Chicago: University of Chicago Press, 1993). Of Mauss' *The Gift*, Derrida says: "[It] speaks of everything but the gift: It deals with economy, exchange, contract (*do ut des*), it speaks of raising the stakes, sacrifice, gift and counter-gift—in short, everything that in the thing itself impels the gift and the annulment of the gift" (p. 24).

28. Derrida takes this analysis much farther. The gift cannot even be recognized for "if the present is present to him as present, this simply recognition suffices to annul the gift. Why? Because it gives back, in the place, let us say, of the thing itself, a symbolic equivalent. . . . The symbolic opens and constitutes the order of exchange and debt, the law or order of circulation in which the gift gets annulled. *Given Time*, p. 13.

29. Here too one must think of Kant. In Kant's aesthetics, one of the distinctive features of beautiful art in contrast to the art of nature is that it can display the ugly. It must be possible, in other words, to display the horrible, perhaps the suffering of the Holocaust for example, in poetic discourse.

30. Paul Celan, *Collected Prose*, trans. Rosmarie Waldrop (Riverdale-on-Hudson: Sheep Meadow Press, 1986), pp. 34–35. The original text appears in *Gesammelte Werke*, III (Frankfurt: Suhrkamp, 1983), p. 186.

31. Krzystof Ziarek, *Inflected Language: Toward a Hermeneutics of Nearness* (Albany: SUNY Press, 1994), p. 135.

32. Celan, "The Meridian," in *Collected Prose*, p. 50; *Gesammelte Werke* III, p. 198.

33. Although Gadamer does not explicitly take up Celan's prose essay "The Meridian," in private conversations he has stressed the importance of this essay for the reading of Celan. What Gadamer says about the turning of breath is stated there succinctly by Celan: "Nobody can tell how long the pause for breath—hope and thought—will last." *Collected Prose*, p. 48; *Gesammelte Werke* III, p. 197.

34. The text in the *Gesammelte Werke* does not follow exactly the text in English. Gadamer modified the German text for its publication in the *Gesammelte Werke*, see "Verstummen die Dichter?" (GW9 362–66).

35. See Joseph Pieper, *Leisure: The Basis of Culture*, trans. Alexander Dru (New York: Pantheon Books, 1964), p. 25.

36. In *Leisure: The Basis of Culture*, Pieper equates celebration with affirmation: "To hold a celebration means to affirm the basic meaningfulness of the universe and a sense of oneness with it, of inclusion with it. In celebrating, in holding feasts upon occasion, man experiences the world in an aspect other than the everyday one" *Leisure*, (p. 30). This is precisely what Gadamer is talking about in his analysis of the festival. See the section "The Temporality of the Aesthetic," in *Truth and Method*, and the essay "The Festive Character of Theater" in *The Relevance of the Beautiful*.

37. "Phenomenological Interpretation with Respect to Aristotle: Indication of the Hermeneutical Situation," p. 361.

38. "Circumspection gives to life its world as interpreted according to those respects in which the world is expected and encountered as the object of concern, in which the world is put to tasks, in which the world is sought as refuge. The respects are available [to factical life], but most of the time not expressly so; factical life, on the path of habit, rather *slips* into these respects more than it expressly takes them on; these respects map out for the movement of care the paths within which this movement is actualized. The interpretedness of the world is factically that interpretedness within which life itself stands. . . . How the world is there, its Dasein, gets temporalized only when factical life takes-a-pause within its concerned movement of dealings. This Dasein of the world is what it is only as having grown from a particular taking-a-pause." "Phenomenological Interpretations with Respect to Aristotle: Indication of the Hermeneutical Situation," p. 363.

39. See "Über leere und erfüllte Zeit" (GW4 137–53).

40. In "Word and Picture" Gadamer writes: "If the work succeeds this means in both cases [both artist and perceiver] that 'it' has come out" (GW8 388).

41. Gadamer, "In Praise of Theory," trans. Dennis Schmidt and Jonathan Steinwand, *ellipsis* 1 (Spring 1990): 97 (GW4 48).

42. Gadamer derives this understanding of nature from Aristotle. See his essay "Die Griechen" (GW3 291). English translation appears as "The Greeks" in *Heidegger's Ways* (HW 147).

43. "In Praise of Theory," p. 98 (GW4 50).

44. Plato, *Phaedo*, trans. Harold Fowler, Loeb Classical Library (Cambridge, MA: Harvard University Press, 1977), 60e. Μουσική means here the arts over which the Muses preside, especially poetry.

45. *Phaedo*, 61a.

46. *Phänomenologische Interpretationen zu Aristoteles: Einführung in die phänomenologische Forschung*, p. 50.

47. See Introduction, p. 17–18.

Glossary of Greek Terms

ἀγορά	agora	place of assembly; Latin *forum*
ἀείδειν	aeidein	to sing
ἀλήθεια	aletheia	truth
ἀνάμνησις	anamnesis	a calling to mind, recollection
ἀρχαί	archai	principle, beginning, source, starting-point
βουλόμενos/βούλεσθαι	boulomenos	to will or wish
γράμματα/γράμμα	grammata	that which is written; a written character
γραφή	graphe	representation by means of lines; writing
διαγωγή	diagoge	tarrying as a passing of life
διάνοια	dianoia	thought
δόξα	doxa	opinion
δύναμις	dynamis	potentiality, potency, power
ἔθos	ethos	custom, habit
εἰδέναι	eidenai	to understand
εἴδωλον	eidolon	shape, image; an idea in the mind
εἰκών	eikon	an image, copy
ἐκφανέστατον	ekphanestaton	that which is most manifest
ἐμπειρία	empeiria	experience

ἔμψυχον/ἔμψυχος	empsychon	having life in one
ἐνέργεια	energeia	actuality, activity
ἐνθέους/ἔνθεος	entheous	full of the god, inspired
ἐπιστήμη	episteme	knowledge, science
ἔπος	epos	a word; a speech, a tale, also a song
ἔργον	ergon	deed, a completed action
ἑρμηνεία	hermeneia	interpretation
ἑρμηνεύειν	hermeneuein	to interpret
ἔτυμον/ἔτυμος	etymon	true, real, actual
ζῶντα/ζῶον	zonta/zoon	a living being
θεωρία	theoria	a looking at, observing
καθόλου	katholou	universally, in general
καλόν/καλός	kalon	the beautiful
κίνησις	kinesis	motion, movement
κυλινδειται/κυλίνδειν	kulindeitai	to role or wallow
λήθη	lethe	a forgetting, forgetfulness
λέγει/λέγειν	legein	to say, tell
λόγος	logos	reason
μάθησις	mathesis	the act of learning
μίμησις	mimesis	imitation
μνήμης/μνήμη	mnemes	memory
Μνημοσύνη	Mnemosyne	Memory, the Mother of the Muses
μουσική	mousike	any art over which the Muses presided
ὁδός	hodos	way, in the sense of method
ὁμολόγειν	homologein	to agree, to say the same
οὐσία	ousia	substance
πάθει μάθος	pathei mathos	to learn through suffering
πεπνυμένα/πνειν	pepnumena	to have breath or soul
ποίησις	poiesis	a making, creating
πόλις	polis	city-state
πρᾶξις	praxis	action
προαίρεσις	prohairesis	choice
ῥᾳστώνη	rastone	rest in the sense of leisure
σοφία	sophia	wisdom
σύνεσις	synesis	good intelligence
τέλος	telos	end, purpose

τέχνη	techne	art in the sense of know-how
ὑπομνήσεως/ὑπόμνησις	hypomneseos	a reminding
φαίνεσθαι	phainesthai	to show itself
φαινόμενον	phainomenon	that which shows itself
φάρμακον	pharmakon	remedy/poison
φωνή	phone	a voice, sound
φρόνησις	phronesis	practical reasonableness
φύσις	physis	nature
χάρις	charis	kindness
ψυχή	psyche	soul

Bibliography

Agamben, Giorgio. *Language and Death*. Trans. Karen Pinkus. Minneapolis: University of Minnesota Press, 1991.

Alejandro, Roberto. *Hermeneutics, Citizenship, and the Public Sphere*. Albany: SUNY Press, 1993.

Ambrosio, Francis J. "Dawn and Dusk: Gadamer and Heidegger on Truth." *Man and World* 19 (1986): 21–53.

———. "Gadamer, Plato, and the Discipline of Dialogue." *International Philosophical Quarterly* 27.1 (1987): 18–32.

Apel, Karl-Otto. *Towards a Transformation of Philosophy*. Trans. Glyn Adey and David Frisby. Boston: Routledge and Kegan Paul, 1980.

Aristotle. *Metaphysics*. Trans. Hugh Tredennick. Loeb Classical Library. Cambridge, MA: Harvard University Press, 1936.

———. *Nicomachean Ethics*. Trans. H. Rackham. Loeb Classical Library. Cambridge, MA: Harvard University Press, 1962.

———. *On Interpretation*. Trans. Hugh Tredennick. Loeb Classical Library. Cambridge, MA: Harvard University Press, 1962.

———. *Politics*. Trans. H. Rackham. Loeb Classical Library. Cambridge, MA: Harvard University Press, 1972.

———. *Posterior Analytics*. Trans. E. S. Forster. Loeb Classical Library. Cambridge, MA: Harvard University Press, 1976.

Beiner, Ronald. *Political Judgment*. Chicago: University of Chicago Press, 1983.

Bernasconi, Robert. "Bridging the Abyss: Heidegger and Gadamer." *Research in Phenomenology* XVI (1986): 1–24.

————. "Heidegger's Destruction of *Phronesis.*" *Southern Journal of Philosophy* 28 (1989): 127–47.

Bernstein, Richard J. *Beyond Objectivism and Relativism.* Philadelphia: University of Pennsylvania Press, 1983.

————. *Philosophical Profiles.* Philadelphia: University of Pennsylvania Press, 1986.

Betti, Emilio. *Allgemeine Auslegungslehre als Methodik der Geisteswissenschaften.* Tübingen: J. C. B. Mohr, 1967.

Bleicher, Josef. *Contemporary Hermeneutics.* London: Routledge and Kegan Paul, 1980.

Bruns, Gerald L. *Hermeneutics: Ancient and Modern.* New Haven: Yale University Press, 1992.

Bubner, Rüdiger. "Is Transcendental Hermeneutics Possible?" *Essays on Explanation and Understanding.* Ed. Juha Manninen and Raimo Tuomela. Dordrecht: Reidel Publishing Co., 1976.

Bultmann, Rudolf. *The Problem of Hermeneutics.* New York: Macmillan, 1955.

Caputo, John D. "Beyond Aestheticism: Derrida's Responsible Anarchy." *Research in Phenomenology* 18 (1988): 59–73.

————. *Radical Hermeneutics.* Bloomington: Indiana University Press, 1987.

Carson, Anne. *Eros: The Bittersweet.* Princeton: Princeton University Press, 1986.

Celan, Paul. *Collected Prose.* Trans. Rosmarie Waldrop. Riverdale-on-Hudson: The Sheep Meadow Press, 1986.

————. *Gesammelte Werke.* 5 vols. Frankfurt: Suhrkamp Verlag, 1983.

Chen, Kuan-Hsing. "Beyond Truth and Method: On Misreading Gadamer's Praxical Hermeneutics." *Quarterly Journal of Speech* 73 (1987): 183–99.

Culler, Jonathan. *On Deconstruction: Theory and Criticism after Structuralism.* Ithaca: Cornell University Press, 1982.

Dahlstrom, Daniel, ed. *Hermeneutics and the Tradition.* Washington DC: The American Catholic Philosophical Association, 1988.

Dallmayr, Fred R. *Polis and Praxis: Exercises in Contemporary Political Theory.* Cambridge, MA: MIT Press, 1984.

Derrida, Jacques. *Dissemination.* Trans. Barbara Johnson. Chicago: University of Chicago Press, 1981.

————. *The Ear of the Other.* Trans. Peggy Kamuf. Lincoln: University of Nebraska Press, 1985.

————. *Given Time: 1. Counterfeit Money*. Trans. Peggy Kamuf. Chicago: University of Chicago Press, 1992.

————. *Margins of Philosophy*. Trans. Alan Bass. Chicago: University of Chicago Press, 1982.

————. *Positions*. Trans. Alan Bass. Chicago: University of Chicago Press, 1981.

Dewey, John. *Reconstruction in Philosophy*. Boston: Beacon Press, 1964.

Dilthey, Wilhelm. *Gesammelte Schriften*. 18 vols. Göttingen: Vanderhoeck & Ruprecht, 1913–67.

————. *Selected Writings*. Trans. H. P. Rickman. Cambridge: Cambridge University Press, 1976.

Dostal, Robert J. "The World Never Lost: The Hermeneutics of Trust." *Philosophy and Phenomenological Research* 47.3 (1987): 413–34.

Eagleton, Terry. *Literary Theory: An Introduction*. Minneapolis: University of Minnesota Press, 1983.

Echeverria, E. J. *Criticism and Commitment*. Amsterdam: Rodopi, 1981.

Eliot, T. S. *Four Quartets*. New York: Harcourt, Brace & World, 1943.

Ermarth, Michael. *Wilhelm Dilthey: The Critique of Historical Reason*. Chicago: University of Chicago Press, 1978

Foster, Mathew. *Gadamer and Practical Philosophy*. Atlanta: The Scholars Press, 1991.

Frank, Manfred. *What is Neostructuralism?* Trans. Sabine Wilke and Richard Gray. Minneapolis: University of Minnesota Press, 1989.

Gadamer, Hans-Georg. "Articulating Transcendence." *The Beginning and the Beyond*. Ed. Fred Lawrence. Chico: Scholars Press, 1984.

————. "Being, Spirit, God." *Heidegger Memorial Lectures*. Ed. Werner Marx. Pittsburgh: Duquesne University Press, 1982. 55–74.

————. "A Classical Text-A Hermeneutic Challenge." *Revue de l'Universite d'Ottawa* (1981): 637–42.

————. "Concerning Empty and Fulfilled Time." Trans. R. P. O'Hara. *Martin Heidegger: In Europe and America*. Ed. Edward G. Ballard and Charles E. Scott. The Hague: Martinus Nijhoff, 1973. 77–89.

————. "The Continuity of History and the Existential Moment." *Philosophy Today* 16 (1972): 230–40.

————. "Culture and Word." *Hermeneutics and Poetic Motion*. Ed. Dennis J. Schmidt. State University of New York at Binghamton, 1990.

————. *Dialogue and Dialectic: Eight Hermeneutical Studies on Plato*. Trans. P. Christopher Smith. New Haven: Yale University Press, 1980.

————, "The Eminent Text and Its Truth." *Bulletin of the Midwest Modern Language Association* 13 (1980): 3–10.

————. *Gesammelte Werke.* 10 vols. Tübingen: J. C. B. Mohr, 1985–1995.

————. *Hans-Georg Gadamer im Gespräch.* Ed. Carsten Dutt. Heidelberg: Universitätsverlag C. Winter, 1993.

————. *Hans-Georg Gadamer on Education, Poetry, and History: Applied Hermeneutics.* Ed. Dieter Misgeld and Graeme Nicholson. Trans. Lawrence Schmidt and Monica Reuss. Albany: SUNY Press, 1992.

————. *Hegel's Dialectic: Five Hermeneutical Studies.* Trans. P. Christopher Smith. New Haven: Yale University Press, 1976.

————. *Heidegger's Ways.* Trans. John Stanley. Albany: SUNY Press, 1994.

————. "Hermeneutics and Social Science." *Cultural Hermeneutics* 2 (1975): 307–16.

————. "The Hermeneutics of Suspicion." *Hermeneutics: Questions and Prospects.* Ed. Gary Shapiro and Alan Sica. Amherst: University of Massachusetts Press, 1984.

————. "Historical Transformations of Reason." *Rationality Today.* Ed. Theodore Geraets. Ottawa: University of Ottawa Press, 1979.

————. *The Idea of the Good in Platonic-Aristotelian Philosophy.* Trans. P. Christopher Smith. New Haven: Yale University Press, 1986.

————. "In Praise of Theory." *ellipsis* 1.1 (1990): 85–100.

————. *Kleine Schriften.* 4 vols. Tübingen: J. C. B. Mohr, 1967–77.

————. *Literature and Philosophy in Dialogue: Essays in German Literary Theory.* Trans. Robert Paslick. Albany: SUNY Press, 1994.

————. *Lob der Theorie.* Frankfurt: Suhrkamp Verlag, 1983.

————. "Notes on Planning for the Future." *Daedalus* 95 (Spring 1966): 572–89.

————. "On the Problematic Character of Aesthetic Understanding." *Graduate Faculty Philosophy Journal* 9.1 (1982): 31–40.

————. *Philosophical Apprenticeships.* Trans. Robert Sullivan. Cambridge, MA: MIT Press, 1985.

————. *Philosophical Hermeneutics.* Trans. David Linge. Berkeley: University of California Press, 1976.

————. "Philosophy and Literature." *Man and World* 18 (1985): 241–59.

————. *Plato's Dialectical Ethics.* Trans. Robert Wallace. New Haven: Yale University Press, 1991.

————. *Platon als Porträtist.* Munich: Verien der Freude und Forderer der Glyptothek und der Antikensammlungen München, 1988.

————. "The Power of Reason." *Man and World* (1970): 5–15.

————. "The Problem of Historical Consciousness." *Graduate Faculty Philosophy Journal* 5.1 (1975): 8–52.

————. *Reason in the Age of Science*. Trans. Frederick Lawrence. Cambridge: The MIT Press, 1981.

————. *The Relevance of the Beautiful and Other Essays*. Ed. Robert Bernasconi. Trans. Nicholas Walker. Cambridge: Cambridge University Press, 1986.

————. "Theory, Technology, Practice: The Task of the Science of Man." *Social Research* 44.3 (1977): 529–61.

————. *Truth and Method*. Trans. Joel Weinsheimer and Donald Marshall. 2nd revised ed. New York: Crossroads Publishing, 1989.

————. "Truth in the Human Sciences." *Hermeneutics and Truth*. Ed. Brice Wachterhauser. Evanston: Northwestern University Press, 1994.

————. *Vernunft im Zeitalter der Wissenschaft*. Frankfurt: Suhrkamp Verlag, 1980.

————. "Von der Wahrheit des Wortes." *Denken und Dichten bei Martin Heidegger*. Messkirch: Der Martin Heidegger Gesellschaft in Messkirch, 1988.

————. "What is Truth?" *Hermeneutics and Truth*. Ed. Brice Wachterhauser. Evanston: Northwestern University Press, 1994.

Gadamer, Hans-Georg, and Paul Ricoeur. "The Conflict of Interpretations." *Phenomenology: Dialogue and Bridges*. Ed. Ronald Bruzina and Bruce Wilshire. Albany: SUNY Press, 1982. 299–320.

Gadamer, Hans-Georg, and Leo Strauss. "Correspondence Concerning Wahrheit und Methode." *Independent Journal of Philosophy* 2 (1978): 5–12.

Gallagher, Shaun. *Hermeneutics and Education*. Albany: SUNY Press, 1992.

Grondin, Jean. *Hermeneutische Wahrheit? Zum Wahrheitsbegriff Hans-Georg Gadamers*. Königstein/Ts.: Forum Academicum, 1982.

————. *Sources of Hermeneutics*. Albany: SUNY Press, 1995.

Habermas, Jürgen. "A Review of Gadamer's Truth and Method." *Understanding and Social Inquiry*. Ed. Fred Dallmayr and Thomas McCarthy. Notre Dame: University of Notre Dame Press, 1977.

Hegel, G. W. F. *Phenomenology of Spirit*. Trans. A. V. Miller. Oxford: Clarendon Press, 1977.

————. *Lectures on the Philosophy of Religion*. 3 vols. Trans. E. B. Spiers and J. B. Anderson. New York: Humanities Press, 1968.

————. *Werke*. 20 vols. Frankfurt: Suhrkamp, 1986.

Heidegger, Martin. *The Basic Problems of Phenomenology*. Trans. Albert Hofstadter. Bloomington: Indiana University Press, 1982.

————. *Basic Writings*. Ed. David F. Krell. New York: Harper & Row, 1977.

————. *Frühe Schriften*. Frankfurt: Vittorio Klostermann, 1972.

————. *Holzwege*. 5th ed. Frankfurt: Vittorio Klostermann, 1972.

————. *Kant and the Problem of Metaphysics*. 4th ed. Trans. Richard Taft. Bloomington: Indiana University Press, 1982.

————. *History of the Concept of time. Prolegomena*. Trans. Theodore Kisiel. Bloomington: Indiana University Press, 1985.

————. *Ontologie (Hermeneutik der Faktizität)*. Gesamtausgabe, vol. 63. Frankfurt: Klostermann, 1988.

————. *Phänomenologische Interpretationen zu Aristoteles*. Gesamtausgabe, vol. 61. Frankfurt: Klostermann, 1985.

————. "Phänomenologische Interpretationen zu Aristoteles (Anzeige der hermeneutischen Situation)." *Dilthey Jahrbuch für Philosophie und Geschichte der Geisteswissenschaften* 6 (1989): 228–74.

————. *Poetry, Language, Thought*. Trans. Albert Hofstadter. New York: Harper & Row, 1971.

————. *Platon: Sophistes*. Gesamtausgabe, vol. 19. Frankfurt: Klostermann, 1992.

————. *Sein und Zeit*. 7th ed. Tübingen: Niemeyer, 1973.

————. *Unterwegs zur Sprache*. Gesamtausgabe, vol. 12. Frankfurt: Klostermann, 1985.

————. *Was Heisst Denken?*. Tübingen: Niemeyer, 1971.

————. *Wegmarken*. 2nd revised ed. Frankfurt: Vittorio Klostermann, 1978.

Hinman, Lawrence. "Quid Facti or Quid Juris: The Fundamental Ambiguity of Gadamer's Understanding of Hermeneutics." *Philosophy and Phenomenological Research* 40 (1980): 512–35.

Hirsch, Eric D., Jr. *Validity in Interpretation*. New Haven: Yale University Press, 1967.

Hollinger, Robert, ed. *Hermeneutics and Praxis*. Notre Dame: University of Notre Dame Press, 1985.

Homer. *The Iliad*. Trans. A. T. Murray. Loeb Classical Library. Cambridge, MA: Harvard University Press, 1960.

————. *The Odyssey of Homer*. Trans. Richard Lattimore. New York: Harper & Row, 1967.

Hoy, David Couzens. *The Critical Circle: Literature and History in Contemporary Hermeneutics*. Berkeley: University of California Press, 1978.
———. "Forgetting the Text: Derrida's Critique of Hermeneutics." *Boundary 2* 8 (1979): 223–35.
Ingram, David. "Hermeneutics and Truth." *Journal of the British Society for Phenomenology* 15.1 (1984): 62–78.
Jauss, Hans Robert. *Question and Answer*. Minneapolis: University of Minnesota Press, 1989.
Kidder, Paulette. "Gadamer and the Platonic *Eidos*." *Philosophy Today* 39.1 (Spring 1995): 83–92.
Kierkegaard, Soren. *Concluding Unscientific Postscript*. Trans. David Swenson and Walter Lowrie. Princeton: Princeton University Press, 1941.
———. *The Concept of Anxiety*. Trans. R. Thomte. Princeton: Princeton University Press, 1980.
———. *Fear and Trembling/Repetition*. Trans. Howard Hong and Edna Hong. Princeton: Princeton University Press, 1983.
Kisiel, Theodore. *The Genesis of Heidegger's Being and time*. Berkeley: University of California Press, 1993.
———. "The Happening of Tradition: The Hermeneutics of Gadamer and Heidegger." *Man and world* 2 (1969): 358–85.
———. "Repetition in Gadamer's Hermeneutics." *Analecta Husserliana*. Vol. 2. Ed. A. Tymieniecka. Dordrecht: Reidel Publishing Co., 1972.
Kisiel, Theodore, and John van Buren, eds. *Reading Heidegger from the Start*. Albany: SUNY Press, 1994.
Kockelmans, Joseph. "Toward an Interpretive or Hermeneutic Social Science." *Graduate Faculty Philosophy Journal* 5 (1975): 73–96.
Leitch, Vincent. *Deconstructive Criticism*. New York: Columbia University Press, 1983.
Madison, Gary. *The Hermeneutics of Postmodernity: Figures and Themes*. Bloomington: Indiana University Press, 1988.
Makkreel, Rudolf. *Dilthey: Philosopher of the Human Studies*. Princeton: Princeton University Press, 1975.
Margolis, Joseph. *Pragmatism Without foundations: Reconciling Realism and Relativism*. Oxford: Basil Blackwell, 1986.
Marx, Werner. *Heidegger and the Tradition*. Trans. Theodore Kisiel and Murray Greene. Evanston: Northwestern University Press, 1971.
Merleau-Ponty, Maurice. *Phenomenology of Perception*. Trans. Colin Smith. London: Routledge and Kegan Paul, 1962.

Michelfelder, Diane P., and Richard E. Palmer, eds. *Dialogue and Deconstruction: The Gadamer-Derrida Encounter.* Albany: SUNY Press, 1989.

Nicholson, Graeme. *Seeing and Reading.* Atlantic Highlands, NJ: Humanities Press, 1984.

Nietzsche, Friedrich. *Sämtliche Werke.* Kritische Studienausgabe. 15 vols. Hrsg. Colli & Montinari. Munich: de Gruyter, 1980.

Onians, Richard. *The Origins of European Thought.* Cambridge: Cambridge University Press, 1989.

Ormiston, Gayle, and Alan Schrift, eds. *Transforming the Hermeneutic Context.* Albany: SUNY Press, 1990.

Palmer, Richard. *Hermeneutics.* Evanston: Northwestern University Press, 1969.

Plato. *Ion.* Trans. W. R. M. Lamb. Loeb Classical Library. Cambridge, MA: Harvard University Press, 1962.

———. *Euthyphro, Apology, Crito, Phaedo, Phaedrus.* Trans. Harold Fowler. Loeb Classical Library. Cambridge, MA: Harvard University Press, 1977.

———. *Philebus.* Trans. Harold Fowler. Loeb Classical Library. Cambridge, MA: Harvard University Press, 1962.

Rasmussen, David. "From Hermeneutics and Critical Theory to Communicative Action and Post-Structuralism." *Critical and Dialectical Phenomenology.* Ed. Donn Welton and Hugh Silverman. Albany: SUNY Press, 1987.

Richardson, William. *Heidegger: Through Phenomenology to Thought.* The Hague: Martinus Nijhoff, 1967.

Ricoeur, Paul. *From Text to Action: Essays on Hermeneutics.* Trans. Kathleen Blamey and John Thompson. Evanston: Northwestern University Press, 1991.

———. *Hermeneutics and the Human Sciences.* Ed. John Thompson. New York: Cambridge University Press, 1981.

———. *Time and Narrative.* 3 vols. Trans. Kathleen Blamey and David Pellauer. Chicago: University of Chicago Press, 1988.

Risser, James. "The Ontology of Hermeneutics." *ellipsis* 1.2 (1991): 209–24.

———. "Poetic Dwelling in Gadamer's Hermeneutics." *Philosophy Today* 38.4 (Winter 1994): 369–79.

———. "Practical Reason, Hermeneutics, and Social Life." *Proceedings of the American Catholic Philosophical Association* 58 (1984): 84–92.

————. "The Remembrance of Truth: The Truth of Remembrance." *Hermeneutics and Truth*. Ed. Brice Wachterhauser. Evanston: Northwestern University Press, 1994. 123–36.

————. "Two Faces of Socrates: Gadamer/Derrida." *Dialogue and Deconstruction*. Ed. Diane Michelfelder and Richard Palmer. Albany: SUNY Press, 1989.

Rodi, Frithjof. "Hermeneutics and the Meaning of Life." *Hermeneutics and Deconstruction*. Ed. Hugh Silverman and Don Ihde. Albany: SUNY Press, 1985.

Rorty, Richard. *The Consequences of Pragmatism*. Minneapolis: University of Minnesota Press, 1982.

————. *Philosophy and the Mirror of Nature*. Princeton: Princeton University Press, 1979.

Rosen, Stanley. *Hermeneutics as Politics*. New York: Oxford University Press, 1987.

Rousseau, Mary. "Recollection as Realization—Remythologizng Plato." *Review of Metaphysics* 45 (December 1981): 337–48.

Sallis, John. *Echoes: After Heidegger*. Bloomington: Indiana University Press, 1990.

Schleiermacher, Friedrich. *Hermeneutics: The Handwritten Manuscripts*. Ed. Heinz Kimmerle. Trans. James Duke and Jack Forstman. Missoula: The Scholars Press, 1977.

Schmidt, Lawrence. *The Epistemology of Hans-Georg Gadamer*. Frankfurt: Peter Lang, 1985.

————, ed. *The Spectator of Relativism: Truth Dialogue, and Phronesis in Philosophical Hermeneutics*. Evanston: Northwestern University Press, 1995.

Schnädelbach, Herbert. *Philosophy in Germany 1831–1933*. Cambridge: Cambridge University Press, 1984.

Schrader, George. "Hermeneutics and Critical Theory." *Critical and Dialectical Phenomenology*. Ed. Donn Welton and Hugh Silverman. Albany: SUNY Press, 1987.

Schrag, Calvin. *Communicative Praxis and the Space of Subjectivity*. Bloomington: Indiana University Press, 1986.

Schweiker, William. *Mimetic Reflections: A Study in Hermeneutics, Theology, and Ethics*. New York: Fordham University Press, 1990.

Seebohm, Thomas. "Boeckh and Dilthey: The Development of Methodical Hermeneutics." *Man and World* 17 (1984): 325–46.

Shapiro, Gary, and Alan Sica, eds. *Hermeneutics: Questions and Prospects*. Amherst: University of Massachusetts Press, 1984.

Sheehan, Thomas. "Getting to the Topic: The New Edition of *Wegmarken*." *Research in Phenomenology* 7 (1977): 299–316.

Silverman, Hugh, ed. *Gadamer and Hermeneutics*. New York: Routledge, Chapman and Hill, 1991.

Smith, P. Christopher. *Hermeneutics and Human Finitude*. New York: Fordham University Press, 1991.

Snell, Bruno. *The Discovery of the Mind*. Trans. T. G. Rosenmeyer. New York: Harper & Row, 1960.

Spanos, William, ed. *Martin Heidegger and the Question of Literature*. Bloomington: Indiana University Press, 1979.

Stack, George. *On Kierkegaard: Philosophical Fragments*. Atlantic Highlands, NJ: Humanities Press, 1976.

Stapleton, Timothy J., ed. *The Question of Hermeneutics: Essays in Honor of Joseph J. Kockelmans*. Boston: Kluwer Academic Publishers, 1994.

Steiner, George. *After Babel: Aspects of Language and Translation*. New York: Oxford University Press, 1975.

Sullivan, Robert R. *Political Thinking: The Early Thinking of Hans-Georg Gadamer*. University Park: The Pennsylvania State University Press, 1989.

Szondi, Peter. *On Textual Understanding and Other Essays*. Trans. Harvey Mendelsohn. Minneapolis: University of Minnesota Press, 1986.

Taylor, Mark C. *Tears*. Albany: SUNY Press, 1990.

Vattimo, Gianni. *The End of Modernity: Nihilism and Hermeneutics in Postmodern Culture*. Trans. John R. Snyder. Baltimore: Johns Hopkins University Press, 1988.

———. "The Truth of Hermeneutics." *Questioning Foundations*. Ed. Hugh Silverman. New York: Routledge, 1993.

Wachterhauser, Brice, ed. *Hermeneutics and Modern Philosophy*. Albany: SUNY Press, 1986.

———. "Prejudice, Reason, Force." *Philosophy* 63 (1988): 231–53.

———, ed. *Hermeneutics and Truth*. Evanston: Northwestern University Press, 1994.

Walsh, George. *The Varieties of Enchantment: Early Greek Views of the Nature and Function of Poetry*. Chapel Hill: University of North Carolina Press, 1984.

Warnke, Georgia. *Gadamer: Hermeneutics, Tradition and Reason*. Stanford: Stanford University Press, 1987.

Watson, Stephen H. *Extensions: Essays on Interpretation, Rationality, and the Closure of Modernism*. Albany: SUNY Press, 1992.

Weinsheimer, Joel C. *Gadamer's Hermeneutics: A Reading of Truth and Method*. New Haven: Yale University Press, 1985.

————. *Philosophical Hermeneutics and Literary Theory*. New Haven: Yale University Press, 1991.

Wright, Kathleen, ed. *Festivals of Interpretation: Essays on Hans-Georg Gadamer's Work*. Albany: SUNY Press, 1990.

Index